Common Property Economics

Common Property Economics presents the theory of natural resource exploitation under the management institution of common property, differentiates common property from open access, and tests the adequacy of resource allocation under common property empirically. Theoretical models demonstrate overexploitation under open access, and the book defines the necessary and sufficient conditions for common property. Stevenson clarifies common property with historical examples, with common property's basis in legal theory, with a contrast to public goods, and with a discussion of the transactions costs of establishing and maintaining common property. Swiss alpine grazing commons are contrasted with grazing in the English open field system, and statistical work using Swiss data compares the performance of common property with that of private property.

Common Property Economics

A General Theory and Land Use Applications

Glenn G. Stevenson

The right of the
University of Cambridge
to print and sell
all manner of books
was granted by
Henry VIII in 1534.
The University has printed
and published continuously
since 1584.

CAMBRIDGE UNIVERSITY PRESS
Cambridge
New York   Port Chester   Melbourne   Sydney

CAMBRIDGE UNIVERSITY PRESS
Cambridge, New York, Melbourne, Madrid, Cape Town, Singapore, São Paulo

Cambridge University Press
The Edinburgh Building, Cambridge CB2 2RU, UK

Published in the United States of America by Cambridge University Press, New York

www.cambridge.org
Information on this title: www.cambridge.org/9780521384414

First published 1991
This digitally printed first paperback version 2005

A catalogue record for this publication is available from the British Library

Library of Congress Cataloguing in Publication data
Stevenson, Glenn G.
Common property economics : a general theory and land use
applications / Glenn G. Stevenson.
p.   cm.
Includes bibliographical references and index.
ISBN 0-521-38441-9
1. Commons.   2. Grazing districts.   3. Right of property.
4. Cooperation.   5. Natural resources, Communal.   6. Land tenure.
7. Commons – Switzerland.   8. Commons – England.   9. Grazing
districts – Switzerland.   10. Grazing districts – England.   I. Title.
HD1286.S74   1991
333.2—dc20   90–49258
                                                        CIP

ISBN-13 978-0-521-38441-4 hardback
ISBN-10 0-521-38441-9 hardback

ISBN-13 978-0-521-02080-0 paperback
ISBN-10 0-521-02080-8 paperback

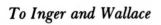
To Inger and Wallace

Contents

Tables and Figures

Tables

Figures

Preface

A preface often justifies an author's having brought pen to paper. I have left that task to my first chapter. Here, I wish to relate how I came to Switzerland and to write this book, discuss how I pursued my research, and thank some people for their part.

Before I left for Switzerland to study the Swiss grazing commons, I had little notion that the inquiry would turn into my doctoral dissertation and no idea that it would become a book on open access, private property, and common property. I simply wished to return to a country that I had glimpsed and for which I had developed an ardency during an undergraduate stay in neighboring Germany. Professor Richard C. Bishop of the University of Wisconsin–Madison discussed with me his interest in the Swiss grazing commons as an example of common property, and given my knowledge of German and desire to revisit the country, the basic ingredients for an application to the Fulbright-Hays program existed. The opportunity to go arose with the awarding of a Swiss government fellowship through this program.

Studying the Swiss commons called on me to travel widely in Switzerland by bus and train and even on foot, speaking with farmers, academics, government officials, and fellow students. I put my bags down in St. Gallen, Switzerland, for most of my stay, living with three Swiss students studying at the Graduate School of Business and Economics in St. Gallen, but I also lived for a period in Bern to be closer to the subject of my most intensive study, the Bernese alpine grazing areas. Because of the gracious welcome I received from the people I moved among, I came to know the Swiss, their country, their language, and their culture as well as an outsider might in two years' time.

I employed a number of methods to reach the two goals that I set out for myself in Switzerland: to understand common property rights systems and to find a way to compare the economic performance of commons and private grazing. Initially I met with specialists in alpine agriculture at the Swiss Federal Department of Agriculture. These men had visited hundreds of alpine grazing areas in the course of a two-decade-long, federally sponsored land registry effort. These experts and the reports they wrote were helpful to me repeatedly. As my research continued, I extended such contacts to the cantonal level and to the universities, gathering the wisdom of authorities on alpine grazing among agriculturalists, economists, ethnologists, and government and cooperative association officials.

To understand the commons rights systems and formulate the commons categorization found in Chapter 4, I tapped the wealth of descriptive material in the university libraries in Zürich, Bern, and St. Gallen. I also visited many alpine grazing areas to observe their conditions and examine the farmers' operations firsthand. I inspected their barns and milk and cheese production facilities; I talked to the farmers about their operations; I even shared some meals and spent some nights with the alpine graziers in their alp huts. I began using a questionnaire to gather consistent data on costs, returns, and rights types from the users, recording my interviews on tape. In addition, I observed user meetings of various types, ranging from small commons user meetings of a half-dozen individuals around a Swiss tavern table to large, open-air meetings of the *Korporation*s of inner Switzerland, in which several hundred farmers participate. I attended town meetings in communities that own grazing areas, *Korporation* legislative and executive body meetings, celebrations before ascensions to the mountain pastures, and other types of commons meetings.

For a year, I searched libraries, government agencies, and private institutes for data on the grazed condition of private and commons grazing areas to compare the impacts of the different property systems. I finally concluded that such data were not available for more than a handful of grazing areas. As a proxy, I decided to use milk yields, which were available from milk producer associations. I subsequently developed intimate ties with personnel at one such organization.

I note as an encouragement to future researchers in foreign environments that part of my success derived precisely from my being an American student studying alpine grazing in Switzerland. I believe that this set of circumstances intrigued the Swiss ("Why would an American want to study *that*?"). Because of this fascination, because I came to them in their own language, because the Swiss generally like Americans, and because the Swiss are an extremely considerate people, I was afforded their fullest attention and hospitality.

Whereas the Swiss research provided the substance for understanding an operating common property system and the data for an empirical comparison with private management, other parts of the book had their beginnings in the United States. My review of open access theory and the development of a theory of common property germinated during my graduate course work and dissertation research at the University of Wisconsin–Madison. Open access theory is well known among economists, but I hope to have added something by tying it together and studying the important question whether excessive inputs come from existing users or new entrants. My development of common property theory builds on the seminal concept from S. V. Ciriacy-Wantrup and subsequent elaborations by Bishop and Bromley. Of course, my development of the theory also incorporates others' ideas from the literature. The evolution of the theory progressed after I joined Oak Ridge National Laboratory in 1984; I continued to change and refine my definitions and my thought on common property from the ideas found in my doctoral work. The book's finishing touch is a description of common grazing under the medieval English open field system and a comparison of it with the Swiss commons. This expansion arose from the suggestion of a reviewer for Cambridge University Press that caused me to delve into intriguing new secondary source research. The resulting chapter, I think, is a nice extension to a contrasting common property system.

I owe thanks to many people, whose whereabouts span two continents. Although the book has undergone extensive revisions since I finished my doctorate, my greatest gratitude is to Richard C. Bishop, my academic mentor and personal friend, whose patience, intellectual curiosity, and personal integrity mark him as an exceptional man. His contribution is embedded in every sentence of my doctoral dissertation, which served as the initial draft of the work before you. Daniel W. Bromley played the role of a second major professor, and his influence throughout the book is considerable. He suggested to me a number of ideas that are developed here, especially in the property rights section of Chapter 3. The third major influence on the work comes from Anthony D. Scott, who initially served as an anonymous reviewer. Professor Scott graciously consented to disclose his name so that I could thank him publicly. His input caused me to rethink and research anew; reformat, prune, and winnow; defend, create, and rewrite throughout the book. I am deeply grateful for his comments.

Other substantive contributions came from Don W. Jones, especially in helping me rewrite Chapter 6 but also in theoretical thought and moral support elsewhere in the book. Arthur Goldberger and Jean-Paul Chavas were helpful in forming some of the econometric questions, although any errors that remain are mine. Matthew Hendryx, an economist and my editor at the press, contributed to the definition of common property. I am indebted also to Colin Day, formerly of Cambridge University Press, whose vision for the book initially got the project off the ground, and to Ina Isobe and Janis Bolster of the Press, who also provided gentle, helpful advice. Alexa Selph was instrumental in preparing a thorough index.

This book would not have been possible without the warm reception of the Swiss people. The Swiss government generously provided the two-year fellowship. In addition, the Swiss people welcomed me with open arms into their offices and homes and onto their agricultural operations to answer my questions. I am forever indebted to them for their graciousness. Particularly the users of the alpine grazing areas, several dozen of whom I could mention, deserve my heartfelt thanks. In the Swiss Department of Agriculture, Mr. Fritz Aeschlimann, Mr. Adrian Imboden, Mr. Andreas Werthemann, and Dr. Josef Von Ah gave me their time to explore my questions and data requirements. Mr. Aeberhardt of the Bernese Milk Producers' Association deserves particular recognition for his aid in gathering information on milk yields from his files. I also thank Mr. Ulrich Peter, Director of the Association, for permission to use the Association's information on milk yields. In the Bernese Cantonal Tax Administration, I am immeasurably indebted to Mr. Würgler of the Agricultural Inspectorate, who personally wrote requests for assessment sheets on alpine grazing lands and gathered hundreds of them into his office. I thank Jack Solock for assistance in data entry and Allison Baldwin for the high-quality graphics throughout. I also acknowledge the support from the University of Wisconsin Graduate School at the dissertation stage.

Finally, general support from friends and colleagues has been invaluable to me. First, I wish to give a word of appreciation to my Swiss roommates, Franz Broger, Martin Noser, Andreas Joost, Jürg Amrein, and Ruedi Reichmuth, for helping an American out of his cultural element and away from his mother tongue. Tom Wilbanks of Oak Ridge National Laboratory provided assistance, Tony Catanese a reviewer's eye, and Shelby Smith-Sanclare and Carl Petrich the moral support of friends. Finally, I especially want to thank Melody Gaye Stone and Dianne Knief, both of whom supported me when I was laboring hard on the dissertation and the book and who have enriched my personal life.

CHAPTER 1

What Is Common Property?

A Confusion of Definition

Since the publication of Garrett Hardin's influential article in *Science* (1968), the "tragedy of the commons" has become a household phrase among economists and others concerned with environmental and natural resource problems. The concept has been used to explain overexploitation in fisheries, overgrazing, air and water pollution, abuse of public lands, population problems, extinction of species, fuelwood depletion, misallocation in oil and natural gas extraction, groundwater depletion, wildlife decline, and other problems of resource misallocation. Yet the rush to explain with a single concept a whole range of natural resource problems—which happen to be similar only in having multiple users—has obscured some important distinctions in the physical characteristics and the manner of use of these resources. We ought not to fall prey to a "tyranny of words," as Leamer (1983) in another context aptly warns, for the "tragedy of the commons" is such a catchy phrase that we are wont to apply it indiscriminately. We look about us and everywhere find resources being used by groups of people in common and are tempted to say, "Aha! Here is another 'tragedy of the commons.' "

What is this "tragedy of the commons"? The next chapter reviews the theory behind it in detail, but I will state it briefly and intuitively here. Where resource use is unlimited, many users are present, and there is excess demand for the resource, overexploitation results. It is said that "everybody's property is nobody's property," as each user rushes to harvest the resource before the next person does. Abuse of the resource occurs because each user, while striving for private gains, can spread some of the costs of his or her use to the other users. Hardin's (1968: 1244) classic description of a grazing commons illustrates this process in simple terms:

As a rational being, each herdsman seeks to maximize his gain. Explicitly or implicitly, more or less consciously, he asks, "What is the utility *to me* of adding one more animal to my herd?" This utility has one negative and one positive component.

1) The positive component is a function of the increment of one animal. Since the herdsman receives all the proceeds from the sale of the additional animal, the positive utility is nearly +1.

2) The negative component is a function of the additional overgrazing created by one more animal. Since, however, the effects of overgrazing are shared by all the herdsmen, the negative utility for any particular decision-making herdsman is only a fraction of −1.

Adding together the component partial utilities, the rational herdsman concludes that the only sensible course for him to pursue is to add another animal to his herd. And another; and another. . . . But this is the conclusion reached by each and every rational herdsman sharing a commons. Therein is the tragedy. Each man is locked into a system that compels him to increase his herd without limit—in a world that is limited.[1]

Although faults exist with some particulars of the reasoning—there is for instance a theoretical limit on the herd's increase—the argument is compelling. How is it then that some commons seem to survive despite the dire predictions of tragedy? For example, the Swiss alpine grazing commons, which serve as the major case study for the current work, have been in use in some cases for a thousand years. If the tragedy of the commons always occurs, then surely it would have transpired in Switzerland by now. Dahlman (1980) points out that common property was the preferred form of land management for grazing across northern Europe for centuries during the Middle Ages. He argues that this was not due to the ignorance of the peasants who used the land, but that it was economically rational. How are these counterexamples reconcilable with Hardin's "tragedy of the commons"?

The answer is quite simple. I have pulled a sleight of hand, but it is casuistry that the literature on "common property" has performed over and over again. Hardin's commons and the grazing commons of Switzerland are two different systems. Indeed, Hardin's commons and many examples of common property ought not to be spoken of in the same breath. What distinguishes them? There are two things, the main one being limitation of entry. The inputs to Hardin's commons may increase until economic exhaustion of the resource occurs. In the common property systems that have survived, people have learned to limit use. The second distinction is that with limited entry often comes coordinated management. There is no coordinated man-

---

[1] Quoted by permission of the author and the American Association for the Advancement of Science. Copyright 1968 by the AAAS.

agement in Hardin's "commons" because no identifiable group has been distinguished as the managers. Where limited entry has been accomplished, the group of included users has the ability to collude and systematize use.

These distinctions seem basic, yet all too many students of resource use institutions have missed them. The class of resources that has been labeled "common property" should more accurately be divided into two subsets. The subset that experiences overuse should be labeled "open access resources," for it is unlimited access that causes the tragedy. The subset that has succeeded by limiting access and employing joint management is *true* common property. For reasons that Chapter 3 makes clear, this subset retains the label "common property" in the present book; in short, only when access has been limited can one talk about "property."

Thus, the condemnation of a potentially viable resource use system, true common property, has been due partially to a problem of semantics. "Common property" has been applied to any natural resource used in common, whether it is an open access resource or a limited access, managed resource. Because the theory in which a tragedy results really applies only to open access resources, rightfully speaking one would talk about the "tragedy of open access." Partly as a result of the semantic problem, however, the belief has grown that any multiple-user system will lead to overexploitation.

This confusion between open access and common property resources has not had benign consequences. Certain authors, launching their reasoning from the assumption that all commonly used resources are overexploited, conclude that there is only one solution: private property.[2] Private property, of course, is one solution to the open access problem. A secure, exclusive right to resource extraction imparts the incentive to the user to utilize the resource at an optimal rate: The private rights holder not only reaps the benefits but also incurs all the costs of additional resource extraction, and a balancing of these benefits and costs leads the user to an optimal extraction rate.[3]

There may be a problem, however, in thinking that private property is the *only* solution to open access. Common property, in which group control over the resource leads to the balancing of benefits and costs, might also be a solution. The ardent private property advocate

---

[2] Defenders of this position include Demsetz (1967), Cheung (1970), Alchian and Demsetz (1973), Anderson and Hill (1977), and Libecap (1981).

[3] Of course, for private property to provide the optimal solution, there must be no divergence between social and private discount rates, no externalities, no imperfect capital markets, and no other market imperfections.

refuses to recognize this possibility because of the belief that individual incentives to cheat will ruin a group solution. This position, however, ignores the incentive that individuals have to collude: Through collusion, the group can increase the size of the joint product that they divide.

It is important to recognize that common property might provide a solution to the open access problem, because certain resource characteristics or social situations may require a common property solution, whereas a private property solution might fail. Consider a fishery, a groundwater aquifer, or certain wide-ranging wildlife. How do we vest private property rights in such natural resources? Short of committing them to a sole owner, which may be completely incompatible with optimal firm size, it is impossible. The resources themselves cannot be physically divided up into individual units. Clearly, if these resources are to be exploited, multiple users must perform the job. To avoid the undesirable results of open access, some type of common property solution must be found.

Thus, the physical characteristics of the natural resource sometimes dictate a common property solution. At other times, the social circumstances do so. Runge (1981) has pointed out that some traditional societies have long depended on group use of a natural resource. Where technological change, population growth, or contact with a nonlocal market economy has rendered traditional use rules incapable of properly allocating the resource, a new solution has to be found. Because of the society's experience with group control over resource use, the people may accept a common property solution more readily than a private one.[4] In such cases, moreover, adverse impacts on wealth and income distribution, which are a regular occurrence when common property is transformed into private property, can also be avoided.[5]

Some agreement between the conventional wisdom that supports

---

[4] Bottomley (1963: 94) provides an example of this in his study of land use in Tripolitania. He advocates increasing the rents accruing from the resource by vesting private property rights in trees, but he urges that the land on which the trees grow remain in tribal control. The land should remain common property because "attempts to violate hallowed rights regarding common land will, no doubt, run into considerable resistance."

[5] The culmination of the enclosure movement in England during the eighteenth and nineteenth centuries is often cited as an example of wealth transfers from poorer to richer classes as commons were converted to private property. One epigram of unknown authorship from the period, quoted in Cheyney (1901: 219), is

> The law locks up the man or woman
> Who steals the goose from off the common
> But leaves the greater villain loose
> Who steals the common from the goose.

private property and a view that backs common property as a solution might be ferreted out. Open access is an undesirable regime under which to exploit a natural resource, at least when extraction becomes intensive. The theory of the next chapter makes this plain. The solution that is often given is to "vest property rights" in the resource in certain users. Vesting property rights means defining who may participate in resource extraction and to what degree, and designating who makes the management decisions regarding the resource. But it is important to note: Common property performs these tasks within the framework of group control, even as private property accomplishes them under individual control. Common property also possesses a set of property rights relationships designed to eliminate open access exploitation. The number of users is limited, each user understands how much of the resource he or she may extract, and decisions about resource allocation are made by some group process. Property rights have been vested in this situation, and they may be adequate to prevent the tragedy of open access. The advocate of vesting property rights who recognizes this may agree that common property provides a viable solution. Those in the mainstream who insist on vesting property rights in scarce resources and the defenders of common property are perhaps not all that far apart.

Thus, although private property can provide the incentives to attain proper resource allocation, it may not be the solution toward which all resource allocation systems must move. To investigate this idea, this book develops theory to characterize common property and examines empirically whether it competes economically with private property.

Objectives

I can summarize the previous discussion by saying that (1) open access and common property regimes are generally confounded with one another, and (2) common property is consequently condemned as inferior to private property. In view of this, the current work's main task is to separate out the three use systems and to look at resource allocation under each. With this general goal in mind, the study has the following objectives:

1. To differentiate open access from common property conceptually and theoretically;
2. To describe real-world, working examples of common property, including mechanisms for resource protection and management;

3. To formulate hypotheses and empirically test whether common property protects the resource as well as private property;
4. To draw conclusions about the efficiency of common property and apply common property principles to other natural resources that can be exploited jointly by a number of economic units.

The Swiss and English Commons

The current work concentrates on the alpine grazing commons of Switzerland as an example of an actual, working common property system. Examining this system provides an understanding of the structure and functioning of a common property institutional setup, as well as supplies information for empirical testing. The study also examines commons grazing in medieval England in order to investigate the commons system in another environment and compare it with the Swiss case.

The alpine grazing areas in Switzerland are seasonal pastures to which cows and other animals are driven in the summer. They lie in the mountains above the villages, which are nestled in the mountain valleys. Fortuitously, different rights systems have developed on different grazing areas. One finds private grazing areas intermixed with common property grazing areas, and thus the opportunity for comparison exists.

The study area for the present work is restricted to the German-speaking part of Switzerland. This encompasses one of the major regions in which alpine grazing occurs. Alpine grazing systems, however, extend beyond this region into French- and Italian-speaking sections of Switzerland, as well as beyond the borders into Germany, Austria, Italy, and France. My limited experience with these other areas indicates that alpine grazing practices there are similar to those described here, but I cannot claim generality for my description to areas beyond the German-speaking part of Switzerland. Moreover, I based the statistical work on an even smaller area, the canton of Bern, Switzerland.[6] The Swiss grazing commons description and statistical investigation are both based on two years of fieldwork in Switzerland.

An integral part of the medieval English open field system was common grazing in the "waste," the meadows after haying, the arable after harvest, the arable during fallow periods, and the balks within

---

[6] The canton is the provincial or state level of government in Switzerland. See Figure 4.1 for a map of the cantons.

the arable. It complemented grain and other food production in the cultivated fields. Although this is unlike the Swiss commons, which integrates into a grazing-dependent economy, the two systems bear many resemblances, as well as provide interesting contrasts.

What's in Store

To begin the investigation, it is helpful to understand the open access resource model that inspires the conclusion that a tragedy results from open access. Knowing precisely the conditions that encourage the tragedy will help us see how common property is different. Chapter 2 reviews several models of open access using graphic and game theoretic approaches and thereby makes the assumptions and results clear. In Chapter 3, I clarify how common property is different and why the term "common property" can be taken to mean something different from open access. The chapter draws mainly on the institutional economics tradition in explicating a theory of common property. In Chapter 4, I describe the working common property system found in the Swiss grazing commons: how it limits entry, what its management tools are, and how decisions are made. Chapter 5 draws the medieval English open field system into the discussion, describing it and contrasting it with the Swiss grazing commons in order to help those more familiar with the English system. Chapter 6 turns to an empirical comparison of the performance of common property with that of private property. This inquiry compares the productivity of the Swiss private and commons grazing areas statistically. Chapter 7 contains conclusions and extensions to other natural resources, drawing on the theoretical chapters of the early part of the book, the descriptive work on the Swiss commons, and the empirical comparison to private property.

CHAPTER 2

Open Access Theory

The economics literature is rife with theory on natural resource use under open access and its results.[1] I will not review this literature exhaustively but rather will present three models that encapsulate the results. Once grounded in the effects of open access, we can proceed to examine how common property is different. The open access models that I wish to review are two graphic open access fisheries models, one of which draws on work by Anderson (1977), and two game theoretic approaches. To corroborate the results of the graphic models, the appendix to this chapter presents a mathematical interpretation by Dasgupta and Heal (1979).

Before we forge into these theories, I define an open access resource and overuse of a resource more precisely. Both of these concepts have different meanings to different scholars, and a common basis will be helpful for the work that follows.

Definition of Open Access

An open access resource is a depletable, fugitive resource characterized by rivalry in exploitation; it is subject to use by any person who has the capability and desire to enter into harvest or extraction of it; and its extraction results in symmetric or asymmetric negative externalities.

The rivalry in production of an open access resource indicates that one agent's extraction of the resource precludes another agent's possession. If one agent catches a fish, another cannot possess the same fish. For some ubiquitous open access resources, such as the air, the relevance of this rivalry in use does not set in until rates of use are

---

[1] A little-known article by Warming ([1911] 1981) is perhaps the earliest more or less accurate description of the open access problem. The modern development of the theory is generally recognized as beginning with Gordon in his 1954 article on fisheries economics. Anderson (1977: chaps. 2 and 3) provides perhaps the most complete description of the static fisheries model. Whereas most of the models have couched exploitation levels in terms of inputs, Haveman (1973) has modeled open access in terms of outputs. See note 3 to this chapter for further references.

high. In the range of use that is of economic concern, however, the resource is scarce and competition between users occurs. Rivalry in extraction indicates that the open access resource is not a pure public good at all potential use rates.

The depletability of an open access resource reflects not only that there is rivalry in exploitation but also that some use rate exists that reduces resource supply to zero. This is true both of strictly exhaustible resources, such as oil and minerals, and of renewable resources, such as fish and trees. Simple physical or economic exhaustion can reduce the former's supply to zero, and sufficiently high use rates can exterminate the latter's capability to reproduce (Ciriacy-Wantrup 1952: 38–40, 256–57; Dasgupta and Heal 1979: 3–4).

The fugitive nature of an open access resource means that it must be "reduced to ownership by capture" (Ciriacy-Wantrup 1952: 141–42). There are no enforceable property rights over the *in situ* resource, as I discuss further in Chapter 3. Hence, as the definition indicates, anyone with the skills, the capital to invest in extraction equipment, and the desire may enter into resource harvest.

The meaning of symmetric versus asymmetric negative externalities also deserves clarification, because this distinction divides open access resources into two groups. The symmetric externality is present in an open access resource in which each entrant to resource use imparts a negative externality to all other producers, but similarly these other producers have negative external effects on the new entrant. The externality is reciprocal or symmetric. Common examples include fisheries, wildlife, open grazing land, groundwater, unregulated wood lots and forests, and common oil and gas pools. The asymmetric externality occurs when production or consumption decisions of economic actors enter the production or utility functions of others while the recipients of the externality do not cause any reciprocal effects. Typically, this situation is labeled simply an externality, and it is illustrated in the classic example of a smoking factory dirtying a nearby laundry's clothes.

The literature on open access resources has concentrated on symmetric externality situations, although the concept of open access can be extended to cover both types of externalities. (Some authors, for example, reason that water pollution, which clearly exemplifies an asymmetric externality, is a problem of firms' having "open access" to a river.) For the purposes of this book, a main one of which is to make a clear distinction between open access and common property, it will be conceptually easier to remain largely confined to symmetric externality situations. This the theory of Chapters 2 and 3 does. Many of the distinctions and comparisons among open access, common property, and private property, however, extend to asymmetric externalities as well.

Definition of Overuse

Because the literature on open access has grown up both within and without economics, the definition of when use of the open access resource becomes excessive has varied. The common, noneconomic definition of overuse is exploitation of the resource beyond carrying capacity, or equivalently, beyond its maximum sustainable yield. We see this use in Hardin's famous article (1968). He talks about an open access grazing area that operates satisfactorily for centuries during which it is used below "carrying capacity." By implication, social and economic problems arise only when use exceeds this level. For many years, however, economists have been trying to substitute another definition for overexploitation. They point out that social policy should be to maximize net economic yield, which in general is not synonymous with maximizing output; that is, it is not the same as utilization at carrying capacity. Economists argue that any level of inputs beyond that which would maximize net return from the resource is overuse.

This is not a major point of contention between economists and noneconomists, because open access resources are often overexploited by either definition. Nevertheless, the level of inputs to resource extraction that causes economic overuse generally differs from the level of inputs that causes physical yield declines. For this work, overuse will mean the former: use that depresses net economic yield below its maximum.

Given these definitions, we turn to two static, graphic fisheries models, the results of which can be generalized to other open access resources.

Graphic Models of Open Access

The two graphic fisheries models that we examine are complementary. The first is an overview at the fishery level, without any view of the dynamics at the level of the firm. The second expands on the results of the first by examining firm-level interactions.

These static fisheries models offer results on equilibria and optima where the goal is to maximize sustainable net economic yield in a single period. Because they are essentially one-period models, they do

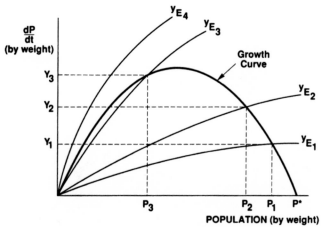

Figure 2.1. Growth Curve of a Typical Fish Population

not weight future net benefits any differently from present net benefits; that is, the discount rate is implicitly zero. Still, for any discount rate less than infinity, dynamic open access models indicate identical conclusions on the relative positions of optimal and open access exploitation levels. Because the static models indicate the correct relative positions of open access and optimal exploitation levels, and because it is sufficient for our purposes to understand the positions of these exploitation levels relative to each other, I confine myself to static open access models.[2]

The General Static Fisheries Model

The static fisheries model was first proposed by Gordon (1954) and refined by Anderson (1977) and others.[3] A graphic treatment of the general model best begins with some simple biology. For many species, the rate of growth of a fish population depends on the standing stock. This relationship is represented in Figure 2.1, where P equals population size by weight and t is time. At low population sizes, population growth dP/dt is low owing to the scarcity of spawners and the low biomass available for growth; at intermediate populations, growth is high owing to large additions to the stock and rapid growth of the

---

[2] The interested reader may refer to Clark (1976) or Anderson (1977) for explications of dynamic open access models.

[3] See, for example, Crutchfield and Zellner (1963: chap. 2); Cheung (1970: sec. 3); Clark (1976: chap. 2); Dasgupta and Heal (1979: 55–63); and Howe (1979: chap. 13). A concise version of the model can be found in Townsend and Wilson (1987).

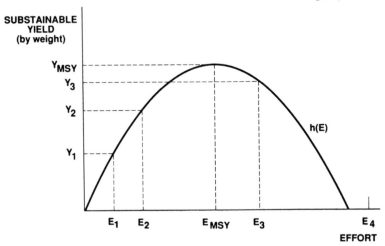

Figure 2.2. The Yield–Effort Function

existing stock; and at high populations, population increase is again slow as environmental constraints become binding. At P^*, the population reaches equilibrium (zero growth), as recruitment (new fish fry) and biomass growth exactly match natural mortality.

Fishing pressure is most often measured by a composite input variable called effort (E); it can be thought of as a fixed-proportion combination of labor, boats, nets, and so forth. At any given level of effort, larger population sizes mean greater catches. In Figure 2.1, fishing yield functions y_E have been drawn to show this relationship. The effort levels in Figure 2.1 are ordered such that $E_1 < E_2 < E_3 < E_4$.

For one of these constant effort catch curves, an equilibrium catch and population pair occurs at the intersection of the growth curve and the catch curve. For effort level E_1, for instance, equilibrium population is P_1 and equilibrium catch is Y_1. This is true because at populations greater than P_1, catch exceeds growth, and population falls; for populations less than P_1, catch is less than growth, and population rises.

As effort increases, that is, as we rotate the y_E curve upward and to the left, two things occur: (1) Equilibrium population decreases monotonically, and (2) catches or "yields" first increase and then decrease. This latter relationship is called the yield–effort function and is graphed in Figure 2.2.

The yield–effort function $h(E)$ of Figure 2.2 indicates that increased effort increases catch up to a point, as just argued. At this point, effort has increased until it is cropping off the maximum growth rate of the

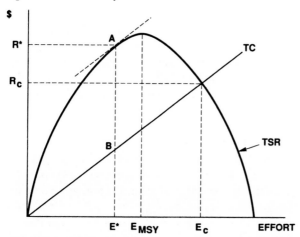

Figure 2.3. Graphic Analysis of an Open Access Fishery

fish, that is, until the maximum sustainable yield (*MSY*) has been reached. If effort is increased further, catch will actually decline because the fish population will be reduced to the point where it grows more slowly.[4] The yield–effort function is an equilibrium concept: The industry settles on $h(E)$ only after a particular level of effort has been maintained for several periods and the growth in the fish population is in equilibrium with natural mortality and human predation.

The model is given economic content in Figure 2.3. Assume that the fishery is one of many such fisheries for the particular species, and that it cannot affect market price no matter how much it supplies. Multiplying total catch by the constant price gives total sustainable revenue (*TSR*). In effect, the yield–effort function in Figure 2.2 is scaled by a factor equal to the price of fish to obtain the total revenue sustainable over time at each level of effort. Thus, as fishing effort increases, catch and revenue increase up to the point E_{MSY}. Further additions to effort cause absolute declines in catch level and total revenue.[5]

---

[4] Crowding effects among the fishermen also eventually have a dampening effect on catch. The primary influence in the downturn of total catch beyond E_{MSY}, however, is the reduced productivity of the resource.

[5] The inverted parabolic shape of the *TSR* function derives from the correspondingly shaped yield–effort function (Figure 2.2). This form of the production function for an open access resource is not essential. Gordon (1954) and Dasgupta and Heal (1979), for instance, use monotonically increasing production functions. The parabolic production function and the functional forms of these other authors, however, all display decreasing rates of resource extraction as effort increases, i.e., $d^2h(E)/dE^2 < 0$, a necessary property for the model (Gordon 1954; Dasgupta and Heal 1979:

Assume that additions to industry effort can be made at constant marginal costs, which implies a linear total cost curve (*TC*), as Figure 2.3 indicates. This does not mean that firms necessarily face constant marginal costs, but we assume it is true for effort added to the industry as a whole. This may mean adding additional identical firms to the industry to increase effort at constant marginal costs. *TC* includes a normal rate of return to capital and labor.

Demonstrating the nonoptimality of open access is now quite easy. The socially optimal level of effort occurs where net revenue is maximized, that is, where the difference between *TSR* and *TC* is greatest. This occurs at *E** in Figure 2.3, where a line tangent to *TSR* is parallel to *TC*, ensuring that *TSR* lies the greatest distance above *TC*. At E^*, however, firms in the industry are earning positive profits, precisely because *TSR* exceeds *TC*. These profits in excess of a normal rate of return will attract the commitment of new inputs to the industry, either by existing firms or by new entrants. The literature is very unclear about the source of excessive inputs to an open access resource, as I discuss in the next section. For the moment, I simply note that additional effort will be expended because of the attractive profit situation in the industry.

As new effort is added, total industry revenues increase, but not in proportion to total industry costs. This can be seen in Figure 2.3, where beyond E^*, *TSR* rises more slowly than *TC*. Nevertheless, additional effort will be supplied as long as positive profits exist. The process stops only when effort has been driven to the point E_c—where total costs and total revenues are equated (*TC* = *TSR*), and no further excess profits can be reaped by additional effort from new or existing fishermen. At this point, the potential rent obtainable from the scarce fishery resource, which reached a maximum at $E = E^*$, has been totally dissipated by the excessive inputs to the industry.

The Firm-Level Graphic Model

To devise appropriate corrective measures, it is important to understand whether expansion of effort comes from new entrants to resource use or from existing users. There is great confusion in the descriptive and graphic literature about the source of excessive inputs

56). The point of resource overexploitation may never be reached at any level of effort if this assumption is not met: If decreasing rates of return to effort do not occur, output can always be increased by adding more inputs, and under constant marginal costs of producing the output, infinite amounts of inputs and outputs would be optimal (Dorfman 1974: 10–11).

in an open access resource. For instance, in his popular model Hardin (1968: 1244) talks of "each herdsman" asking himself:

"What is the utility *to me* of adding one more animal to my herd?" . . .

Adding together the component partial utilities, the rational herdsman concludes that the only sensible course for him to pursue is to add another animal to his herd. And another; and another. . . . But this is the conclusion reached by each and every rational herdsman sharing a commons.

Thus, excessive inputs here come from within the group, even if the group is fixed in size. Similarly, Davidson (1963: 94) in describing the common oil pool problem writes:

If there is more than one producer from a common pool, then adjacent producers are in danger of losing all "their" oil to their neighbors. Hence, it is in the self-interest of each producer to attempt to bring to the surface as much crude oil as quickly as possible, before his neighbor draws off more oil.

Howe (1979: 244–45), whose notation for the socially optimal rate of output is X^*, on the other hand writes:

[Assume] X^* could be induced or enforced. . . . Since price has been equated to the firm's marginal cost, each *existing* firm is maximizing its profit. X^* appears to be a stable competitive equilibrium, except that a pure economic profit is being generated. . . . If the firms constituting the industry at X^* shared among themselves the *exclusive right of access* to the resource, they would, indeed, protect this rent on the early units of production by refusing to expand output and by . . . refusing admission to any more firms. . . . However, the firms that would exist at X^* cannot keep other firms out, simply because of open access to the resource. Other firms, observing the excess profits being made in this particular resource, are attracted to enter the industry, expanding the rate of output beyond X^*.

Howe obviously blames excessive inputs on new entrants and not at all on expansion by existing resource users. This is the same explanation given by Clark (1976: 26), whose notation for the open access level of effort is E_∞:

No level of effort $E < E_\infty$ can be maintained indefinitely, because of the open-access condition: at such an effort level the fishermen would earn a profit, *additional fishermen* would be attracted to the fishery, and effort would increase. (Emphasis added)

Some authors, Gordon (1954) and Turvey (1964) being examples, do not specify at all how superoptimal inputs enter the industry. Others, such as Haveman (1973: 280), vaguely refer to both avenues. Haveman, also using X^* as the socially optimal rate of output, says:

As long as there exists open access to the resource stock, the existence of quasi-rent at X^* will induce entry of additional firms and resources.

In another paragraph (p. 281) he states:

With free and open access to the resource by any and all potential entrants, additional resources are artificially attracted into the activity.

A liberal interpretation of his first quotation indicates that additional inputs come both from entry and from existing firms. The second quotation is less clear. This reflects the general confusion about the source of excessive inputs in much of the literature.

It turns out that the excessive effort can come from either source, depending on certain conditions. If the number of firms is greater than one, but limited, excess inputs will come from existing firms, contrary to Howe's argument. If the number of firms is unlimited, excessive effort will come *only* from new entrants in the long run. A graphic analysis in the remainder of this section and a mathematical treatment in the appendix to this chapter show these conclusions.

The source of excess inputs can be isolated by focusing the discussion at the level of the firm. By precisely specifying firm revenue and cost conditions, and by varying the number of firms, firm effort, and industry effort, we can shed light on firm entry and exit from the industry and the implications for industry optimality. The graphic treatment here is an adaptation from Anderson (1977: chap. 3).

Consider each fishing firm as being a *producer of effort*, where effort is regarded as an intermediate good. Conceptually, the firm applies this intermediate good to the fishery to produce the final output, fish. This construct is useful because a firm can "produce" effort at costs that are independent of total industry effort: The cost of effort depends only on outlays for boats, crew, and so on, which are assumed to have constant prices. In contrast, the costs to the firm of producing a certain amount of fish depend upon the production level of the rest of the industry, because industry marginal and average product curves decline as industry output increases, reflecting the external diseconomies of open access.

Given this construct, we can draw a set of short-run[6] firm cost curves of effort. Anderson (1977) assumes that these cost curves take the U-shape of traditional production theory, and that they are identical for all firms (Figure 2.4a). Implicitly, he assumes that the long-run cost curves *for the firm* take the gentle U-shape of traditional production theory.[7] Figure 2.4a pictures the short-run average vari-

---

[6] The short run is that period during which firms cannot adjust the fixed input component of effort, and new firms cannot enter the fishery.

[7] Anderson does not state this as an assumption, but it is necessary to arrive at a determinant firm size and a determinant number of firms in the industry as discussed shortly. Anderson ignores the fact that beyond his single set of firm short-run cost curves there is a set of long-run cost curves for the firm reflecting that period during

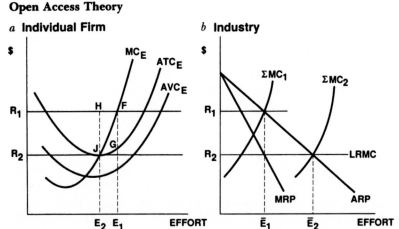

Figure 2.4. Firm-Level Analysis of Entry, Exit, Firm Size, and Firm Number

able cost of effort (AVC_E) and average total cost of effort (ATC_E). All costs include a reasonable rate of return to the factors constituting effort.

The summation of the individual firms' marginal cost of effort curves (MC_E) above the AVC_E curves gives the industry supply schedule for effort in the short run. Figure 2.4*b* gives two possible industry supply schedules, which correspond to different numbers of firms: ΣMC_1 and ΣMC_2. Figure 2.4*b* also shows the industry average revenue product (ARP) curve that is associated with the total sustainable revenue curve in Figure 2.3. ARP is linear because the TSR curve is assumed to be quadratic (i.e., it forms an inverted parabola). The industry ARP, which each firm faces, is similar to a demand curve from price theory, because the industry ARP determines the individual firm's unit return on effort. Therefore, short-run equilibrium effort and unit return on effort will settle at the intersection of the industry supply and the industry ARP curves.

We turn now to the dynamics of open access equilibrium. First

which fixed inputs are also adjustable. The long-run ATC_E curve is the well-known envelope of all short-run ATC_E curves. Anderson's omission is excusable, for it would make the graphic analysis unnecessarily complicated to consider the changes in firms' sizes as they obtained optimal scale (minimized short-run ATC_E) in response to each change in industry effort and consequent changes in total, average, and marginal revenues. Although it is a shortcut, it simplifies matters greatly to consider the short-run cost curves of Figure 2.4*a* to be those at the minimum of the long-run ATC_E curve. This means that right from the beginning and throughout the analysis the fishing firm has the optimal scale of fixed inputs; that is, it has the size of a firm found at eventual industry equilibrium.

imagine that ΣMC_1 is the industry supply curve of effort. Total industry effort will be $\bar{E}_1$ and return on effort will equal R_1. Figure 2.4a indicates that each individual fisherman, equating MC_E with R_1, supplies E_1 units of effort and earns profit FG. In the long run, this profit will attract new entrants to the fishery and push the industry supply curve of effort to the right. As effort increases, the fish population declines and ARP will decrease. Individual firms, equating MC_E to ARP, will move back down their MC_E curves, *contracting* their individual contributions to effort. Thus, while the number of firms increases, effort per firm decreases. In the industry as a whole, however, the former outweighs the latter, since total industry effort expands. Entry will continue as long as supernormal profits exist. Therefore, the process stops only when the industry supply schedule in Figure 2.4b has been pushed to ΣMC_2, the industry applies $\bar{E}_2$ units of effort, and ARP has been depressed to R_2. Individual firm effort in Figure 2.4a will have contracted to E_2, and no abnormal profits will be earned ($ARP = ATC_E$). At this point, firms are smaller (expending less effort), and total industry effort is greater. A determinant number of firms exists in the industry, and each has a determinant size, as measured by effort expended. They are also operating at their most efficient levels, at the minimums of their ATC_E curves.

Using Figure 2.4, we can also investigate the optimal level of effort for the firm and for the industry. Figure 2.4b shows long-run marginal cost ($LRMC$) as horizontal, because additions to industry effort may be achieved at constant marginal costs by adding firms to the industry. The optimal industry output occurs where marginal revenue product equals marginal input cost. This occurs at $\bar{E}_1$ in Figure 2.4b. Again, open access equilibrium effort $\bar{E}_2$ exceeds optimal effort $\bar{E}_1$.

The number of firms must be reduced to curtail effort from $\bar{E}_2$ to $\bar{E}_1$. This is because at the open access equilibrium $\bar{E}_2$, firms produce at their most efficient points, the minimum of their ATC_E curves, as shown above. To produce the optimal $\bar{E}_1$ units of effort, with each firm producing at its most efficient rate E_2, the number of firms must be reduced. If this reduction can be achieved, each firm will receive rent HJ per unit of effort.

Limiting entry to the correct number of firms, however, is not sufficient. The final step to ensure optimality is also to limit the effort expended by each firm to its optimal rate E_2. This is necessary, because the firms are no longer in equilibrium by supplying E_2 units of effort each. Cutting industry effort to $\bar{E}_1$ increases the standing fish population and raises ARP to R_1. As a result, unit return on effort R_1 exceeds MC_E by HJ. There is an incentive for each existing firm to expand effort, moving up the MC_E curve in Figure 2.4a, until MC_E equals ARP, at which point each would still be enjoying positive rent FG. But if the firms are allowed to do this, not only would they no longer be producing at the minimums of their ATC_E curves, but they would expand the industry supply of effort beyond ΣMC_1 (but to a level less than ΣMC_2). Industry effort would exceed the optimal $\bar{E}_1$ (but be less than the open access $\bar{E}_2$). Of course, ARP would fall and the firms would readjust effort yet again. So the process would continue in successively smaller adjustments of individual firm effort and industry ARP until an equilibrium was reached. In this equilibrium, however, firm and industry amounts of effort would exceed the optimal amounts. Positive rents would still accrue to each firm, but these rents would not be at their maximums. Thus, limiting the number of firms is not sufficient for ensuring optimal amounts of inputs. The amount of inputs per firm must also be restricted.

In summary, I have shown four results that will be helpful in comparing open access with common property, results that the mathematical treatment in the chapter appendix corroborates.

The first is the complete dissipation of rent at open access equilibrium.

Second, the externality that firms impose on one another under open access leads individual firms to *contract* their effort as industry effort expands. The source of excessive effort under complete open access—when both inputs and number of firms are unlimited—becomes clear: It comes from entry of new firms.

Third, if the number of firms is limited to less than the number reached at open access equilibrium, positive rent will accrue, *even without restricting input from these firms*. However, firm and total industry inputs will not be optimal; rather they will expand to some point between the optimal and the open access amounts. Nor will resource rent be at its maximum. Thus, "limited user open access," where the number of firms is restricted but their input levels are not, also leads to nonoptimality. The nonoptimality is simply not as severe as under complete open access.

Finally, it is therefore necessary to limit not only the number of firms but also their input levels, if the socially optimal amount of effort and the rent associated with it are to be realized. The incentive always exists, however, to expand beyond these limits. Because of the rent available, excluded firms want to enter and existing firms strain against restrictions under an incentive to expand inputs.

Game Theoretic Models of Open Access

Open access also can be presented in game theoretic terms, and expressing it in this structure leads to new insights. Commonly, open access has been represented by the "prisoner's dilemma" game, a version of which I reproduce here so that all readers have a common basis for the discussion in this book. However, I will also discuss an alternative, two-person, nonzero-sum game that gives some different results and additional understanding of the open access problem.

The prisoner's dilemma can be shown to represent open access[8] if we imagine two cattle owners who use a grazing area that is at its maximum economic yield. Each grazier has the choice of either adding a head of cattle or not adding a head, and the graziers may not collaborate. Assume that the marginal revenue product for the grazing area is −$2 per animal, and that this is composed of −$6 in reduced output from other animals in both graziers' herds and +$4 in value from the animal added.[9] Assume identical players and individual herds, so that the loss in value of outputs from existing animals from adding a head divides equally between graziers (i.e., −$3 each). For simplicity, assume these values are constant for the first two animals grazed beyond the optimum.[10]

Given these assumptions, Figure 2.5 gives payoffs for the game. If both Herdsman 1 and Herdsman 2 decide not to add an animal (the lower right-hand box in the game) there will be no loss to either one; both payoffs are zero. If Herdsman 1 adds, but Herdsman 2 does not,

---

[8] The assumption of a constant number of herdsmen (i.e., two) confines this model to the situation of limited user open access, i.e., a limited number of firms but open access toward inputs. This is also true of the second game in this section, in which the number of herdsmen is greater than two, but constant.

[9] Assume that the marginal revenue product to the grazing area (− $2) and the value of the additional animal (+ $4) are net of costs of providing the animal, e.g., purchase price, supplementary feed costs, veterinary costs, etc.

[10] These assumptions are arbitrary, but they meet a set of conditions that make the open access herding example a prisoner's dilemma. These conditions are

$$c_i < b_i < 0 < a_i \text{ and } a_i + c_i < 0,$$

where c_i = the loss to each individual's existing herd (or one-half the total loss to both individuals' existing herds) from adding an animal (this equals − $3 in the example); b_i = the marginal revenue product of an additional animal to the grazing area, composed of both a negative component of reduced existing herd output and a positive component of the additional animal's output (− $2 in the example); a_i = the *net* private gain from adding an animal when the other individual does not add an animal, also composed of a negative and a positive component (+ $1 in the example; see text); and i = 1, 2 for Herdsman 1 and Herdsman 2. The last condition, $a_i + c_i < 0$, must be met, because if it is not, the net private gain from adding an animal a_i exceeds the loss to the other individual's herd c_i when only one individual adds animals. This would indicate that fewer animals stock the grazing area than are economically optimal at the beginning of the game.

		HERDSMAN 2	
		ADDS	DOES NOT ADD
HERDSMAN 1	ADDS	(-2,-2)	(1,-3)
	DOES NOT ADD	(-3,1)	(0,0)

Figure 2.5. The Open Access Problem as a Prisoner's Dilemma

the former will gain the value of the additional animal less the costs he imposes on the rest of his own herd ($4 − $3 = $1). Herdsman 1 enjoys a net gain, which is necessary, for otherwise he would not make this move in the absence of Herdsman 2's adding an animal. Herdsman 2's loss is greater here than in any other scenario, because he has not added an animal to offset costs imposed on him ($0 − $3 = −$3). This is the upper right-hand box in the game. Reverse payoffs occur if Herdsman 2 adds a head while Herdsman 1 does not (the lower left-hand box); Herdsman 1 incurs his greatest loss while Herdsman 2 faces his sole chance for gain. Finally, if both add a head of cattle, losses to each are moderate because they are offset by the value each herdsman gains from the additional animal he grazes ($4 − $6 = −$2), but the total loss to the grazing area is greatest.

Playing the game without collusion results in both herdsmen's choosing to add a head of cattle, even though it causes losses to both of them and their mutual restraint would have resulted in losses to neither. Consider the problem from Herdsman 1's standpoint. If Herdsman 2 adds a head (first column), Herdsman 1 finds that he minimizes losses by adding a head: In absolute value terms −$2 is less than −$3. Considering his possibilities if Herdsman 2 does not add a head (second column), Herdsman 1 still decides to add a head, since +$1 > $0. That is, he stands to gain rather than standing pat with no loss. Thus, Herdsman 1's dominant strategy—the strategy he pursues no matter what Herdsman 2 chooses—is to add a head. Since the game is symmetric, Herdsman 2 will make the same choice. Both add a head and the tragedy of open access occurs. Moreover, after each has added a head, if the private gains and losses from adding a head of cattle shift only slightly from those assumed here, the herdsmen will add more cattle in future plays of the game. This will continue until private gains and losses shift enough to reach an open access equilibrium as described in the graphic model.

This game theoretic explanation of open access is simple and well known, and I give it mainly to introduce a more realistic version of the game that gives some new insight into open access and common property. In this alternative game, which I have adapted from Muhsam ([1973] 1977), the number of herdsmen is expanded to $h > 2$, but it still is played as a two-person game. Herdsman 1, now called "our individual herdsman," plays against a collective second player, "all other herdsmen."

Assume that each of the h herdsmen has an average-sized herd of n cattle when the grazing area is optimally stocked. Define also $N = nh$ to be the total number of animals on the grazing area at the economic optimum, and let the net economic value of each animal be 1 at this point. In accordance with the discussion of the economic and physical yield optimums in the section on resource overuse earlier in this chapter, I define these quantities and values at the input level (number of cattle)[11] where the net economic yield is at a maximum. Moreover, the value that each of the animals has at this point (i.e., unity) is defined as a *net* value so that the summation over all animals gives the maximum total *net* value of the herd (i.e., N), by definition the economic optimum. In this way, costs are subsumed into the model.

Let us assume that the percentage decrease in the net value of each head of cattle as a result of adding a head of cattle beyond the grazing optimum is a. Also suppose that this percentage remains constant no matter how many head are added beyond the optimum. Although unrealistic, this is a conservative assumption because the decrement in value[12] per head likely would increase as more cattle are added. If the failure of open access can be shown with a constant percentage, it would also occur under the more realistic assumption of progressively worsening overexploitation costs.

As a preliminary step in viewing the game, it is useful to derive a condition that indicates when overgrazing has occurred. I call this condition the overgrazing constraint. If x extra head are added beyond the grazing optimum, assuming a is constant, the value of each head will be $1 - ax$. The total number of cattle will be $N + x$, and the total value of the herd

---

[11] To make the parallels clear between a fishery and a grazing area, consider what elements in each example are the inputs, the resource base, and the outputs. In a fishery, the inputs (effort) are boats, nets, labor, etc.; the resource is the fishing grounds or, some would say, the fish themselves; and the output consists of the fish. In the grazing example, the inputs are cattle (capital applied), labor, fencing, etc.; the resource is the grass; and the output is milk, meat, wool, hides, etc., depending on the product used from the animals. Thus, I consider the cattle as *inputs*, not outputs.

[12] Here, as often below, I simply substitute "value" for "net value," but the reader should understand that I always mean "net value."

$(N + x)(1 - ax).$ (2.1)

By definition, overgrazing occurs if the addition of an extra head decreases the total net value of the herd found in expression (2.1). Also by definition, this occurs when x increases from $x = 0$ to $x - 1$. Therefore, the value of expression (2.1) must be lower when $x = 1$ than when $x = 0$:

$(N + 1)(1 - a) < N.$ (2.2)

Condition (2.2) can be rewritten as

$$a > \frac{1}{N + 1}.$$ (2.3)

Condition (2.3), a definitional constraint on the value of a, can be called the overgrazing constraint. To interpret (2.3), substitute the approximately equal condition

$$a > \frac{1}{N},$$ (2.4)

for if (2.4) holds, then (2.3) also holds. Condition (2.4) (and by approximation the overgrazing constraint) says that if the percentage drop in value of each head of cattle exceeds the percentage of total *herd* value that one head of cattle represents ($1/N$), then overgrazing has occurred. When this condition is met, as it is at or beyond the optimum, the addition of one animal adds less to total herd value than the sum of the losses in value incurred by all other animals in the herd.

With these definitions, we can construct the open access model as another two-person, nonzero-sum game. Again, the game is played between "our individual herdsman" and the collective of "all other herdsmen." Our individual herdsman decides between adding another head of cattle and not adding another head, while all other herdsmen decide between adding $h - 1$ head and zero head of cattle. In reality, all other herdsmen could pursue a variety of strategies, ranging from adding zero to adding $h - 1$ head of cattle, but the results are insensitive to all these possible strategies, as will be proved below (see note 14).

The payoff matrix for our individual herdsman is shown in Figure 2.6. Each element is found by comparing the value of our individual herdsman's herd before and after the other players have decided to add or not to add animals. For example, the upper left-hand element is found first by taking the size of the individual herdsman's herd after he has added an animal; this is $n + 1$ if he started with an

ALL OTHER HERDSMEN

		ADD	DO NOT ADD
OUR INDIVIDUAL HERDSMAN	**ADDS**	$1 - a(N + h)$	$1 - a(n + 1)$
	DOES NOT ADD	$- a(N - n)$	0

Figure 2.6. Muhsam's Game for Our Individual Herdsman

average-sized herd. We multiply by the value of an animal after all have added a head of cattle, namely by $(1 - ah)$. Thus, our individual herdsman's herd has value $(n + 1)(1 - ah)$. The herd's initial value was n. Therefore, our individual herdsman's payoff is $(n + 1)(1 - ah) - n = 1 - a(N + h)$. The other elements are found analogously.

Now compare the choices available to our individual herdsman. If all other herdsmen do not add an animal, the possible payoffs to our individual herdsman are found in the right-hand column. He will add an animal if $1 - a(n + 1) > 0$, that is, if

$$a < \frac{1}{n + 1}. \tag{2.5}$$

Roughly speaking, condition (2.5) indicates that our individual herdsman will add an animal if the percentage decrease in value of each of his animals is less than the value of the additional animal divided up over his $n + 1$ animals. Under these conditions the additional animal will at least cover all of the losses in value of his other animals.[13] We may assume, at least over some range of values of N, that these conditions hold. Condition (2.5) becomes another restriction on the value of a for the model to represent the open access problem.

If all other herdsmen add an animal, the payoffs to our individual herdsman are contained in the left-hand column of Figure 2.6. The herdsman will add an animal if $1 - a(N + h) > - a(N - n)$, which can be rewritten as

$$a < \frac{1}{n + h}. \tag{2.6}$$

This condition is even more restrictive on the value of a than (2.5), since

---

[13] This is only a rough interpretation because the numerator of $1/(n + 1)$ only approximates the value of an animal. At herd size $N + 1$, an animal has value $1 - a$, not a value of 1.

$$a < \frac{1}{n + h} < \frac{1}{n + 1}.$$

Therefore, if we assume that (2.6) holds, by implication (2.5) also holds. Unfortunately, there is no good economic interpretation of (2.6) that I can see. However, putting (2.3) and (2.6) together yields the restrictions on the value of a necessary for the model to work for our individual herdsman:

$$\frac{1}{N + 1} < a < \frac{1}{n + h}. \tag{2.7}$$

To sum up, if (2.6) holds, which means (2.5) also holds, then our individual herdsman *always* decides to add an animal, independent of the decision made by all other herdsmen.[14] He will add a head of cattle if the others do not, because he stands to profit by doing so: The upper right-hand cell in Figure 2.6 is greater than zero under our assumptions. He will also add an animal if the others do so, because he will minimize losses: The upper left-hand cell is less negative than the lower left-hand cell in Figure 2.6, under our assumptions. Our individual herdsman's strategy of adding a head of cattle dominates the strategy of not adding a head. This is the "strict dominance of individual strategies" also found in the prisoner's dilemma.

It hardly needs pointing out that, assuming all herdsmen make the same rational decision, all will add a head of cattle. This naturally means that the range will be overgrazed, because there will be $N + h$ head on a range that was at economic carrying capacity with only N head. Again, as in the prisoner's dilemma, it is entirely possible that at $N + h$ head on the range, the values of the model parameters—in particular, the value of a in relation to the other parameters in (2.7)—will be such that the independent decisions by all herdsmen will be again to add more animals.

So far, this two-person, nonzero-sum game has yielded results identical to those of the prisoner's dilemma. Results diverge, however, when we consider the decision of all other herdsmen. Not only is it to our individual herdsman's advantage if all other herdsmen do not add a head of cattle—because then he can make a profit by adding to

---

[14] In fact, we now can see the analytical equivalence of assuming that all other herdsmen have only two choices, adding no head or adding $h - 1$ head of cattle, with them having the variety of choices of adding between 0 and $h - 1$ head. Since our individual herdsman finds it to his advantage to add a head of cattle whether the others add 0 or $h - 1$ head, he will find it advantageous if they add any number between 0 and $h - 1$. Therefore, we needed only to consider the two extreme choices available to all other herdsmen.

his own herd—but it is to the advantage of all other herdsmen (as a collective) if they do *not* add. This can be seen by examining the payoff matrix for the second player, all other herdsmen, in Figure 2.7. Elements in this figure are derived in the same fashion as those in Figure 2.6. For instance, for the upper left-hand element, the initial value of the herd of all other herdsmen is subtracted from the value of their (larger) herd after all h herdsmen have added an animal:

$$(n + 1)(h - 1)(1 - ah) - n(h - 1) = (h - 1)[1 - a(N + h)].$$

Now look line by line at the choices of all other herdsmen. If our individual herdsman does not add a head of cattle (bottom line), all other herdsmen incur a loss if they each add a head of cattle, whereas they suffer no loss if they refrain from increasing their herds. They incur a loss by adding a head, because for most values of the model parameters, $(h - 1)[1 - a(h - 1)(n + 1)] < 0$, which is equivalent to

$$\frac{1}{(h - 1)(n + 1)} < a. \tag{2.8}$$

Condition (2.8) holds for most values of the model parameters, because $(h - 1) \cong h$ and $(n + 1) \cong n$, making (2.8) approximately the same as condition (2.4), $1/N < a$, which in turn approximates the overgrazing constraint (2.3), as argued above. Strictly speaking, (2.8) must be added as a new restriction on the value of a, because $1/[(h - 1)(n + 1)]$ may be greater than, less than, or equal to $1/(nh + 1)$, the previous lower bound on a required by conditions (2.3) and (2.7).

On the other hand, if our individual herdsman does add an extra animal (top line), all other herdsmen minimize their losses by each choosing *not* to add another head of cattle. This is true because, in general,

$$(h - 1)[1 - a(N + h)] < -a(N - n). \tag{2.9}$$

Condition (2.9) is generally true, because (2.8) was true for most values of the model parameters. Condition (2.9) is equivalent to

$$\frac{1}{(h - 1)(n + 1) + 1} < a,$$

which is certainly true, if (2.8) holds, because

$$\frac{1}{(h - 1)(n + 1) + 1} < \frac{1}{(h - 1)(n + 1)} < a.$$

Thus, given the assumptions in (2.7) and (2.8), all other herdsmen pick the optimal strategy by *not* adding to their herd, no matter what our individual herdsman does.

ALL OTHER HERDSMEN

	ADD	DO NOT ADD
ADDS	$(h - 1)[1 - a(N + h)]$	$- a(N - n)$
DOES NOT ADD	$(h - 1)[1 - a(h - 1)(n + 1)]$	0

(row header for the left of the table: **OUR INDIVIDUAL HERDSMAN**)

Figure 2.7. Muhsam's Game for All Other Herdsmen

The situation, then, is paradoxical. It is in the best interest of our individual herdsman to convince all other herdsmen not to add an animal, because he then avoids losses and could even make a profit. Further, it is in the best interest of all other herdsmen as a group to be convinced of precisely that—not to add any animals.[15] Ironically, it is then in the best interest of our individual herdsman to add an animal. Because any herdsman can be considered our individual herdsman, there is a constant incentive for any individual to disregard any pact made by all herdsmen not to add animals beyond the optimal use rate of the resource.

This reemphasizes the essential nature of the open access problem. Agents are better off with an agreement to limit entry than with no agreement, yet under any agreement, there exists a constant incentive for individuals to break it. This result comes from the strict dominance of individual strategies and lack of assurance in collusive agreements. Still, group solutions do exist for the problem, a matter that we will take up in Chapter 3. As we will see, both enforcement and assurance in collusive agreements can play important roles in providing better outcomes.

Underinvestment in Common Improvements

Besides overinvestment in the private inputs necessary to extract the resource and dissipation of the economic rent attributable to the resource, several other effects have been ascribed to open access for

---

[15] These circumstances indicate that this two-person, nonzero-sum game is not a prisoner's dilemma, because both players do not have the same dominant strategy. The reason is that the two players do not have symmetric payoff matrices, as they do in the prisoner's dilemma. Because the second player is a collective of many individuals who impose costs on one another, they end up worse off as a group if they decide to add animals than if they refrain. Only in the limiting case where $h = 2$ does the game collapse to a true prisoner's dilemma, as can be shown by substituting $h = 2$ into Figure 2.7.

which no rigorous models, but rather intuitive arguments, have been given. One of these is particularly relevant to empirical work discussed in this book.[16]

The notion is that investment in common improvements to the resource will be lacking. Several rationales can be given for this idea, and I discuss them more completely in subsequent paragraphs. The simplest reason, however, is that no user in an open access situation can be assured of reaping the benefits of improvements to the resource before others do so. If a herdsman fertilizes an open access grazing area, there is nothing to prevent other herdsmen's animals from consuming much of the increase in grass. As a consequence, there is insufficient motivation to invest in the improvement.

The lack of incentive to invest in the resource results from a divergence between the party who incurs costs and those who reap benefits. The idea that inadequate resource use results has a long history. It goes back, in fact, to Adam Smith himself, although not as part of a discussion of open access. Smith ([1786] 1880: bk. 3, chap. 2), and other classical economists after him (Say [1821] 1964: bk. 2, chap. 9; Mill 1878: bk. 2, chap. 8), discussed the economic acceptability of share tenancy, the land tenure system in which a tenant paid land rent by delivering a set proportion of the gross product to the landowner.[17] Typically, rent was 50 percent of the produce. The classical economists decried the lack of incentive under this system, because it reduced the fruits of the tenant's labor by half. This reduced not only the incentive to labor but also the inducement to invest in the land. Half of any increase in yield that a farmer's investment might coax from the land would be shared with the landlord, and the dampening effect on tenant investment was obvious. The same effect also would discourage the landlord from any investment that he contemplated, for he too would give up half the investment's benefit—in his case to the tenant. The parallel to open access is clear: Benefits resulting from improvements that one party makes may accrue to another; consequently, the improvements probably will not be made.

Both nineteenth- and twentieth-century economists also attacked

---

[16] Other effects of open access not described here have also been discussed by Bottomley (1963), Cheung (1970), and Anderson (1977: 173–74). They include the ideas that inputs and outputs may be different under open access than under a system of coordinated management; rent on the land may decline because the input–output mix is suboptimal even before entry dissipates rents; the misallocation of inputs and outputs may have side effects on adjoining resources managed under private or cooperative means; and technological innovations will be introduced too quickly under open access.

[17] Some of the classical economists used the French term for share tenants, *metayers*.

other types of rental tenure (e.g., fixed rent) for providing insufficient incentive to improvement (Sidgwick 1883: bk. 2, chap. 7; Ely
1914: pt. 1, chap. 13; Pigou 1932: pt. 2, chap. 9). A lack of investment
incentive exists, they argued, whenever there is no arrangement between the tenant and the landlord to compensate the tenant for improvements at termination of the contract (and the contract duration
is insufficient to allow recovery of investment costs).

Although the classical and early neoclassical economists spoke regularly of tenancy problems, they referred less frequently to the problem of underinvestment in common improvements to open access
resources. The idea nevertheless emerged as early as the beginning of
the nineteenth century:

Capital and industry [i.e., labor] will be expended upon [land] in vain, if all
are equally privileged to make use of it; and no one will be fool enough to
make the outlay, unless assured of reaping the benefit. (Say [1821] 1964: bk.
2, chap. 9)

Natural agents, like land, would not yield nearly so much if they were
not subject to appropriation and if the proprietors were not assured
of exclusive benefits from them (Say [1821] 1964: bk. 1, chap. 5). The
certainty of enjoying the undivided benefit of one's land, labor, and
capital, and of one's skill and economy, was cited as one of the surest
inducements to promote productivity and "accumulation" (Say [1821]
1964: bk. 1, chap. 14; Mill 1878: bk. 1, chap. 13). Indeed, even a
person excluded from the use of others' goods is better off living in a
system of appropriation than if the system did not exist at all, because
that person abides in a community that has benefited from the inducements to labor and accumulation of capital that result from exclusive property (Sidgwick 1883: bk. 3, chap. 6).

The idea of underinvestment in common improvements to jointly
used resources emerges with greater clarity with Ely (1914: pt. 1,
chap. 15). Ely cites the oyster beds in Chesapeake Bay, where the
taking of oysters had long been free to all. Private property or long
individual leases in oyster beds are necessary, he asserts, to avoid the
"principle of the twentieth man." If nineteen well-meaning men
cultivate (i.e., invest in) the oysters, but the twentieth does not, the
latter can invade the beds and destroy all oyster cultivation. Ely calls
for a system that assures reward to the one who puts forth effort and
invests capital.

Until now, I have spoken of underinvestment in common improvements as resulting from only a single phenomenon—lack of assurance
of reaping benefits. Actually, it may result from one of several separate but related circumstances. First, as already explained, an individ-

ual who invests in resource improvements may receive some benefit from the investment but may not be able to capture all benefits. The leakage of benefits to others reduces or destroys the incentive to invest. Viewed in a slightly different light, this is a typical positive externality. One may fertilize the land for oneself, but in doing so one generates fertilization externalities for others. It is well known that, from the standpoint of social optimality, private agents underinvest in activities that generate positive externalities.

The second set of circumstances is closely akin but not completely equivalent to the first. Some larger resource improvement projects may exist that would have net benefits to all users in the group, but their benefits to a single individual do not exceed total costs. This may occur if there is lumpiness or a public goods nature in the investment. Examples might be a large barn or watering troughs on a grazing area. Because private costs exceed private benefits, no single individual would be willing to provide improvements at personal expense, even though the project is economic for the group as a whole. Both this case and the previous instance, in which benefits are fugitive, represent circumstances in which the private cost of the investment exceeds the private return. The individual will be unwilling to contribute to the investment unless some arrangement is devised by which all share improvement costs (Ostrom 1977; Ostrom and Ostrom 1977).

Viewed in a certain manner, Scott's (1955) article on the economic objectives of fishery management presents yet a third way in which underinvestment occurs in common improvements. Scott emphasized that the economic objective for jointly exploited resources should be not to maximize single-period resource rent but rather to maximize the return from the resource over present and future periods. In order to do this, users must take into account the effect of current resource extraction on future extraction possibilities. The link between present and future is clear when we are talking about a renewable resource such as fish, because the resource reproduces. The connection often also holds for nonrenewable resources, for which present exploitation may increase future extraction costs. In addition, in both cases, discounting links the present with the future. Therefore, for both physical and financial reasons, users should consider the balance between extraction and conservation of the resource. In an open access situation, however, the competition for the resource causes users to ignore the so-called user cost, the present value of forgone future extraction benefits or increased future extraction costs caused by current resource exploitation. This is equivalent to saying that they ignore the potential returns from investing in (i.e., conserving) the resource. In yet another way, underinvestment in the jointly exploited resource occurs.

Thus, we have a long history of argument and a number of reasons for suspecting underinvestment in common improvements to open access resources. This, in addition to overexploitation of the resource, is a primary problem that any system of joint resource management must address.

Summary

To this point, I have described one-half of the open access–common property dichotomy, having defined open access and explained its consequences in theoretical detail. Open access resources have been defined as depletable, fugitive resources that are open to extraction by anyone, whose extraction is rival, and whose exploitation leads to negative externalities for other users of the resource. Although the externalities may be either symmetric or asymmetric, most of the literature on open access concentrates on resource use exhibiting symmetric externalities.

The theory that we have reviewed has indicated the undeniable conclusions of superfluous input levels and resource overuse under open access. We further have been able to pinpoint the source of excessive inputs, namely, existing firms in the short run and in limited user open access situations, and entering firms in the long run in complete open access situations. Therefore, limits on both the number of firms and their individual input levels are necessary to attain socially optimal resource rents. As a corollary, there is always an incentive to increase one's input level beyond the limits, even though this leads to declines in overall group welfare.

Open access also leads to underinvestment in common improvements to the resource base, which could increase the benefits to all who extract the resource. This underinvestment results from a divergence between those who invest in the improvements and those who reap the benefits, from a mismatch of the scale of some investments and the amount of potential individual benefit, and from a lack of incentive to invest in the resource for future benefits because of a competitive rush for the resource in the present.

This description of open access and its results has given us a strong foundation for understanding common property, to which we turn in Chapter 3.

Appendix: A Mathematical Treatment of Open Access

This appendix presents a mathematical model that corroborates the results of the graphic model of open access resources presented in this chapter. The mathematical model confirms the results on excessive investment and rent dissipation, as well as pinpoints the source of excessive inputs, that is, whether superoptimal inputs come from existing firms competing for the costless resource or from new entrants attracted by excess profits in the industry. The model shows again that (1) superoptimal inputs will come from existing firms if the number of firms is limited below the number that would occur at complete open access equilibrium, and (2) excessive inputs will come from new entrants if access is completely open. In the former case all rent is not dissipated, whereas in the latter it is. In addition, the mathematical model reaches one conclusion that differs from the results of the graphic model, namely, (3) open access equilibrium is reached only as the number of firms goes to infinity and each firm contributes only an infinitesimal amount of effort. This result occurs because of an implicit assumption about constant marginal costs of producing effort at the firm level. This assumption of course differs from Anderson's (1977) assumption of U-shaped cost curves for the firm. The model is an adaptation from Dasgupta and Heal (1979: chap. 3).

We begin by assuming that N firms extract the resource, for example, fish. Although the number of firms is initially fixed, this assumption will be relaxed later. To extract the resource, each of the N firms applies an amount of variable input x_i, $i = 1, \ldots, N$. The x_i can be considered the number of boats introduced by firm i, although the variable input is assumed perfectly divisible. Total inputs[18] to the fishery area

$$X = \sum_{i=1}^{N} x_i.$$

Also assume that total harvest from the fishery Y is a function of X:

$$Y = F(X),$$

where

$F(0) = 0;$
$F'(X) > 0;$
$F''(X) < 0;$
$F(X)$ is bounded above.

---

[18] To preserve Dasgupta and Heal's notation, total inputs to the fishery are noted as X. This replaces the notation E used in the graphic presentation.

These assumptions are not identical to those of the graphic analysis; in particular, $F'(X)$ never turns negative. The crucial assumption, however, is $F''(X) < 0$—diminishing returns on variable inputs (see note 5, this chapter)—and this we find in both presentations. The assumptions imply that average product lies above marginal product:

$$\frac{F(X)}{X} > F'(X) \tag{2.10}$$

and that average product goes to zero:

$$\lim_{X \to \infty} \frac{F(X)}{X} = 0. \tag{2.11}$$

Denote by X_{N-i} the inputs of all other firms besides a single representative firm, such that $x_i + X_{N-i} = X$, and define y_i as the ith firm's catch. We assume that a vessel of the ith firm catches fish at the rate of the average product:

$$y_i = x_i \frac{F(X)}{X} = x_i \frac{F(X_{N-i} + x_i)}{X_{N-i} + x_i}.$$

Suppose the markets for catch and inputs (boats) are perfectly competitive, so that the prices for both are constant at all levels of input and output. Take catch to be the numeraire good and r to equal the rental rate of boats. If all firms are identical and firm i supposes that every other firm will introduce $\hat{x}$ vessels, then firm i will attain its goal of maximizing profits by choosing x_i to maximize

$$y_i - rx_i = \frac{x_i F[(X_{N-i} + x_i)]}{X_{N-i} + x_i} - rx_i = \frac{x_i F[(N-1)\hat{x} + x_i]}{(N-1)\hat{x} + x_i} - rx_i.$$

By differentiating with respect to x_i and setting the result equal to zero, we obtain the condition for profit maximization:

$$\frac{(N-1)\hat{x}F[(N-1)\hat{x} + x_i]}{[(N-1)\hat{x} + x_i]^2} + \frac{x_i F'[(N-1)\hat{x} + x_i]}{(N-1)\hat{x} + x_i} = r. \tag{2.12}$$

Because all firms are identical, they will make the same profit-maximizing decision, and $x_i = \hat{x}$ for all i under open access (unlimited inputs, limited number of firms). If we make this substitution in (2.12), the open access equilibrium number of boats per firm $\hat{x}$ will be the solution to the equation:

$$\frac{F(Nx)}{Nx} - \frac{1}{N}\left[\frac{F(Nx)}{Nx} - F'(Nx)\right] = r. \tag{2.13}$$

In equilibrium, $Nx = X$, so the open access equilibrium number of total vessels in the fishery $\hat{X}$ is the solution to

$$\frac{F(X)}{X} - \frac{1}{N}\left[\frac{F(X)}{X} - F'(X)\right] = r. \tag{2.14}$$

A positive solution value $\hat{X}$ to (2.14) exists if $F'(0) > r$; that is, in Figure 2.3, if the slope of the *TC* curve is less than the slope of *TSR* at zero inputs.

To nail down the nonoptimality of open access, we must derive the condition for the socially optimal amount of inputs and compare it to (2.14). The Pareto efficient amount of inputs per firm is the solution to the maximization with respect to x of total net revenue:

$$\max_{x} \; F\,(Nx) - rNx.$$

Employing the calculus as before, we obtain the optimality condition

$$F'(Nx) = r, \tag{2.15}$$

which alternatively may be written

$$F'(X) = r. \tag{2.16}$$

Denote the solution values to (2.15) and (2.16) as $\bar{x}$ and $\bar{X}$, respectively. Because of the identicalness of firms and the potential for upsetting the optimal solution if rent is divided unequally, $\bar{X}$ will equal $N\bar{x}$. Equations (2.15) and (2.16) are equivalent restatements of the familiar condition for profit maximization that the value of the marginal product must equal the rental rate of the input.

It remains to compare the open access equilibrium condition (2.14) with the efficiency condition (2.16). After substituting its solution value $\hat{X}$ and subtracting $F'(\hat{X})$ from both sides, (2.14) can be transformed to

$$r - F'(\hat{X}) = \frac{N-1}{N}\left[\frac{F(\hat{X})}{\hat{X}} - F'(\hat{X})\right]. \tag{2.17}$$

Using (2.10), we can see that the right-hand side of (2.17) is positive. Therefore,

$$r - F'(\hat{X}) > 0,$$

or equivalently,

$$r > F'(\hat{X}).$$

Recalling the optimality condition (2.16), $r = F'(\bar{X})$, we now have

$$F'(\hat{X}) < F'(\bar{X}).$$

Since we have assumed diminishing marginal rates of extraction, that is, $F''(X) < 0$, $F'(\hat{X})$ can be less than $F'(\bar{X})$ if and only if

$$\hat{X} > \tilde{X},$$

or equivalently,

$$\hat{x} > \tilde{x}.$$

Thus, open access (unrestricted inputs, limited number of firms) leads to an excessive total number of inputs and an excessive number of inputs per firm. These conclusions correspond to those of the graphic analysis.

The mathematics also confirm another conclusion from the graphic model. If access is limited to N firms, where N is less than the open access number of firms, rents will accrue to each firm, even if the amount of inputs remains unrestricted. As we shall see, open access equilibrium occurs in the current model only as N goes to infinity; thus N needs only to be restricted to any number less than infinity for positive rents to accrue. Mathematically, we show this by rearranging (2.14) and using (2.10) to obtain

$$\frac{F(X)}{X} - r = \frac{1}{N}\left[\frac{F(X)}{X} - F'(X)\right] > 0,$$

which implies

$$\frac{F(X)}{X} - r > 0.$$

Average revenue product less unit input cost is strictly positive, indicating positive profits. The result does not depend on N. Thus, even though optimal rents are obtained only by restricting industry inputs to $\tilde{X}$, some rents accrue if only the number of firms is limited.

Finally, we look mathematically at complete open access, where not only input levels but also the number of firms is unrestricted. This means relaxing the assumption that the number of firms is fixed at N. However, because firms will earn positive profits for any $N < \infty$, new entrants theoretically will be attracted to the industry at any level of N. For results on complete open access, therefore, one must examine what happens as N goes to infinity. The main result can be seen if we substitute the equilibrium open access solution $\hat{X}$ into (2.14) and evaluate its left-hand side as N goes to infinity:

$$\lim_{N\to\infty}\left\{\frac{F(\hat{X})}{\hat{X}} - \frac{1}{N}\left[\frac{F(\hat{X})}{\hat{X}} - F'(\hat{X})\right]\right\} = r. \qquad (2.18)$$

One's immediate impulse is to evaluate the left-hand side of (2.18) by treating $\hat{X}$ as a constant. However, $\hat{X}$ changes as N changes. Therefore, we must examine $\hat{X}$ as N goes to infinity first. To do this, define the left-hand side of (2.14) as $G(\hat{X}, N)$:

$$G\,(\hat{X}, N) \equiv \frac{F(\hat{X})}{\hat{X}} - \frac{1}{N}\left[\frac{F(\hat{X})}{\hat{X}} - F'(\hat{X})\right] = r, \tag{2.19}$$

and regard N as continuous. In equilibrium, then, we have[19]

$$\frac{d\hat{X}}{dN} = -\frac{\dfrac{\partial G}{\partial N}}{\dfrac{\partial G}{\partial \hat{X}}}. \tag{2.20}$$

Finding the partial derivatives on the right-hand side shows that[20]

[19] To show (2.20), start with the equilibrium condition (2.19):

$$G(\hat{X}, N) = r. \tag{a}$$

Differentiate totally with respect to N:

$$\frac{dG}{dN} = 0, \tag{b}$$

which is true because r is a constant. Since $\hat{X}$ is a function of N, the general formula for the total derivative is

$$\frac{dG}{dN} = \frac{\partial G}{\partial N} + \frac{\partial G}{\partial \hat{X}}\frac{d\hat{X}}{dN}. \tag{c}$$

Equate (b) and (c):

$$0 = \frac{\partial G}{\partial N} + \frac{\partial G}{\partial \hat{X}}\frac{d\hat{X}}{dN}.$$

Solve for $\dfrac{d\hat{X}}{dN}$:

$$\frac{d\hat{X}}{dN} = -\frac{\dfrac{\partial G}{\partial N}}{\dfrac{\partial G}{\partial \hat{X}}}.$$

[20] To show (2.21), first find the signs of the partial derivatives:

$$\frac{\partial G}{\partial N} = \frac{\dfrac{F(\hat{X})}{\hat{X}} - F'(\hat{X})}{N^2} > 0 \text{ using equation (2.10);}$$

$$\frac{\partial G}{\partial \hat{X}} = \frac{\hat{X}F'(\hat{X}) - F(\hat{X})}{\hat{X}^2} - \frac{1}{N}\left[\frac{\hat{X}F'(\hat{X}) - F(\hat{X})}{\hat{X}^2} - F''(\hat{X})\right]$$

$$= \frac{1}{\hat{X}}\left[F'(\hat{X}) - \frac{F(\hat{X})}{\hat{X}}\right] - \frac{1}{N}\frac{1}{\hat{X}}\left[F'(\hat{X}) - \frac{F(\hat{X})}{\hat{X}}\right] + \frac{1}{N}F''(\hat{X}) < 0,$$

where in the last equation, I have used (2.10) and the assumption $F''(\hat{X}) < 0$. Therefore, using these signs on the partial derivatives,

$$\frac{d\hat{X}}{dN} = -\frac{\dfrac{\partial G}{\partial N}}{\dfrac{\partial G}{\partial \hat{X}}} > 0.$$

$$\frac{d\hat{X}}{dN} > 0. \qquad (2.21)$$

Thus, $\hat{X}$ is monotonically increasing in N. However, it must be bounded from above.[21] We know this because (2.14) holds at equilibrium for *any* N. If $\hat{X}$ were not bounded, then

$$\lim_{\substack{X \to \infty \\ N \to \infty}} G(\hat{X}, N) = \lim_{\substack{X \to \infty \\ N \to \infty}} \left\{ \frac{F(\hat{X})}{\hat{X}} - \frac{1}{N} \left[\frac{F(\hat{X})}{\hat{X}} - F'(\hat{X}) \right] \right\} = 0,$$

where (2.11) helps to evaluate the limit. But a value of zero for this limit violates (2.14), which requires the limit to equal r. Hence $\hat{X}$ must be bounded from above. Since $\hat{X}$ is monotonically increasing in N and yet bounded from above, we conclude that $\hat{X}$ tends to a finite limit as N goes to infinity.

Since $\hat{X}$ has a finite limit, it is acceptable to treat it as a constant equal to its limiting value in (2.18). It is then easy to evaluate (2.18), and we find that as N grows arbitrarily large

$$\frac{F(\hat{X})}{\hat{X}} = r.$$

That is, the average revenue product equals the rental rate of effort; all excess profits (rents) to the resource are dissipated. Furthermore, each firm introduces only an infinitesimal amount of effort at the open access equilibrium; because $\hat{X}$ tends to a finite value, $\hat{x} = (1/N)\hat{X}$ will tend to an infinitesimal quantity as N goes to infinity.

The results of the mathematical model differ from those of the graphic model in one significant way. The mathematical model predicts an infinite number of firms, each expending infinitesimal effort at open access equilibrium; the graphic model indicates a finite number of firms, each expending a finite amount of effort at open access equilibrium. These differences can be explained by divergent assumptions about the cost function for producing effort. The graphic model uses traditional U-shaped cost curves at the firm level, although industry effort enjoys constant returns to scale (constant marginal costs). Such cost curves lead to a definite number of firms producing at the minimums of their average cost curves in equilibrium. The mathematical model, in contrast, incorporates no explicit assumptions about the form of the cost of effort function. The model assumes constant returns to scale in total industry input X and the size of the catchment area S, and that the variable input x_i is perfectly divisible and supplied

---

[21] $\hat{X}$ being bounded from above means that a finite open access equilibrium input level exists.

by a perfectly competitive (constant price) industry. The model's results depend on a "crowding of vessels" (Dasgupta and Heal 1979: 56) or the population dynamics of the fish, as I have argued. Although it is an assumption, we might take all this to mean that firms in the mathematical model enjoy constant returns to scale in producing effort from x_i, even though they face diminishing returns in producing fish when effort is applied to the fishery. Now the presence of constant returns to scale (constant marginal costs) at the firm level leads to the classic indeterminacy problem. The firm has no optimal size nor is there a determinant number of firms in an industry, although industry supply is determinant (Viner 1931; Samuelson 1947: 78–80; Henderson and Quandt 1971: 79–84). Thus, under constant returns to scale, the industry's entire output may be produced efficiently by one, several, many, or, theoretically, an infinite number of firms. Although an assumption of constant returns to scale in effort does not necessitate an infinite number of firms each producing an infinitesimal amount of effort, it is at least consistent with this result.

Despite these differences, both models point to the several identical conclusions mentioned in the body of this chapter: Rent is completely dissipated at open access equilibrium; firms contract their effort as industry effort expands; if the number of firms is limited below open access equilibrium, positive rents accrue—even if inputs are not restricted; and it is necessary to limit both the number of firms and their input levels to attain the socially optimal level of inputs to the jointly used resource.

CHAPTER 3

Common Property

In Chapter 2, I referred to the problem of unrestricted entry and use of a resource as the problem of open access. Frequently, others have labeled such resource use "common property."[1] I contend, however, that "common property" and "open access" should not be used synonymously. They are two separate resource use regimes, and the distinctions between them deserve to be understood. In this chapter, I make explicit the differences between open access and common property.[2]

This chapter has a second major goal. Some authors in discussing open access offer private property as the best or only solution to the problem (Demsetz 1967; Cheung 1970; Ault and Rutman 1979). Private property is indeed one solution to the inefficiencies of open access. Private property is not the only or necessarily the best solution to open access problems, however. Several other ways to correct open access distortions exist, and a subset of them forms the class of common property. This chapter defends the theory that common property, once defined and distinguished from open access, may represent a solution to open access.

Definition of Common Property

I will begin by presenting a formal definition of common property, which is characterized by seven points that constitute a set of necessary and sufficient conditions for common property. The conditions are individually necessary because a resource managed under common property must meet all seven of them. The conditions are jointly

---

[1] The equating of open access with common property is best illustrated by a quotation, of which many similar examples exist. North and Thomas (1977: 234) in their description of hunting and gathering societies state: "The natural resources, whether the animals to be hunted, or vegetation to be gathered, were initially held as common property. This type of property rights implies free access by all to the resource."

[2] I do not claim credit for the distinction between open access and common property. Ciriacy-Wantrup (1971) and Ciriacy-Wantrup and Bishop (1975) made the distinction quite some time ago.

sufficient for common property because all other resource use regimes (in particular, various forms of open access and private property) fail to meet at least one of the conditions.

Let us proceed to the definition. Common property is a form of resource ownership with the following characteristics:

1. The resource unit has bounds that are well defined by physical, biological, and social parameters.
2. There is a well-delineated group of users, who are distinct from persons excluded from resource use.
3. Multiple included users participate in resource extraction.
4. Explicit or implicit well-understood rules exist among users regarding their rights and their duties to one another about resource extraction.
5. Users share joint, nonexclusive entitlement to the *in situ* or fugitive resource prior to its capture or use.
6. Users compete for the resource, and thereby impose negative externalities on one another.
7. A well-delineated group of rights holders exists, which may or may not coincide with the group of users.

Bounded Resource Condition

Point 1 is included because it is necessary in any particular case to know the answer to the question, "What is the resource?" The boundaries of the resource catchment area are sometimes defined by physical or biological parameters, sometimes by social conventions, and sometimes by a combination of these. For example, a fish population is defined by biological characteristics; groundwater and oil pools are circumscribed by physical properties; grazing lands are delimited by the social convention of property lines. An example of physical and social parameters interacting to define the resource is provided by alpine grazing. Sometimes a mountain ridge or the limit of grass growth on a rocky escarpment will provide the property line that humans draw.

The term "common property," it should be emphasized, refers to a social institution, not to a physical or intangible object. The resource is the physical or intangible asset that a group can own and manage by common property. The demarcation of the resource, however, must be included in the definition of the social institution of common property. The institution cannot exist without the resource that it controls.

Well-delineated Group of Users Condition

Point 2 in the definition specifies that there are two groups with a relationship to the resource: included users and excluded persons. The first group consists of an identifiable, countable number of users, the second of a set of persons who do not have the right to use. This of course contrasts to open access, where everyone is a potential user. In limiting cases, such as the atmosphere or the oceans, there eventually may be examples of common property in which there are no excluded users. For such cases, however, all of the other criteria for common property must be established, a feat that has not been accomplished by any example of global common property to date.

Multiple Users Condition

Point 3 indicates that common property is utilized by two or more people. It excludes the degenerate group of one person. The use or control of a resource by a single person is associated primarily with private property.

Well-understood Rules Condition

Point 4 states that rules exist within the included group of users to guide resource extraction. The most important of these rules—important because it helps distinguish common property from open access—is some method to control who may take how much of the resource. Rights to use, however, are not necessarily rights to equal amounts of the resource. Indeed, it is the exceptional case when all users have equal rights to exploit the resource. Other rules may include how rights are transferred, what financial obligation a user has to the group, what work requirement he or she has, and how the rules themselves are changed.

The rules may be formal and explicit or they may be informal and implicitly accepted. In traditional societies, the users themselves may put into place the institutional structure to govern and manage the resource. Such rule structures are often informal and involve implicit understandings, although formal rule structures such as the Swiss grazing commons discussed in Chapter 4 also have evolved in traditional contexts. In an industrialized society setting up a new common property framework, the government may have a hand in implementing rules to govern resource use, where such rules are generally formal, written regulations with legal force.

The rules and conventions of resource extraction under common property always appeal to some authority higher than the individual user or any subset of users. This authority is often explicit, taking the form of a chief, a medieval manor court, a democratic governing body of the commons, a government agency that regulates the commons, and so on. In cases in which the rules of resource extraction are traditional and implicit, however, this authority may be no more (and no less) than the group consciousness and peer pressure.

Joint, Nonexclusive Entitlement Condition

Point 5 inspires two discussions, one about an essential difference between common and private property and the other about the relationship of common property to a public good.

First, let us examine joint, nonexclusive entitlement's implication for the difference between common and private property. Under private property, the *in situ* resource can be said to belong to a particular real or legal person. This person can have secure expectations about possessing particular physical units as well as particular amounts of the resource. Common property resources, however, are fugitive resources. A physical unit of the resource in its *in situ* or fugitive state cannot be associated with a particular user as its owner (Ciriacy-Wantrup 1952: 141–42). Under common property, users may have secure expectations about possessing certain amounts of the resource, but not about possessing particular physical units. The joint, nonexclusive entitlement condition means that participants in a common property arrangement have simultaneous, ex ante (prior to capture) claims on any particular unit of the resource. Therefore, an essential step in the use of common property resources (except those that have a public goods character) is that they be "reduced" to sole ownership through capture. For example, by capturing a fish, a user converts the resource from joint, nonexclusive entitlement to sole ownership.

The distinction between common property and public goods requires a lengthier discussion than is appropriate for understanding joint, nonexclusive entitlement. I will take up this discussion subsequently. For now, two points are relevant. First, some resources that may be managed as common property have a public goods character, such as parks, natural harbors, and so on. They do not exhibit rivalry at low and moderate levels of use. For such resources, reducing the resource to sole ownership through capture does not apply, as it does to resources that exhibit rivalry in extraction. Second, these resources do exhibit joint, nonexclusive entitlement, because all participants who use the resource have an ex ante claim to benefits from the resource, where "ex ante" here means prior to use rather than prior to capture. For these reasons, reduction to sole ownership through capture is not a necessary condition for common property, but joint, nonexclusive entitlement is.

Competitive Users Condition

Embedded in Point 6 are two closely related ideas. The first is simply that the multiple users compete for the resource. This does not mean that they may not cooperate to limit resource extraction (see Point 4) or that they may not cooperate in such ways as making mutual capital investments to assist each other in resource extraction. Rather, Point 6 differentiates common property from a corporation, in which two or more users found an enterprise to exploit a resource by pooling their real and financial assets and skills in order to enjoy a common return. Although some aspects of a common property institution may include pooled ownership, for example, buildings, equipment, and other inputs, some inputs and/or outputs remain in the ownership of the individual participant. The model for common property lies more in a cooperative than in a corporation. Competing users under common property come together to cooperate rather than to become corporate.[3]

The second implication of Point 6 is that one user's extraction of the resource generates negative externalities for other users. In this sense, common property is like open access. The difference lies in the extent to which externalities are generated. As I discuss in the section of this chapter entitled "The Private Property, Common Property, Open Access Trichotomy," the well-delineated group of users and the well-understood rules among them, Points 2 and 4, can control the negative externalities at an appropriate level.

Like those under open access, the externalities under common property may be either reciprocal or nonreciprocal. On the one hand, extractors of the resource may impose negative externalities of like kind upon each other. Such reciprocal externalities occur most often in cases where all users of the common property resource are alike in their reason for exploiting the resource. Typically, they are producers utilizing, for instance, a grazing commons, a fishery, a groundwater

---

[3] A borderline case is the unitized oil pool. Below I include this case as a form of common property, despite exploitation that occurs under unified management. To me, a unitized oil pool is common rather than corporate property, because separate actors with disparate, competing goals *cooperate* to extract the resource.

basin, a common forest, or something similar. On the other hand, common property externalities may be nonreciprocal, as they are between the two essentially different classes of users in such problems as air and water pollution. In the pollution case, one set of users exploits the resource as a sink for pollutants, while the other set of users utilizes the resource for consumption—breathing, drinking, re-creating, and so on. Generally, this situation is viewed as one set of users being the generators and the other the receivers of the exter-nality. The incidence of an externality, however, is entirely dependent on who holds the property rights to the resource. Not only can a smoking factory be considered to be imposing an externality on neigh-boring residents, but neighboring residents can also be considered to be imposing an externality on a factory required to install pollution control devices (Coase 1960). Therefore, the designations "genera-tors" and "recipients" of the externality are in some sense arbitrary, depending entirely on who has property rights to the air. Therefore, users of the resource might be considered all who make some claim on it, and resource systems in which the resource is put to multiple uses could be brought under management schemes in which various types of users become the included group (Point 2 in the definition of common property). The rules they set up for use would constitute the rights and duties of common property.

Unfortunately, expanding common property to include situations of divergent user types and nonreciprocal externalities complicates the analysis considerably. Therefore, as in the analysis of open access in Chapter 2, I will confine myself largely to reciprocal externality situations in discussing common property and contrasting it with open access and private property.

Rights Holders Condition

Point 7 recognizes that the resource users and resource owners are not always coincident. Common property rights holders, for instance, may rent their resource use rights to the actual users. Where rights holders and users diverge, however, the rights holders condition re-quires that the rights holders be a group of people who fulfill the other institutional criteria of common property. Nevertheless, Point 7 is not meant to preclude the situation in which a government entity coordinates or imposes the rules regarding resource extraction on users and rights holders.

Point 7 also differentiates common property from property tenure in which a private owner grants rights to a group to use a resource.

For instance, a private owner does not set up common property in a field when he rents it to a church for its picnic, even if the church as the user group passes all of the other institutional criteria for common property. The contract between the private owner and the group is still the primary arbiter of resource use, not the implicit or explicit rules of the group.

An Excluded Condition: Coequal Rights

Before leaving the definition of common property, I wish to discuss a concept that is related to the definition, but that I have not included in it. Ciriacy-Wantrup and Bishop (1975), pioneers in common property theory, indicate that participants in a common property system have "coequal" rights to use. In practical terms, this means that users share fluctuations in availability of the resource proportionally according to each user's basic right to use or historical pattern of use. It does *not* mean that users have rights to equal amounts of the resource. For example, under coequal rights, a common property fishery regulated by quotas or transferable licenses would follow the rule of proportionate reductions in historical catch rights during bad fishing years. In the commons grazing in the European Alps, where one may graze the same number of animal units from year to year, proportionate adjustments in use for good or bad years are made by lengthening or shortening the grazing season.

S. V. Ciriacy-Wantrup included coequal rights as a necessary condition for common property because he rejected such rights systems as the appropriations doctrine in Western water law from the class of common property (Bishop 1983). This doctrine is based on the principle of first-in-time, first-in-right. The first user to withdraw an amount of water and put it to beneficial use establishes a right to use that amount of water in future periods, as long as the full amount of water continues to be put to beneficial use. Subsequent users may establish rights by withdrawing further water, but the chronological order in which the water is first withdrawn determines each user's right to future water. In particular, in dry years, junior rights holders may be cut off completely, whereas users who established their rights earlier have access to their full amount of water.

Ciriacy-Wantrup excluded this type of allocation system from common property. Yet if members of the resource user group agree among themselves to allocate the resource in an inegalitarian manner, or, in an extreme case, if the group agrees to give only one of its members the entire resource harvest in times of shortage, why should we not call this common property?[4] Users have agreed upon well-defined rules between the group and outsiders as well as within the group, and if the other conditions are met, then one might hold to a definition of common property without an egalitarian allocation rule under resource fluctuations. Although many resources exploited jointly exhibit coequal rights to use, whether they are fisheries or wildlife, groundwater or grazing areas, certain common use resource systems with well-defined rights and duties among users and nonusers exhibit inegalitarian allocation mechanisms, notably irrigation systems. For this reason, I do not include coequal use as a necessary condition for defining common property.

Synoptic Definition

In closing this section, I give a less formal definition of common property that includes the salient points from the seven above. *Common property is a form of resource management in which a well-delineated group of competing users participates in extraction or use of a jointly held, fugitive resource according to explicitly or implicitly understood rules about who may take how much of the resource.* There are two reasons for defining common property in this way, in contrast to the frequent usage that equates it to open access. One is historical and one is rooted in the meaning of the word "property." The following two sections elaborate on these reasons.

The Historical Record of Common Property

Historically, the commons has not represented a system of open access exploitation (Clawson 1974; Juergensmeyer and Wadley 1974; Ciriacy-Wantrup and Bishop 1975; Dahlman 1980). As Clawson (1974: 60) points out:

> Property owned in common, whether land or other kinds, has not by any means always been freely open to any user, nor is property owned in common today in many parts of the world open to any user. Social controls of many kinds have existed, and do exist, to limit and govern the use of property owned in common. Such social controls often regulate the intensity of use. Property owned in common has not invariably been used in an exploitative way.

Examples of natural resources that have been used in common without overuse abound in history and prehistory.[5] Prehistoric hunt-

---

[4] I am indebted to Robin Cantor for this point.

[5] Besides examples cited in the text, other accounts of historical and modern common

ing and gathering societies used land communally under regulation by tribal heads, closed seasons, social taboos on marriage and lactation, and fission of tribal groups. These institutions managed the resources on a sustained yield basis, and common ownership, far from being the cause of overexploitation, may have been the primary reason for preservation of resources (Ciriacy-Wantrup and Bishop 1975).

Common grazing land and communal forests in Europe offer other long-standing examples of group-managed, limited access resources. Some of the community forests in Europe provided models of good forest management, precisely because they were managed for the community. Grazing commons were often limited to residents of a certain village or hamlet, or only to descendants of original residents from a specific prior date. Further regulation of grazing took the form of opening and closing dates, limitation of animals to the number for which an individual could provide forage through the winter, or outright stinting.

Common grazing also occurred in the open field system of England, a system that we will view in detail in comparisons with the Swiss grazing commons in Chapter 5. English common grazing, rather than a maladaptation, may well have been the most efficient production method that stood alongside individual cropping in the arable, given the economies of scale in cattle grazing relative to crop planting (Dahlman 1980: 7).

The English commons system apparently sprang from previously open access land, because at very early dates all members of a community had equal access to common lands (Juergensmeyer and Wadley 1974). Because of limited resources and growing population, however, such liberties of use changed into exclusive rights to use during prefeudal and feudal times. These rights to use were based on long-standing residency, property holdings, and rights of certain feudal classes, and they excluded outsiders:

The Englishman's rights . . . were the rights he enjoyed as a member of some particular class and community.

He lived under customs and enjoyed franchises which might be peculiar to his native town or even his native parish. . . . And every village and township would no doubt be as anxious to exclude strangers from its woods and pastures as to preserve its ordinary members' rights in them against encroachment from within or from above. [Pollock 1896: 18]

property resource patterns are given in Hoskins and Stamp (1963), Rhoades and Thompson (1975), Netting (1976), Panel on Common Property Resource Management (1986), and McCay and Acheson (1987).

... Common rights in general, consist of privileges of use, i.e., the liberty of taking sand and gravel, of pasture, of cutting underbrush, etc., according to the customs of the particular neighborhood, and naturally depend upon the resources of the neighborhood. ...

... [I]t was entirely possible that not all the members of a given village with common lands shared equally, or even at all, in the use and enjoyment of the lands. Those to whom the common lands originally belonged (and their heirs) retained their rights over the common. In addition, others, perhaps of another village or even members of the same village who had moved in after the common originated but who lacked rights by descent, might have only one or another of the rights of common, e.g., the right of pasturage, or of turbary. (Juergensmeyer and Wadley 1974: 363–64)

Moving to another time and part of the world, the peasant fishermen of Bahia in northeastern Brazil provide another example of common property resource management (Cordell 1978). Before the technological innovation of nylon nets, they pursued a common property fishery based much more on implicit rules and traditions than on explicit, codified regulations. These traditions had arisen because natural limits had prevented the expansion of estuary fishing. Knowledge of tidal rhythms as influenced by lunar periodicity was very important in locating different fish species in the estuary. The knowledge of tides, fishing grounds, and types of nets to set was confined to a certain number of boat captains and judiciously passed on to only a certain number of apprentices. The possession of this knowledge established implicit but definite property rights claims over lunar-tide fishing areas. Violation of implicit rules was prevented by social pressure from the community of fishermen, and disputes were settled by being aired before this community. Fishing decorum included trading of favors, such as the use of each others' fishing grounds, in a cooperative but controlled fashion.

To summarize, open access has not been the modus operandi of many historical commons. They at least limited the number of users, and some of them limited the amount of exploitation allowed by each individual user. Because of these historical practices, many of which can still be observed to this day, it is incorrect to equate common property with open access.

The Meaning of Property

The second reason for using "common property" to indicate an institution of joint ownership lies in the meaning of property and its distinction from nonproperty. Property's existence in an object entails rights and duties for property holders and nonproperty holders alike.

In our case, property implies rights and duties for both participants and nonparticipants in resource extraction; the absence of rights and duties means that the institution of property does not exist. As I will show, open access exhibits the complete absence of ex ante (prior to capture) rights and duties, and therefore it constitutes the total absence of property. Common property, on the other hand, as the word "property" implies, involves ex ante rights for the rights holders— even if they are multiple rather than single—and duties for nonproperty holders. It is therefore important to distinguish common property from open access. This section elaborates these ideas by explaining the meaning of rights and duties, the class of rights called property rights, and their application to the distinction between open access and common property.[6]

The first step toward understanding rights is to examine the nature of the connection between persons involved in an ethical or legal relationship. A widely recognized classification of such relationships consists of the four Hohfeldian correlates:

right/duty,
liberty/no right,[7]
power/liability,
immunity/no power.

Each of the four correlate pairs indicates how one person stands in relation to another person in an ethical or legal relationship and what the reciprocal relationship is. The pairs are invariably linked. For instance, the first correlate pair indicates that if one party has a right, the other necessarily has a duty. Where duty is absent, no right exists.

The most important set of correlates for our purposes is the right/ duty pair. A *right* is a claim by one individual or institution (the right holder) on another (the duty bearer) for an act or forbearance, such that if the act or forbearance is not performed, it would be morally or legally acceptable to use coercion to extract compliance or compensation in lieu of it (Becker 1977: 11). A *duty*, as the complement (or correlate) to a right, is the obligation of the duty bearer to perform the act or forbearance. Thus, if one agent has the right to expect an act or a forbearance from another, the other necessarily has the duty, in a moral or legal sense, to act or forbear.

---

[6] This section, up to the application to common property and open access, is based on work on the meaning of property rights by several philosophers and legal scholars, including Hohfeld (1919), Hallowell (1943), Honoré (1961), and Becker (1977: chap. 2).

[7] Hohfeld (1919) uses the word "privilege" instead of "liberty" in the second correlate pair. Becker (1977) uses the term "liberty," which I also adopt.

The liberty/no right correlate pair is also important for our analysis. A *liberty* is a legal or ethical freedom to perform or not to perform an act without any duty incumbent on another person. It also means that others have no right to require the person at liberty to perform or forbear from the act; that is, others hold *no right* as the correlate to the person's liberty. Competitive situations provide an example. Each competitor is at liberty to win; no one has the duty to let another win; each competitor has no right to stop another from winning (if the winner follows the rules of the game) (Becker 1977: 12).[8]

Now I narrow the discussion to *property rights*, in order to show how they exist in common property but not in an open access situation. Whereas rights are relationships between persons, property rights are specifically relationships between persons regarding use of a thing—whether corporeal or incorporeal (Hallowell 1943; Becker 1977: 22). Various rights, duties, liberties, powers, immunities, and liabilities combine to define a person's property rights (ownership rights) in a thing and how another person is morally or legally required to act with regard to the thing (Ely 1914: 106; Honoré 1961; Becker 1977: 19).[9] The existence and observance of these rights, duties, and other relationships distinguishes property from nonproperty, as well as one type of property from another.

One of the most fundamental rights of complete, liberal ownership is the right to possess, which is the right to exclusive physical control or the right to exclude others from the use or benefits of a thing (Becker 1977: 19). Possession is important in the comparison between open access and common property, because fugitive resources under open access are not possessed, whereas they are possessed under com-

---

[8] The other two Hohfeldian correlate pairs are not important for our analysis of common property. Briefly, however, the power/liability correlates refer to the situation in which one party has the *power* to change the rights, duties, liberties, powers, or immunities of another person at will. An example is a person's power to alter his or her last will and testament. The heirs' *liability* lies in the fact that they must respect their changed legal status toward the bequeathed goods. The immunity/no power correlates refer to the situation in which the first party is *immune* from a power possessed by the second party, who logically has *no power* in that specific case. An example is that creditors generally have power to seize possessions for unpaid debts; a person in bankruptcy proceedings, however, is immune from such power.

[9] The rights, duties, liberties, powers, and immunities that define the degree of ownership are the right to possess; the right to personal use; the right to manage (i.e., to decide how and by whom a thing shall be used); the right to income through forgoing personal use and allowing others to use a thing; the powers to alienate, consume, waste, modify, or destroy a thing; an immunity from expropriation; the power to bequeath; the rights regarding term of ownership; the duty to forbear from using the thing in ways harmful to others; the liability to expropriation for unpaid debt; and rights and duties regarding the reversion of lapsed ownership rights (Honoré 1961; Becker 1977: 19).

mon property. Becker (1977: 21) elaborates on the right to possess as follows:

The right to possess is to be sharply distinguished from mere protection of possession once achieved—that is, it is a claim right to have possession, not merely a power to acquire or a liberty to keep. If I have a right to possess a thing, others do not merely have "no right" that I not possess it; they have a duty not to interfere with my possession.

This points directly to the property rights distinction between open access and common property. Ownership, if it includes the right to possess, implies the positive right of holding the object and the negative right of excluding others from its possession, even if the object is not yet held. Under open access, however, neither of these rights is present. No one has the right to exclude another from extracting the resource; hence the negative, exclusionary right is not present. Nor is there any security of possessing either particular physical units or a certain amount of the resource; hence the positive right of holding the object also is not present. Thus, there is no ownership, at least not ownership that includes the fundamental right of possession.

This point is important, so I will put it another way. In an open access fishery, no one is secure in the claim to certain fish or even to a certain amount of fish, because someone else may capture them first. Thus, there is no right holder with a claim to possess certain fish or a certain amount of fish. Necessarily, there is also no correlate duty bearer who should forbear capture of fish. With no right/duty relationship in an open access resource, there is *no property* and there are *no owners*. Resources in this situation are *res nullius*, unowned resources (Ciriacy-Wantrup 1971).[10]

Common property, on the other hand, *is* property. It has a definable set of users who have the right to exclude others from possession, use, and enjoyment of benefits. Excluded persons have the duty to observe the rights of the included users to extract the resource. Furthermore, in a well-functioning common property situation, the users have certain rights and duties among themselves with respect to possession, use, and enjoyment of benefits from the resource (Bromley 1989: 205). For example, in a regulated groundwater regime, all participants have the right to pump water at specified rates; they also have the correlate duty of not exceeding their assigned rate so as not to interfere with others' water extraction.

[10] In fact, open access is better characterized by the liberty/no right correlates (Bromley 1989: 203–5). A user is at liberty to catch what he wants. Other users have no right to prevent him. At the same time, however, they have no duty to allow capture. They may possess the fish if they capture them first.

Moreover, the rights and duties in true common property go beyond the right of possession. Under common property, the right to use, the right to manage, the right to income, an immunity from expropriation, the power to bequeath, and the absence of any term of ownership rights all often reside to varying degrees with the individual or the group. With definite right and duty relationships among all parties concerned—both users and nonusers—regarding the object in question, it is possible to talk about owners and their *property* (i.e., their rights in the object). Such property rights represent *res communes,* common property (Ciriacy-Wantrup 1971).

In summary, then, an implicit distinction between open access and common property lies in the concept of property and its requirement of well-defined rights and duties. Open access does not represent property; common property does. An open access resource does not have owners; common property does.

Limited User Open Access

A qualification is necessary to define common property clearly. Ciriacy-Wantrup (1971) has pointed out that not only has open access been confused with common property but so has a type of resource use pattern that I have called limited user open access (see Chapter 2). Under limited user open access, property rights have been established for a limited number of users, but the property rights among these users remain ill-defined. The most common example of this type of resource is oil and gas pools. Groundwater is also sometimes utilized under this regime, and some forms of limited entry programs in fisheries result in such a property rights structure. The included users are only "quasi-owners" of the resource. They have exclusive rights *to extract* the resource, but not exclusive rights to a certain amount of the resource extracted. Any included user may exploit the resource at any rate desired.

As the models of Chapter 2 indicate, if only the number of users is restricted but not their input levels, the users will expand total inputs beyond the optimal level. The nonoptimality may not be as severe as when complete open access in both inputs and the number of firms is allowed. Nevertheless, limited user open access leads to some expansion of inputs beyond the optimal amount. The lack of individual input controls leaves the property rights structure indefinitely defined, and users are therefore free to follow individual incentives to overexploit the resource. For this reason, I follow Ciriacy-Wantrup (1971) and confine my definition of common property to situations of clearly defined property rights between users and nonusers *and* among the users themselves. This excludes the situation of limited user open access.

As mentioned, unregulated extraction from common oil and gas pools provides an example of limited user open access. Economically excessive extraction rates result from the "rule of capture" prevailing among the limited number of users (Davidson 1963). In order to establish a full set of extraction rights and duties that lead to optimal resource exploitation, compulsory field unitization has long been proposed as an alternative to unrestricted pumping or inefficient government regulation of extraction rates (Davidson 1963; Wiggins and Libecap 1985). Unitization of the fields would

"require the organization of companies or cooperatives in which all surface owners would share on an equitable basis" [Rostow 1948: 45]. The advantage of such an operation would be to void the rule of capture. (Davidson 1963: 97)

This is a common property solution. The user group would make production decisions to maximize joint profit. Then, by deciding how to divide up the oil or profits among existing users, the group would effectively establish definite property rights.

Another example arises from the establishment of the offshore, two-hundred-mile, exclusive economic zones (EEZs). Before the extension of national claims to two hundred miles, the fish in waters beyond twelve miles (for most countries) constituted an open access resource. Anyone from any country could exploit them. No one had the right to possess the fish before anyone else; no one had the duty to forbear capture. The founding of the EEZs represented the first step toward establishing property rights. There came into being a group of included users (domestic and specially permitted foreign fishers) and a group of excluded users (all unpermitted foreigners). The included users have rights to capture, and the excluded persons have duties to forbear from fishing. Property rights must be defined more strictly, however, to say that full common property has been established. Rights must be set among the included users. This means establishing rights to certain amounts of fish and the simultaneous, correlate duty of not capturing more than permitted amounts.

Common Property and Public Goods

Understanding common property also requires a grasp of the distinction between common property and a public good. Common property and public goods are similar in that both are held by a group. For common property, the joint, nonexclusive entitlement condition indicates that resource owners have a joint claim on the resource prior to capture or use. The public that supplies a public good similarly has a shared claim on its benefits as a result of providing it through, say, tax collections. However, here the similarities between common property and public goods end.

The essential distinction between a public good and common property lies in a public good's being a type of good or service, while common property is a resource management method. A public good lies among a set of goods types that vary in their degrees of rivalry and excludability in consumption. A public good is the particular case in which consumption of the good is nonrival (two or more may enjoy benefits simultaneously) and exclusion from benefits cannot be enforced.[11] Common property, in contrast, lies on a spectrum of ownership and management forms that ranges from open access to private property. (This ownership spectrum is developed further in the section entitled "The Private Property, Common Property, Open Access Trichotomy.") In fact, because common property is a resource management institution, different types of goods or resources, including public goods, may be managed under it. For example, land, a commodity subject to rivalry in use and exclusion of others from use, may be managed under common property; at the same time, goods or resources with greater public goods character, such as a park or a natural harbor, may also be managed as common property. Nevertheless, as I have discussed, some degree of excludability must be present to define a common property resource adequately.

The conditions of excludability and rivalry both provide contrasts between pure public goods and common property. Pure public goods, with their extremely high costs of exclusion from benefits, are generally supplied under open access conditions rather than conditions that resemble common property. Because it is nearly impossible to

---

[11] This is not to say that nonrivalry in consumption and nonexcludability from benefits are strictly technical characteristics that define a public good. Exclusion from benefits, for example, can be enforced for almost any good if high enough costs are incurred; conceptually at least, even the purest public goods could be supplied privately. Thus, whether a good is supplied as a public good depends on human decisions about costs and is not strictly determined by technical characteristics. In this sense, the choice between providing a good publicly and supplying it privately can be said to be an institutional choice, just as the choice between managing a resource by common property and managing it by private property can be an institutional one. Still, the probability of a good's being supplied as a public good depends on the costs of exclusion, which *are* a technical characteristic under a given state of technology. Thus, one can classify some goods as more prone to be public and others as more likely to be private.

exclude anyone from enjoying benefits, no attempt is made to define included and excluded user groups. Likewise, complete nonrivalry in consumption, also characteristic of a pure public good, generally does not apply to a common property resource. There are two cases. If the resource can be reduced to sole ownership by capture, then one person's extraction of a unit of the resource clearly precludes another's possession of that unit; there is absolute rivalry in extraction. If the resource exhibits a public goods nature at low and moderate levels of use, but congestion occurs at higher levels of use, users may institute common property–like limitations on use. Significantly, it is precisely the congestion that negates its public goods nature that calls forth common property limitations on use. That is, only the lack of a *pure* public goods nature, nonrivalry at all levels of use, is compatible with the need for common property management.[12]

In contrast to benefits from public goods, benefits from common property resources that exhibit rivalry in extraction can be enjoyed only after the resource has been captured. Joint, nonexclusive entitlement implies that owners of a common property resource possess a *potential* benefit, contingent upon capture or efforts to use the resource. In contrast, beneficiaries of a pure public good, such as national defense, enjoy *actual* benefits even though the good remains under joint, nonexclusive possession.

Another difference between public goods and common property resources lies in the fact that public goods generally are artificially manufactured goods that may be supplied in discretionary amounts. In fact, much of public goods theory relates to how much of a public good to provide. In contrast, common property resources generally are natural resources whose growth or extraction must be managed to obtain optimal use rates. This contrast extends subtly to such examples as parks and natural harbors, which are potential common property resources that traditionally have also been considered public goods. Public goods theory concerns itself with how much to invest in providing these types of amenities—how much of the resource to set aside and how many improvements to provide to make the resource accessible and usable. Common property theory, in contrast, discusses how to manage their use—how intensely to allow use and by whom.

---

[12] Alternatively, one might say that pure public goods that exhibit no rivalry at any level of use, whose benefits therefore accrue to the whole public, are common property whose user group is everybody. No management of use rates is necessary, because there is complete lack of rivalry in use. At the same time, the whole user group pays for general resource supply and management through taxation and government representation. Admittedly, in this interpretation, the distinction between common property and a public good blurs.

To conclude, not only may goods that can be reduced to sole ownership through capture be managed under common property, but so can some public goods. It is now clear that these are impure public goods, because they are subject to congestion and some form of exclusion. I have given the examples of parks and natural harbors. Potentially, a scenic vista could fall into this category. Because both public goods and goods that can be reduced to sole ownership may be common property, the process of capture that reduces a unit of the resource to sole ownership is not a necessary defining characteristic for common property. Although effort may be needed to capture benefits from a common property resource that has a public goods nature—a person may have to travel to a park, a harbor, or a scenic site to profit from it—deriving benefits does not necessarily compete with others' demands for benefits or exclude others from enjoying benefits, as long as use is controlled below the level of congestion. Thus, reducing the resource to sole ownership to enjoy benefits does not come into the question for a common property resource with a public goods nature. This said, most of the treatment in the rest of this book concentrates on fugitive resources that can be reduced to sole ownership through capture.

Multiple-Resource Common Property Systems

To round out the definition of common property, I wish to make clear that the institution manifests itself in diverse ways. It may stand alone or be integrated into larger resource management systems. Users in the simplest form of common property employ one technical process to harvest a resource that delivers a single resource commodity or service in one contiguous location. A single-gear, single-species fishery is a good example. More complicated common property systems exist, however. The users may be involved in extraction of several common property resources with one or more techniques simultaneously—as in multiple-gear, single-species or multiple-gear, multiple-species fisheries. The common property resource may deliver multiple services to different types of users. A future example might be the atmosphere, if it is ever fully controlled to accept various pollutants from varying sources at levels that match its varying assimilative capacities. Common property use also can complement other resource management forms in a system. The English open field system was such a system of resource management, in which crop cultivation occurred mainly under individual tenancy intermixed with and complemented by grazing under common property. In all of these cases, however, analysis is eased without loss of generality if the problem is reduced to the harvest of a single resource commodity, although not necessarily by a uniform technology. This is my approach in discussing common property throughout the rest of this book.

The Private Property, Common Property, Open Access Trichotomy

The preceding sections have concentrated on drawing the distinction between open access and common property in some detail. In the subsequent sections of this chapter, I wish to argue how common property may present a potential solution to the open access problem.

First let us set open access and common property into a larger framework that includes private property. In some ways, common property is like private property: The resource has a definable set of users who may be declared its owners, outsiders are excluded from use, and the users control resource extraction to increase the (joint) net product in order to benefit themselves. Thus, both private property and common property meet the well-delineated group of users and well-understood rules conditions, Points 2 and 4, in the definition of common property.[13] In other ways, common property has properties of open access: Both have multiple users and both contain the incentive for individuals to increase their output beyond the individual share that would produce the joint maximum net product. Thus, open access exhibits the joint, nonexclusive entitlement and the competitive users conditions, Points 5 and 6 of common property's definition, without the controls of the other conditions in the definition. For these reasons, common property might be considered to lie between private property and open access.

The degree of exclusivity in property rights to the *in situ* resource varies under the three systems. Under private property, property rights in the resource (the right to extract it, the right to possess it, the right to alienate it, and so on) are vested in one real or legal person. Under common property, the right to any given physical unit is less well defined. Rather, rights generally are specified in terms of total amounts of inputs or outputs that the user may apply or extract. Which particular units are extracted in fulfilling the quota are immaterial. The next loosest definition of property rights is limited user open access. Under this regime, rights are vested in a certain group of

---

[13] Of course, for private property an individual user or firm replaces the group of users.

users, but the users have no rights among themselves, either to possess specific physical units or to extract a set amount of the resource. Finally, exclusivity of property rights is lost altogether under open access, where there is neither a definable group of rights holders nor any link between users and physical units or amounts of the resource extracted.

Thus, there is more than just a dichotomy between open access and private property. If limited user open access is grouped with complete open access, there is at least a trichotomy. Common property should not simply be lumped with other group use situations.

Not only is common property distinct from open access and from private property, but it can be a solution to the open access problem, even as private property is. Each of the resource use regimes being discussed has two characteristics that govern extraction rates. How each resource use system is defined on each of these characteristics determines whether controlled extraction rates are achievable. The two characteristics are existence or nonexistence of an included and an excluded group, and existence or nonexistence of constraints on included user extraction rates, as is shown in Figure 3.1. Open access is defined by the lack of constraints on both the number of users and the amount that each user may extract. The models of Chapter 2 made it clear that this is a formula for disastrous overuse. Even if only one of the limitation characteristics is left unfettered, as under limited user open access, exploitation expands beyond the desired rate. Under common property, however, both of the problem-causing characteristics of open access are remedied. Group size is limited and rights and duties to limit extraction are defined among the included users. Private property also limits the number of resource managers

PROPERTY INSTITUTION

	1	2	3	
			OPEN ACCESS	
	PRIVATE PROPERTY	**COMMON PROPERTY**	**LIMITED USER**	**UNLIMITED USER**
GROUP LIMITATION	ONE PERSON	MEMBERS ONLY	MEMBERS ONLY	OPEN TO ANYONE
EXTRACTION LIMITATION	EXTRACTION LIMITED BY INDIVIDUAL DECISION	EXTRACTION LIMITED BY RULES	EXTRACTION UNLIMITED	EXTRACTION UNLIMITED

Figure 3.1. A Trichotomy of Resource Use Regimes

(to one) and controls extraction rates (through the individual's optimization decision). Therefore, although common property stands between open access and private property in the ways already mentioned, it is like private property in the two vital areas of having a defined group and having limited individual use rates. Because both of these regimes eliminate the two main problems of open access, common property may stand beside private property as a solution to the open access problem.

Common Property in the Economics Literature

Some authors, but by no means all, have ignored the existence of common property institutions. This problem has been made no less severe by the frequent confusion of common property with open access. Witness, for example, Demsetz (1967: 354):

Several idealized forms of ownership must be distinguished at the outset. These are communal ownership, private ownership, and state ownership.
. . . Communal ownership means that the community denies to the state or to individual citizens the right to interfere with any person's exercise of communally-owned rights. Private ownership implies that the community recognizes the right of the owner to exclude others from exercising the owner's private rights. State ownership implies that the state may exclude any from the use of a right as long as the state follows accepted political procedures for determining who may not use state-owned property.

Demsetz's "communal ownership" refers to an open access situation, despite his use of the terms "rights" and "ownership," which as we have seen cannot exist in an open access resource. This is clear because he goes on to speak of *everyone's* having the "right" to use the resource, a failure to "concentrate the cost" of extraction on the user, and consequent overuse of the resource. Thus, because Demsetz explicitly ignores state ownership in his subsequent discussion, he recognizes only a dichotomy of tenure systems: private property and open access.

Cheung (1970: 64) is another who, while recognizing the possibility of common property, labels this ownership pattern less than optimal. It purportedly yields lower rent than sole ownership:

Consider three alternative arrangements. The first arrangement is a group of individuals forming a tribe, a clan or a union so as to exclude "outsiders" from competing for the use of a non-exclusive resource. In this arrangement each "insider" is free to use the resource as he pleases and derive income therefrom. According to our analysis, the fewer the insiders, the greater will be the "rent" captured by each. . . .
The second arrangement involves not only the exclusion of outsiders, but,

as in some cooperatives, there is central regulation of the amounts of work and income for the insiders. The third arrangement is private property rights governing all resources, where the property rights are exclusively delineated and enforced, and where resource use is guided by contracting in the marketplace.

All three arrangements are costly. While it appears that these costs are lowest for the first type and highest for the third, the gains from each arrangement are in a reverse order.

One must agree with Cheung that the first arrangement yields the lowest rent. Both Anderson's graphic model in Chapter 2 and Dasgupta and Heal's mathematical model in its appendix showed that limiting the number of users but not their input levels leads to some excessive inputs and overuse of the resource. Cheung, however, makes no argument to support his contention that the second arrangement, which describes common property, necessarily yields lower benefits than private property. Indeed, as I argue in the next section and the appendix to this chapter, solutions to open access based on quota and licensing schemes prove that proper limitation of inputs via "central regulation" can lead to the same optimal results as private property. Whether central regulation or private property is more costly is an empirical question that depends on characteristics of the resource.

Although it may seem that other authors repeatedly advocate private property as the sole private solution to open access, many mention, or at least leave room for, common property as a solution. Since definition of property rights is a characteristic of common property, just as it is of private property, many authors might admit to the common property solution even though they primarily had private property in mind when writing. Ault and Rutman (1979: 173) provide an example of this. They describe the transition in many tribal African land use systems from open access when land was plentiful to the division of land into private property when land scarcity emerged and go on to state:

In order to insure that the individual invests in the land and limits the size of the herd, the land tenure system must change so that individual rights to land are defined, assigned, and transferable.

Not all common property systems would meet Ault and Rutman's requirement of transferable property rights (e.g., strict quota systems do not). Some common property systems, however, do define and assign individual, transferable rights to use. Even though Ault and Rutman were probably trying to describe private property, they might assent to the appropriateness of certain common property arrangements.

Other authors acknowledge the possibility of common property solutions much more freely. Even Gordon (1954: 134), who began the modern theoretical debate on open access resources, has this to say:

The older anthropological study was prone to regard resource tenure in common [i.e., open access], with unrestricted exploitation as a "lower" stage of development comparative with private and group property rights. However, more complete annals of primitive cultures reveal common tenure [i.e., open access] to be quite rare, even in hunting and gathering societies. Property rights in some form predominate by far, and, most important, their existence may be easily explained in terms of the necessity for orderly exploitation and conservation of the resource. Environmental conditions make necessary some vehicle which will prevent the resources of the community at large from being destroyed by excessive exploitation. Private or group land tenure accomplishes this end in an easily understandable fashion.

Scott (1955: 116), who went so far as to subtitle his article "The Objectives of Sole Ownership," recognizes the possibility of common property:

The mere existence of the institution of private property is not sufficient to insure the efficient management of natural resources; the property must be allocated on a *scale* sufficient to insure that one management has complete control of the asset. In this paper, for example, I shall show that . . . sole ownership of the fishery is . . . necessary. . . . [An] immense sole ownership organization [might be] . . . a cooperative, a government board, a private corporation, or an international authority.

Bottomley (1963: 94) also advocates a couple of tenure systems for Tripolitania that have common property character:

Attempts to violate hallowed rights regarding common [i.e., open access] land will, no doubt, run into considerable resistance. It may be that the only politically feasible solution lies in a grafting of the characteristics of private holdings on to common [i.e., open access] land without actually forcing enclosures upon the Arab tribes. In other words, a way must be found of ensuring investors a full return on the capital which they expend regardless of the land tenure system which obtains.

Perhaps the existing tribal structure can be adapted to some cooperative orcharding venture but the formation of such organizations may prove difficult and growth will probably be more rapid if it occurs on the soil of individual enterprise; if, that is to say, the tribesmen, and even outsiders, are able to exercise their entrepreneurial ability to direct self-interest rather than through the cooperative alone. But this requires the alienation to the individual of certain rights pertaining to the common land; the right for the individual to plant trees upon the common land and to harvest them for a predetermined period, subject only to a payment for the use of the land to the members of the tribe, or to some pre-arranged agreement for repurchase by the tribe. In other words, *secure* mutual agreements need to be made between the tribe and the individual so that the fruits of investment will belong to the individual and the rents for the land whereon the investment has been made will belong to the tribe as a whole.

I wish to emphasize that the cooperative orcharding arrangement is not the only example of common property here. The proposed arrangement in which trees would be privately held also exemplifies a common property arrangement *in the land.* Although the capital inputs, the trees, would remain private—much as have cows and other livestock in traditional common property systems of Europe—the land would remain under group control—again like common property in Europe.

Finally, Weitzman (1974: 230–31) illustrates that common property schemes might be considered variants on private property rights. He contrasts two systems: free access and private ownership. His "private ownership" category, however, is not exhausted by cases of sole ownership. Rather, he seems to include various common property schemes:

> There is even a way of envisioning PO [private ownership] in terms of producer cooperatives which take a lease on property at the competitive rental price and determine their membership size by maximizing the dividend of net revenue (after payment of rent) per variable factor member. The solution is the same as before [under individual private ownership of the resource] if rentals have been accurately determined.
>
> It is also conceptually irrelevant to the determination of an optimal allocation whether PO is regarded as based on competitive *private* ownership of property or on efficiently organized government *public* ownership. . . .
>
> Thus, for the model building purposes of theoretically characterizing efficient allocation, who owns property and what factor is thought of as hiring the other in the economic system we are calling PO is somewhat arbitrary. Which arrangement is in fact to be employed would largely depend on institutional considerations and on tradition.

In summary, some economists have not recognized the existence of common property as an institutional form between private property and open access, but have acknowledged only private property as an alternative to open access. This is by no means true of all economists, however, not even some of those steeped in neoclassical traditions. Some of these call only for some type of property rights arrangements in open access resources, which common property as well as private property can provide. Others outwardly admit to the possible success of certain group solutions. Perhaps the war being waged between advocates of private property rights and the proponents of institutional alternatives to private property is unnecessary.[14] Both sides support the vesting of some type of clearly defined property rights in the resource to prevent the "tragedy of open access." Since there is agreement on this point, it is only one more step to realize that the particular form of property rights might best be designed to match the characteristics of the resource being exploited and the people doing the exploiting.

Neoclassical Justifications of Common Property

Until now, justification of common property's adequacy has been confined to citing characteristics that it shares with private property and its persistence in history. In this section, I defend common property by referring to neoclassical proofs of group solutions. In subsequent sections, we will look at property rights and institutional arguments.

Six neoclassical solutions to the open access problem have been suggested: private property, input quotas, input rights, output quotas, output rights, and taxation. Four of these—the ones involving quotas and rights—can be considered common property solutions. Although an appendix to this chapter offers formal proofs, in this section I give some intuitive grounds for the optimality of these solutions and explain how they can be considered common property.

Input Quotas

In a system of quotas on inputs, participants collude to limit their total inputs for resource extraction to the amount that yields the maximum sustainable net revenue, E^* in Chapter 2. The participants use some nonmarket, nonprice mechanism to allocate individual quotas. In the simplest case, individual quotas are set at E^*/N, where N is the number of permitted resource harvesters. The quota on inputs scheme works properly if a rigid production function exists between the inputs applied and the amount of resource extracted. Together, the limitation on inputs and the fixed production relationship effectively vest rights to a certain amount of the resource. The scheme

---

[14] A group of institutional economists and political scientists has emerged who defend common property as a practical solution to open access. These authors include Ciriacy-Wantrup and Bishop (1975), Runge (1981, 1986), Bromley (1986), and Ostrom (1986), although this is not an exhaustive list. I have not reviewed their work here because it presents arguments that overlap with many of those presented elsewhere in this chapter.

meets the conditions of common property because the number of users has been limited (to N) and their individual resource extraction rates have been restricted by limiting inputs. By definition, the arrangement is optimal when the summation of the individual quotas equals E^*. The Bahia swamp dwellers described in the section entitled "The Historical Record of Common Property" implicitly followed a quota on inputs scheme.

There are two problems with this solution. First, the incentive remains to cheat on the system by introducing more than E^*/N inputs (or whatever the individual input quotas are) and increasing the personal rent while others hold to their limits. Although the input quotas confine the common property resource users to the optimal solution (figuratively speaking, the southeastern box of the game theoretic diagram of Figures 2.5 to 2.7), there is a constant incentive in this position for some player to cheat on the agreement. The optimal amount of inputs will not be introduced if some members of the commons decide not to be honest and devise a method of hiding extraction effort.

Not only may members cheat on the optimal solution directly, but the second problem with input quotas is that they may expend excess effort indirectly through factor substitution. Until now, the analysis has assumed a composite input, effort or vessels or some other conglomerate variable input. In reality, production processes most often depend on various inputs. Unless the production process is simple and depends heavily or exclusively on only one or two inputs, or unless factor ratios must be maintained in strict proportions for technical reasons, putting quotas on certain inputs can result in factor substitution toward other inputs (Dorfman 1974). For instance, if the number of boats in a fishery is limited, larger boats and crews, or more nets and fuel, may be substituted. In this case, limitation of inputs fails as a viable common property solution.

Input Rights

Input rights, or licensing of inputs, as Dasgupta and Heal (1979) have called them, are also designed to limit resource extraction through limiting inputs. However, they operate differently from quotas. Either the unified user group or the government issues or sells rights for inputs, which in total allow a certain amount of industry effort, say $\bar{E}$. The authority then allows a competitive market to develop for the rights to apply effort. Each of the N firms must decide how many rights it will buy. If N is large enough and if $\bar{E} < E_c$, where E_c is the number of inputs introduced at open access equilibrium, then a competitively determined, positive license price will develop. Call it $\bar{r}$. This price is determined in a market for rights, where the derived demand curve for rights is a function of resource rents obtainable by applying inputs to extract the resource and the supply curve of rights is inelastically set at $\bar{E}$. The cost of the rights $\bar{r}$ is added to other variable input costs, and the higher costs lead to reduced effort. Thus, the cost of a right and a decentralized market mechanism, not a rigid quota, limit effort. Ideally, of course, the authority that issues rights would set $\bar{E}$ equal to E^* and let the market mechanism operate to develop a rights price such that the optimal number of inputs is introduced. A formal proof that this leads to optimal results is contained in the appendix to this chapter.

Input rights also vest a claim to a certain proportion of the resource's productive capacity by virtue of a rigid relationship between inputs applied and resource extraction, and hence they also may be weak if input substitution can circumvent the rights requirement. The solution, however, corresponds closely to the practice of many alpine grazing commons of Switzerland. In this situation, a limited number of users holds grazing rights, where the number of rights held indicates how many animal units may be grazed. These grazing rights are often tradable on the market. This, together with the fact that the cows can be thought of as the capital input, makes the grazing rights identical in principle to the concept of input rights. Because a rather rigid production relationship exists between the primary capital input (cows) and the amount of resource extracted (grass), the limitation on inputs effectively prevents resource overexploitation.

Output Quotas and Output Rights

Two other solutions for the open access problem from neoclassical economics are output quotas and output rights. I make the distinction between nontransferable output quotas and transferable output rights, consistent with the distinction between nontransferability and transferability in input quotas and input rights. The literature has mentioned output limitation schemes for common pool resource extraction much less frequently (e.g., Christy 1973; Crommelin, Pearse, and Scott 1978) than input limitation schemes.[15] To my knowledge

[15] The literature in tradable output rights for pollution control, which might be termed a common property solution for asymmetric externalities, is of course well developed. See, for instance, Dales (1968: 93–97), Montgomery (1972), Atkinson and Tietenberg (1982), Krupnick, Oates, and Van De Verg (1983), and McGartland and Oates (1985).

only Moloney and Pearse (1979) have modeled output rights. The lack of attention in the theoretical literature is odd, because a number of countries and state and provincial governments have implemented output quotas or output rights in fisheries.

Output quotas put a direct limitation on the amount of the resource each user may harvest such that the total amount harvested is socially optimal (maximizes resource rent). More interesting is the output rights system, because of the transferability of the rights. In an output rights system applied to a fishery, the rights-issuing authority determines a total allowable catch $\bar{Y}$, issues rights to individual fishermen, and allows a market to develop in catch rights. Again, the rights-issuing authority sets the total number of rights at the level that maximizes societal net revenues. The price of a catch right will develop to equal the societal shadow price of additional resource extraction, that is, the loss in rent of expanding output beyond the societal optimum. A formal proof is provided in the appendix to this chapter.

Quotas on outputs and output rights constitute direct common property methods of preventing resource overexploitation. There is no need to assume a rigid production relationship between inputs and outputs to get the correct amount of output under this scheme. This has some notable advantages. The users cannot use input substitution to avoid the restriction on exploiting the resource, as they can under input quotas or input rights. In fact, this system encourages producers to determine their own input mixes, and it allows them to install technological changes, both of which encourage efficiency. Firms will use the optimal amount of inputs if they are cost minimizers. Nevertheless, enforcing output rights can be equally as difficult as enforcing input quotas or input rights. Whereas the latter allow input substitution to avoid the restriction, the incentive exists to misrepresent real harvest figures under output limitations. Black markets in the product can also develop. Finally, in some situations—grazing as an example—a limit on outputs (grass harvested) is difficult to implement, and one preferably implements input quotas or input rights.

It is worth noting that a private owner might use any of these quota or rights methods. A sole owner of a fishery, for instance, might use quotas or tradable rights to control lessees in the fishery.[16] The concept of common property, however, does not include the use of quo-

---

[16] The sole owner would maximize his return from the fishery by limiting the number of lessees and their effort or catch to the optimal levels and charging a rental fee that extracted the resource rent. The lessees would be willing to fish as long as the sole owner left to them at least the normal rate of return on capital and labor.

tas or rights by a private owner, because the possession of the resource and decisions about its exploitation lie in a single person's hands. This violates the multiple users condition, Point 3, and the condition of joint, nonexclusive entitlement prior to capture, Point 5, of the definition of common property. Moreover, as long as a sole owner can enforce limitations, the decisions about external costs that actors in a common property system impose upon each other do not lie with a group of rights holders, Point 7 of the definition. Thus, if a private owner applies a quota or a tradable rights method to a group-used resource, the institution cannot be called common property. When a group or government employs these methods, however, the institution is common property.

Institutionalist Justifications of Common Property

Since the late 1960s, the property rights and institutional schools of economics have debated the emergence, the efficiency, and the stability of common property. Until Dahlman (1980), the property rights school held a disapproving opinion of group solutions, whereas the institutional school looked more favorably on their potential. In this section, I draw on some of the arguments from both schools to explore the incentives and transactions costs of two phases of a property rights system: establishing it and operating it. Common property may make sense for some natural resources, because the establishment incentives and transactions costs may favor it over private property, while the operating incentives and transactions costs are conducive to common property's stability.

Establishing Common Property

The property rights paradigm. Several authors of the so-called property rights school have developed various shades of the idea that economic circumstances can explain the emergence of property rights (Demsetz 1967; Pejovich 1972; Alchian and Demsetz 1973; Anderson and Hill 1977; Dahlman 1980). This notion has been labeled "the property rights paradigm." Its main idea is that new private property rights in objects emerge when the benefits of claiming rights exceed the costs of negotiating and enforcing those rights. The value of assets and the cost of protecting assets vary over time, because of changes in technology, relative factor scarcities, tastes and preferences, governmental regulation, and so forth. As these values and costs change, the marginal benefits and marginal costs of defining property rights shift, so that agents gain or lose interest in defining and enforcing rights in the assets (Anderson and Hill 1977). A reduction in cost, such as the lower cost of enforcing property lines in the nineteenth-century American West caused by the invention of barbed wire, or an increase in benefits, such as land's increased value owing to scarcity, may increase definition and enforcement of property rights.

The majority of supporters of the property rights paradigm believe that more property rights definition and enforcement activity means efforts to increase the level of *private* property. Dahlman (1980), however, has extended the property rights paradigm to show that changes in the benefits and costs of controlling assets that lead to increased incentives to control the assets do not determine the *type* of property rights that emerge. Rather, characteristics of the resources, economies of scale involved in the technologies to exploit them, and other economic factors affect the property rights structure. Depending on resource and social characteristics, one incentive system will yield a better economic outcome than another. Hence, actors choose different property rights systems, depending on their efficiency characteristics, to manage different resources (Dahlman 1980: 3).

For example, in the open field system in feudal England, people used two different property rights structures for farming and grazing land: narrow, scattered strips under individual husbandry for crops and large, undivided commons for grazing. Dahlman (1980: 7) argues that these were not inefficient, anomalous practices undertaken by backward peasants unable to see the error in their ways. After all, people used these methods across northern Europe for centuries. Rather, the key to the property rights structures and the agricultural practices lay in varying optimal scales. In the medieval era, livestock production exhibited greater economies of scale than did crop production. Family-centered production using individual plots could not have exploited the full economies of scale in grazing, whereas it could do so in arable cultivation. Therefore, the peasants left grazing lands in large tracts, utilizing them in common, to exploit the economies of scale in grazing. Simultaneously, they divided the arable into small strips—some just fractions of an acre—to fit the technological capabilities available in crop cultivation.

This then explains the existence of, and even the efficiency of, common property in grazing:

If the grazing grounds were owned privately, the large-scale grazing areas desired could only be attained by continual transaction between the farmers involved: collective ownership completely bypasses the problem. (Dahlman 1980: 7)

General economic theory does not imply the universal inefficiency of communal ownership and collective control. On the contrary, correctly applied economic theory will predict that, under certain conditions with respect to transactions and decisions costs, such arrangements will be superior to private ownership and individual control. (Dahlman 1980: 6)

Extending these ideas to the present, we can recognize that the physical attributes and costs of exploitation for at least one class of natural resources preclude private property rights for them. This class is common pool resources, such as groundwater, underground oil and gas, and fish and wildlife.[17] Private property can take two forms: dividing a resource into individual, privately controlled units and sole ownership of the entire resource base. Common pool resources are not physically amenable to the first of these solutions, being divided into pieces and put under private property in their *in situ* state (Dasgupta and Heal 1979: 65; Runge 1981). The technology to control separate units of these resources prior to their capture is extremely costly or does not exist. Therefore, the only private property solution for such resources is sole ownership of the entire resource base. Yet sole ownership for these resources may be impractical for reasons of high cost of instituting and maintaining sole ownership. First, the immense physical scale that some of these resources encompass, such as the wide range of migratory fowl and pelagic fishes or the extent of the atmosphere, makes the control of these resources by a sole owner infeasible, because the costs of control by a sole owner would be virtually infinite. Second, the scale of the resource might not match the optimal scale of production for a single firm; that is, the firm would not be able to extract the rent-maximizing amount of the resource while operating at the minimum on its average total cost curve. In such a case, multiple firms might be able to extract the resource efficiently, but their exploitation would have to be coordinated to avoid the problems of open access. In sum, extending Dahlman's property rights argument indicates that the physical attributes and the costs of exploitation render common pool resources unsuitable for division into individual units on the one hand and unworkable for sole ownership on the other. That is to say, private property

[17] By "common pool resources" I mean the class of resources that are physically unamenable to division into individual, private units prior to capture. *Common pool*, a type of resource, should not be confused with *common property*, a resource management institution. Common pool resources may be exploited under either open access or common property conditions.

rights in general are infeasible for them. In contrast, it is frequently possible to vest common property rights in common pool resources in order to achieve satisfactory use. As examples, input or output rights may be used for fisheries and pollution control; pumping agreements (output quotas) may be applied to groundwater and oil and gas pools.

In addition, some natural resources may be exploited under common property that are not of a common pool nature, resources that could be divided into individual units and used under private control. Land and forests are prime examples. Dahlman's argument at the beginning of this section, playing heavily on the concept of economies of scale, already indicates that certain resource configurations and technological constraints may result in common property's being a preferable arrangement, even when the resource could be privatized. The Swiss grazing commons provide another example. Some Swiss common property grazing areas are found in remote locations, where transportation costs and the risks of individual husbandry favor the scale economies of cooperative use over the incentives of private management.

Thus, whether the resources are common pool or amenable to privatization, particular natural resource configurations, technological constraints, and transactions costs may make common property a superior solution to private property.

Social and institutional effects. Besides the physical attributes of the resource and the technological aspects of its exploitation, social and institutional factors influence the establishment of property rights. These include costs of negotiation and institutional and cultural inertia.

Perhaps the most widely recognized barrier to establishing group solutions consists of the costs of negotiation. Establishment transactions costs of this type include (1) uncertainty about one's potential contribution to production without an agreement; (2) the inability to communicate to others one's knowledge about one's reserves of the resource (oil pools, etc.) or one's ability to capture the resource (fisheries, etc.); (3) the costs generated by holdouts and concessions made to them to bring them into the agreement; and (4) the administrative and time costs of negotiating. Often private property advocates contend that these costs of negotiation are a prohibitive deterrent to collective solutions (e.g., Demsetz 1967: 354–55). This is apparently true in some cases. Without government intervention, negotiators for many oil reservoir unitization schemes have failed to reach agreement

(Wiggins and Libecap 1985). As the prisoner's dilemma and the open access resource models indicate, however, negotiations may yield gains to all concerned when the starting point is open access and the resource is about to be or already is overexploited. Given the existence of establishment transactions costs, the question is an empirical one: Do the benefits of collusion—the recovery of lost resource rents—exceed the establishment transactions costs? If so, there are incentives to negotiate and potentially to reach agreement. Common property solutions will emerge in some cases and fail in others. Therefore, failure need not be a foregone conclusion, as some private property advocates maintain. Moreover, where a group solution does not emerge on its own, government intervention to promote it may be an acceptable substitute.

Finally, institutional and cultural inertia may favor converting an open access resource to common rather than to private property. For instance, even if the physical extent of the resource is confined to a space that makes sole ownership theoretically feasible, previous institutional patterns for the resource may make sole ownership unachievable. Even for a resource as large as a fishery on one of the Great Lakes, one can at least imagine a government concession for sole exploitation rights. Yet the history in this area of many independent commercial fishermen makes the political practicality of the idea doubtful. In this case, the administrative and social costs of conversion probably would be prohibitive. As another example, it may be inappropriate to impose certain property rights structures on certain cultures at a particular point in their evolution (Ely 1914: 266, 297–98; Ciriacy-Wantrup 1952: 146). Bottomley (1963) has already provided an example of this inappropriateness, in which he recommends avoiding the violation of "hallowed rights" in land that would occur if a private property approach in tree planting in Tripolitania were undertaken. Instead, he recommends what amounts to a common property solution. In some other cases in the developing world, the attempt to impose private property in other natural resources has not increased efficiency but rather has led to social disruption and even increased resource abuse (Runge 1986). Even in developed countries, historical instances of establishing private property have given rise to rather large costs. The costs associated with legislative acts, disenfranchisement, and social upheaval that accompanied the English enclosure movement provide an example. In sum, there is no a priori reason to believe that establishment costs of converting an open access resource to private property are less than those associated with establishing common property.

Maintaining Common Property

As I have mentioned, in the game theoretic formulation of the open access problem, even if collusion leads to the joint-welfare-maximizing solution (the lower right-hand box in Figures 2.5–2.7), there remains the incentive for both players to break the agreement. Similarly, at the optimal total input level in the models of open access, there is always the incentive of increased profits' luring each individual firm to expand inputs and production beyond its allotted amount. How stable, then, is a common property solution?

The answer lies in the transactions costs of enforcing the solution and other incentives that tend to stabilize the solution. Specifically, stability of group solutions requires one or both of two elements— coercive enforcement and assurance of cooperation by other users. Enforcement is a conventional answer, given most often by economists who put limited faith in common property solutions. Assurance is a theme usually found among institutional economists who consider common property a viable alternative to private property in its own right. Here I examine each of these approaches to stability.

Stability through enforcement. First, let us consider enforcement. Assume that the problems of reaching a solution have been overcome. Collusion has been allowed and establishment transactions costs are low enough for players to reach and maintain a joint-welfare maximum if they wish. Alternatively, assume that the government can locate the optimal level of inputs and outputs and can allocate these quantities among firms. The question then is, what is to keep the participants at this optimal point? In the context of the conventional wisdom, the answer is enforcement: enforcement tough enough to overcome the incentive to cheat.

I use enforcement in a rather general sense. It can take different forms, depending upon the form of the common property. If the common property system is that of the Bahia swamp dwellers, then enforcement is composed mainly of informal, extralegal procedures and group pressure. If the common property system is that of the Swiss grazing areas, then enforcement means not only group social pressure but policing by an elected overseer and fines for violations as well. If the common property is that of a provincial or state quota-restricted fishery, then enforcement takes the form of a watchdog agency with the full powers of the state and courts to back it up.

In a comparison of common property to private property on enforcement, several points are worth noting. First, whereas the difficulty of enforcing common property rights is explicit in most formulations of the idea, the costs of enforcing private property often remain hidden and implicit in suggestions that it is the best solution. Yet private property rights can be violated just as can common property rights. Trespass or theft violates private property rights; overuse violates common property rights. To be sure, some form of enforcement may be necessary to ensure common property solutions. Large costs, however, both private and social, also are incurred to protect private property rights. Personal costs such as fencing, locks, security guards, court cases, and so on are associated with protecting private property. If these personal measures do not succeed, then the enforcement powers of the state can be brought to bear, a process that also engenders costs. Thus, enforcement is necessary not only to stabilize the unsteady joint-profit-maximizing solution to the prisoner's dilemma, but also to secure private property rights. Criticism of common property for its need to incur enforcement costs to stabilize an unsteady solution is unbalanced if it takes no account of the investment that society and individuals make in protecting private property.

Differences probably do lie in incentives to provide enforcement, however. Whereas under private property individuals are willing to incur some costs of enforcement, under common property the group or outside agents must support a greater proportion of enforcement costs. This is because, even as individuals cannot capture all benefits from investments in improvements to a common property resource, they cannot capture all benefits of enforcement. Still, there is no general reason to suspect that total enforcement costs are greater or less under common property than under private property. In fact, enforcement costs are likely to be less for some resources under private property and less for other resources under common property.

Finally, the costliness of enforcing property rights depends on the type and degree of property rights socialization that takes place in a society. If particular property rights configurations are justified and legitimatized in the prevailing social mores, people will observe them more readily, lowering establishment and enforcement costs. Although private property is the primary form of property rights sanctioned through socialization in most industrialized Western nations, this does not mean that alternatives have not been equally as legitimate in other times or places. For this reason, common property may not require large enforcement costs in certain cultural situations.

Stability through assurance. The idea that enforcement is the way to stabilize common property arises from the assumption that individual incentives strongly and invariably lead participants to defect. The idea that stability can occur through assurance questions the validity of this assumption.

Runge (1981, 1986) has attacked the adequacy of the prisoner's dilemma as a model for studying group use, saying that it does not adequately reflect the interdependencies of joint use. As part of the definition of the prisoner's dilemma, the players make decisions independently. Runge argues that real-world commons do not exhibit such independent, separable decisions. Rather, commons users condition their decisions on expectations of others' behavior. A common range ties the users' welfare and decision making together (Runge 1981: 599).

Runge proposes adopting a new model, the "assurance problem" (Sen 1967). He argues that assurance of what others will do allows better decisions, and that the possibility for better decisions gives an incentive to make and keep agreements. Groups, recognizing the advantage to all of capturing resource rents and the potential disaster to the group economy of noncooperation, choose the Pareto optimal solution. This approach also proposes that the incentives involved make the solutions inherently stable, that no incentive remains to defect from optimal solutions once reached.

Runge uses models that reflect interdependencies of decision making and involve no incentives to individuals to defect from the optimum once reached. There is no reason, however, to jump to totally new frameworks to model the benefits of assurance, as Runge does.[18] The problem of assurance can be modeled within the original context of the prisoner's dilemma by allowing adjustment of individual strategies once the other player's move is known. This, after all, is similar to the real world in resource extraction. Assume that each player is assured that the other player will refrain from overexploitation, if he or she also refrains. Let us further assume that maverick behavior on either person's part will simply trigger overexploitation by the other.

[18] To model assurance, Runge uses the "battle of the sexes" (Luce and Raiffa 1957; Bacharach 1977; Runge 1981) and an n-person model without strictly dominant strategies (Runge 1986: fig. 2). By using these models to represent real-world interdependencies, however, Runge emasculates another part of the group use problem, the incentive to cheat. In the models of the assurance problem that Runge presents, there is no incentive to cheat once an agreement has been reached. Is there, however, incentive to cheat on the group agreement in a real-world common property solution? Clearly, the answer is yes. The incentive to cheat, if not actual cheating behavior, always persists. The incentive to increase catch in a controlled fishery, to increase pumping from a controlled groundwater aquifer, to graze one more animal on a commons, is ever present. It is just a question of whether the incentive for the individual to stick to the group solution is greater.

What will the solution be? Assuming collusion is possible, the answer is obvious. The joint-maximizing decision will be reached. It is not possible to end up in either the upper right-hand or the lower left-hand box of the prisoner's dilemma payoff matrix (Figure 2.5), where one player is defecting while the other cooperates, because adjustment of strategies is allowed. In addition, both players prefer the lower right-hand to the upper left-hand box, so the former will be chosen. Therefore, given the *assurance* of restraint on the other's part, together with the *assurance* that maverick behavior will simply cause the other to defect as well, each will show restraint. The incentive to cheat is still present, because the lower left- and upper right-hand boxes are still technologically feasible. It is just that the incentive not to cheat is greater. The incentive to obtain a share of the joint maximum profit can be sufficient within the prisoner's dilemma with adjustable strategies to overcome the individual incentive to cheat (Bishop and Milliman 1983). Add to this the real-world desires of individuals to conform to group norms and pressure, and we come to the same conclusion as does Runge (1981: 603):

The benefits possible in the short term may be more than offset by costs arising within the group from breaking the institutional rule. In the absence of strictly dominant individual strategies, recognized interdependence makes the costs of reputation loss high. Pecuniary costs imposed by the group on its own noncooperative members also may occur. . . . These costs, plus reductions in the attainable set if such antisocial behavior "sets a trend" for others, plus the opportunity costs of innovating new rules, may well exceed the expense of stinting on the range.

These conclusions are strengthened by the fact that a certain amount of uncertainty about others' strategies can lead to cooperation (Kreps, Milgrom, Roberts, and Wilson 1982; Braden 1985). If individuals assign any probability at all to the possibility that others will view cooperation as being in their long-term self-interest, they may experiment with the cooperation strategy, in turn inducing others to follow suit. Experiments with finitely repeated prisoner's dilemmas have shown patterns of cooperation among players, at least for some of the time (Kreps et al. 1982).

In conclusion, then, to the extent that assurance and tit-for-tat strategies obtain, common property can be viewed as a stable solution to open access in and of itself. Runge has moved us forward by taking a close look at the conventional assumption of independent self-maximizers in a noncollusive prisoner's dilemma as an adequate model for the commons. Through his work and the ideas presented here—that a *collusive* prisoner's dilemma can lead to stability—we are closer to understanding how historical common property systems, once they have evolved, have sometimes survived for centuries.

Summary

I began this chapter by carefully differentiating common property from open access. Both its role in history and its nature as a property institution imply limited use by a definable group of co-owners. Therefore, common property may offer an alternative to private property as a solution to the open access problem. Open access has two characteristics that lead to nonoptimality, and resource users must handle both of them to find acceptable solutions. Both (1) a lack of limitations on the *number of users* who enter into resource extraction and (2) a lack of limitations on the *number of inputs* that each user applies cause inefficiency. Common property addresses both problems. It limits the number of users who are allowed to exploit the resource, and in a well-functioning common property situation, some mechanism is used to limit the amount of inputs that each user may apply or the outputs that each may extract.

As a resource management institution, common property lies between open access and private property. Like open access, it exhibits the incentives inherent in group use, but it imposes the resource control characteristics of private property. It differs from a public good, which also involves group use, because it is a resource use regime whereas a public good is a type of good or service. Some resources that display a public goods character can be managed as common property.

The rules for controlling common property may be imposed from outside or generated within the group. They range from the neoclassical solutions of input or output quotas and rights to far less formal solutions embodied in a set of customs among users. Common property is the preferred solution to open access when the resource is unamenable to being split into individually controlled units, the control costs of sole ownership are prohibitive, or the technological characteristics of production (e.g., economies of scale) favor it over private property. It may also be preferred when social or cultural factors favor a group over an individualistic solution. Once common property is established, enforcement and assurance are elements that can secure its stability. Whereas enforcement may arise from inside or outside the group, assurance arises from inherent incentives within the group to keep agreements.

In view of all this, one is encouraged to ask: Does common property empirically provide an adequate solution to the open access problem? After a look in Chapters 4 and 5 at how the Swiss and English constructed common property institutions, I will take up this question. Chapters 6 and 7 describe and draw conclusions from empirical work comparing common property with private property in Switzerland.

Appendix: Proofs of Solutions to Open Access

This appendix includes formal proofs of the optimality of the input quotas, input rights, and output rights schemes. A proof of private property's optimality is also included, since it is the standard against which we measure common property's adequacy. Much of the treatment is an adaptation of the approach in Dasgupta and Heal (1979: chap. 3). The output rights proof is a variation of the approach in Moloney and Pearse (1979).

Private Property

Private property as a solution to the nonoptimality of open access can take two forms: (1) putting the entire resource recovery area under a sole owner or (2) splitting the resource grounds into private plots. We will examine both cases.

If there is only one firm in the industry, it will introduce the optimal number of inputs. We can see this by noticing that for $N = 1$, competitive equilibrium conditions (2.13) and (2.14) in the appendix to Chapter 2 reduce to the optimality conditions (2.15) and (2.16), respectively. Thus, a sole owner manages the resource optimally, and the problem of unrestricted inputs arises only if $N > 1$. The sole owner allocates correctly, because he or she considers all costs and benefits of additional resource extraction and internalizes the costs that were imposed on other users under open access.

An assumption of constant returns to scale in producing effort, which, I argued in the appendix to Chapter 2, is consistent with the results of the mathematical model, also facilitates the conclusion that a sole owner can operate an entire fishery optimally. If constant returns to scale do not obtain, scale diseconomies may make the costs of sole ownership prohibitive. For larger fisheries, it is difficult to imagine a single firm producing all industry effort under the U-shaped cost conditions that Anderson (1977) assumes. On the other hand, if increasing returns to scale were to prevail, the other private property solution of splitting the resource into private plots would not be optimal. Thus, private property solutions are not as straightforward as simple mathematical models present them.

Nevertheless, to show mathematically the optimality (under constant returns to scale) of splitting the resource grounds, let us assume that the resource grounds can be divided into N equally productive plots. We must now explicitly introduce the size of the resource catchment area into the production function. Define the production function as

$$Y = H(X, S),$$

where S denotes the size of the entire resource grounds. Our earlier analysis ignored S because it was a constant $\bar{S}$. This, along with an implicit assumption that H exhibits constant returns to scale in X and S, allowed us to reduce the production function to a single variable:

$$Y = H(X, \bar{S}) = H\left(\frac{X}{\bar{S}}, 1\right) = H(X, 1) \equiv F(X),$$

where the second-to-the-last step is taken by normalizing $\bar{S}$ to 1.

We now alter S by dividing the resource area up into N plots. Note that this is the crucial assumption for this solution, particularly because some resources, such as fisheries, large oil pools, and wildlife, do not lend themselves to being divided up. By making this assumption, we essentially assume away the reciprocal externality. If, however, it is possible to divide the grounds into N plots, the production possibilities facing a particular user would be

$$y_i = H\left(x_i, \frac{\bar{S}}{N}\right).$$

Here x_i denotes the input level of user i. Recalling the assumption of constant returns to scale for H and the normalization $\bar{S} = 1$, we have

$$y_i = H\left(x_i, \frac{\bar{S}}{N}\right) = \frac{1}{N} H(Nx_i, \bar{S}) = \frac{1}{N} H(Nx_i, 1) = \frac{1}{N} F(Nx_i).$$

If we use these production possibilities for the individual firm and take the recovered resource to be the numeraire good, the individual firm's profit is given by

$$\frac{1}{N} F(Nx) - rx,$$

where again r is the rental rate for inputs (boats) and the i subscript has been suppressed because all firms are identical. Maximizing this function with respect to x gives

$$F'(Nx) = r. \tag{3.1}$$

Condition (3.1) is identical to the optimality condition (2.15) in the appendix to Chapter 2. This proves that competitive profit maximization under the regime of N private plots leads to optimal results.

Input Quotas

Another solution to open access is a system of quotas on inputs. The formal proof of the optimality of this solution is implicit in the derivation of the optimality conditions (2.15) and (2.16) in the appendix to Chapter 2. There it was noted that the socially optimal (Pareto efficient) amount of inputs is the solution to the maximization with respect to x of resource rent:

$$\max_{x} F(Nx) - rNx.$$

The first-order condition for this problem is

$$F'(Nx) = r. \tag{3.2}$$

Again, let $\bar{x}$ be the value of x that satisfies equation (3.2). The quota on inputs system consists of participants in resource recovery colluding to limit themselves to $\bar{x}$ units of input each. (Alternatively, the government may impose this limit on them.) If each firm introduces $\bar{x}$ units of input, by the definition of $\bar{x}$ and condition (3.2), the optimal resource rent will be realized. Each firm will extract $F(N\bar{x})/N$ amount of the resource and enjoy $(1/N)^{\text{th}}$ of the maximal rent.

Input Rights

The third solution sometimes mentioned for the open access problem is input rights. This too is a scheme to limit inputs, although unlike quotas, rights are assumed to be tradable.

To formalize an input rights scheme, assume that (1) the management agency issues $\bar{X} < \hat{X}$ rights, where $\hat{X}$ is the amount of inputs introduced at open access equilibrium; (2) there are N firms; and (3) the firms are identical. To find the inverse derived demand function for rights—that is, the competitive license price $\bar{r}$ as a function of x_i—we need to find an expression for the ith firm's profit function. This profit function will take the standard form of revenues minus costs. On the revenue side, the ith firm must make an assumption about how many vessels all other firms will introduce, because its average product is affected by the open access externality from other firms. If it assumes that all other firms will introduce $\bar{x}$ inputs each, its revenues will be

$$x_i \frac{F[(N-1)\bar{x}+x_i]}{(N-1)\bar{x}+x_i},$$

where x_i is the number of inputs it introduces, the ratio term is its average product, and the output (captured resource) price equals one. On the cost side, an operator will regard the equilibrium price of a right as an expense to be added to the purchase price of the input. Hence total costs are

$$(r+\bar{r})x_i.$$

The profit function then is

$$\pi = x_i \frac{F[(N-1)\bar{x}+x_i]}{(N-1)\bar{x}+x_i} - (r+\bar{r})x_i. \tag{3.3}$$

To maximize profits, equation (3.3) is maximized with respect to x_i. As a result, the operator will chose x_i such that

$$\frac{(N-1)\bar{x}F[(N-1)\bar{x}+x_i]}{[(N-1)\bar{x}+x_i]^2} + \frac{x_i F'[(N-1)\bar{x}+x_i]}{(N-1)\bar{x}+x_i} = r+\bar{r}. \tag{3.4}$$

Since all firms are identical, in equilibrium $x_i = \bar{x}$, and (3.4) reduces to

$$\frac{(N-1)\bar{x}F(N\bar{x})}{(N\bar{x})^2} + \frac{F'(N\bar{x})}{N} = r+\bar{r}. \tag{3.5}$$

Equation (3.5) implicitly defines the demand for rights $N\bar{x}$ as a function of their price $\bar{r}$ and the cost of a unit of effort r. The supply of rights is $\bar{X}$. Equating demand and supply, we have $N\bar{x} = \bar{X}$ as a condition of equilibrium that may be substituted into (3.5). Solving for the equilibrium price of a right:

$$\bar{r} = \frac{(N-1)}{N}\left[\frac{F(N\bar{x})}{N\bar{x}} + \frac{F'(N\bar{x})}{N}\right] - r, \tag{3.6}$$

where $N\bar{x} = \bar{X}$.

This shows that the equilibrium price of a right is a function of the number of rights issued $\bar{X}$, and the cost of effort r. Presumably, the issuing agency will want to issue rights only for the optimal number of inputs, that is, set $\bar{X}$ equal to $\hat{X}$, where the optimality condition (2.16) in the appendix to Chapter 2 defines $\hat{X}$. Given identical firms, $\hat{X} = N\hat{x}$. Moreover, the cost of effort r can be eliminated from (3.6), because at the optimal level of effort $\hat{X}$, $r = F'(N\hat{x})$ by the optimality conditions (2.15) and (2.16). Equation (3.6), then, can be rewritten to give $\hat{r}$, the equilibrium price of a right when the optimal number of rights is issued:

$$\tilde{r} = \frac{(N-1)}{N}\left[\frac{F(N\tilde{x})}{N\tilde{x}} - F'(N\tilde{x})\right].$$

Faced with this cost of an input right, the individual resource user will introduce the optimal amount of inputs. The rights-issuing agent, however, needs only to determine the correct number of rights $\tilde{X}$ to introduce, and $\tilde{r}$ will develop by market processes. The revenue from the sale of rights may be collected by the government or user cooperative, or it may be capitalized into the value of the firms if the rights are initially issued free of charge.

Output Rights

A fourth solution for open access based on neoclassical economics consists of transferable output rights. The proof of optimality given here is based on a 1979 article by Moloney and Pearse that develops output rights for a fishery. In such an output rights system, the rights-setting authority determines a total allowable catch $\tilde{Y}$, issues rights to individual fishers, and allows a market to develop in catch rights. Properly constructed, this market in rights will not only encourage individual and industry efficiency but also lead individual decisions to the social optimum.

To begin, define a net revenue function $R_i(y_i, P)$, where y_i is the catch of firm i and P is the fish population.[19] The function $R_i(y_i, P)$ gives net revenues that accrue to a fishing operation from the resource rent only; it excludes any costs or revenues from the purchase or sale of catch rights. The control variable for the individual fisher is the catch rate y_i; independent of any transferable rights scheme, the fisher would want to maximize $R_i(y_i, P)$ by adjusting y_i. Define L_i as the number of rights that the ith firm holds. Further, let m be the market

---

[19] Moloney and Pearse (1979) use the notation H_i for a firm's catch and X for the fish population level. This would be confusing here, given notation used elsewhere in this book. I have altered H_i to y_i and X to P to make my notation clear. Also, in my equation (3.9), the function $G(\cdot)$ is the same as Moloney and Pearse's $F(\cdot)$.

Population P appears in the net revenue function, because the catch rate for an individual fisher depends not only on input level x_i, but also on the population level: $y_i = y_i(x_i, P)$. Imagine, for instance, that the net revenue function takes the form

$$R_i(y_i, P) = py_i - C_i(y_i),$$

where P is the price of fish and $C_i(\cdot)$ is the cost of harvest for the ith firm. Net revenue depends on the fish population P because y_i (which depends on P) appears in both revenues and costs. The influence of the fish population on an individual's catch was incorporated differently into the previous mathematical model (in the appendix to Chapter 2). There the input level of all other firms, which affects population level, was included in the individual fisherman's production function:

$$y_i = x_i F(X_{N-i} + x_i)/(X_{N-i} + x_i).$$

price for a right. Because a fisherman must hold L_i rights to catch y_i fish, $R_i(y_i, P) = R_i(L_i, P)$. It is obvious that the ith fisher will retain his holdings of rights only if

$$\partial R_i(L_i, P)/\partial L_i = \partial R_i(y_i, P)/\partial y_i \geq m. \tag{3.7}$$

Indeed, if the strict inequality in (3.7) holds, the fisher will be a purchaser of rights. In the event that

$$\partial R_i(L_i, P)/\partial L_i = \partial R_i(y_i, P)/\partial y_i < m, \tag{3.8}$$

the fisher would sell rights, because a right's value in the market exceeds its marginal value in catching fish. The fisher is in equilibrium if and only if there is equality between his marginal net revenues and the price of a right.

Through the operation of the market in rights, an equilibrium price m^* will develop. The market equilibrium will also be characterized by $\partial R_i/\partial L_i = m^*$ for all i, because then and only then is each fisher in equilibrium as just described. All fishermen will be maximizing profits subject to incurring the cost of the rights and holding to the overall constraint on output:

$$\bar{Y} = \sum_{i=1}^{N} L_i.$$

Of course, the only problem is setting $\bar{Y}$ optimally. In keeping with this book's emphasis on static models, I will derive the conditions for a static social optimum. Define the population growth curve in Figure 2.1 as

$$\frac{dP}{dt} = G(P). \tag{3.9}$$

When fishing mortality is added:

$$\frac{dP}{dt} = G(P) - \sum_{i=1}^{N} L_i. \tag{3.10}$$

In equilibrium, natural population growth just equals catch, so

$$\frac{dP}{dt} = 0,$$

and (3.10) becomes

$$G(P) - \sum_{i=1}^{N} y_i = 0. \tag{3.11}$$

For the individual fisher, there is no advantage in holding either more or fewer rights than he catches fish, so in equilibrium $L_i = y_i$. Substitute this into equation (3.11) to get the constraint for a static optimization problem,

$$G(P) - \sum_{i=1}^{N} L_i,$$

and also into the net revenue function,

$$R_i(y_i, P) = R_i(L_i, P).$$

Thus, to attain the social optimum, we wish to maximize total net revenues

$$\sum_{i=1}^{N} R_i(L_i, P),$$

subject to the constraint

$$G(P) = \sum_{i=1}^{N} L_i.$$

This can be performed by maximizing the Lagrangean function

$$\max_{L_i, P, \lambda} V = \sum_{i=1}^{N} R_i(L_i, P) + \lambda[G(P) - \sum_{i=1}^{N} L_i].$$

The optimal solution will meet the first-order conditions:

$$\frac{\partial R_i}{\partial L_i} = \lambda \qquad (i = 1, 2, \ldots, N)$$

$$\sum_{i=1}^{N} \frac{\partial R_i}{\partial P} = -\lambda G'(P)$$

$$\sum_{i=1}^{N} L_i = G(P).$$

The Lagrangean multiplier λ can be interpreted as the shadow price of a right. Since, as argued above, $\partial R_i/\partial L_i = m^*$, the first-order conditions imply

$$m^* = \partial R_i/\partial L_i = \lambda.$$

That is, $m^* = \lambda$; the equilibrium market price of a right will equal its societal shadow price. Therefore, private actions responding to the price m^* will lead to the social optimum. The rights-setting authority need only set the correct number of rights

$$\sum_{i=1}^{N} L_i = G(P)$$

such that

$$\sum_{i=1}^{N} \partial R_i/\partial P = -\lambda G'(P)$$

and

$$\partial R_i/\partial L_i = \lambda$$

for all i. In reality, λ cannot be observed and the quantities $\partial R_i/\partial L_i$ for all i would require large quantities of information, especially if N is large. Practically speaking, the number of rights that maximizes social net revenue can be set only by trial and error, perhaps by the rights-setting authority buying and selling into the market.

CHAPTER 4

The Swiss Grazing Commons

This chapter describes the practices, rights systems, history, management tools, and governance of Swiss alpine grazing. Although I emphasize common property, private property is also discussed. Because there may be two audiences for this material, I have arranged it to allow the reader to decide how much of it to read. One audience, I suspect, will be interested primarily in the distinctions between open access and common property and the idea that common property may present a solution to resource use that rivals that of private property. For this audience, who may not be interested in an exhaustive description of Swiss alpine grazing, I provide a summary section on how the Swiss have avoided the open access problem. For the second audience, interested institutional economists, economic historians, geographers, and anthropologists, I provide a detailed treatment of Swiss grazing practices to which many English-speaking scholars may otherwise have no access.

The following section is a brief introduction on alpine grazing for all readers. Subsequently, I present the summary on limited entry and methods of resource protection. At this point, those interested only in the debate on open access and common and private property can proceed to Chapter 5 without loss of continuity. The remainder of the chapter gives a full description of the rights systems, history, management tools, and governance of Swiss grazing commons.[1]

---

[1] I base this chapter on both primary and secondary sources. My primary sources include regulations written for the alpine grazing areas; constitutions written for the larger organizations that own multiple grazing areas; a contract written between a renter and a grazing area owner; several dozen interviews of users, government officials, and university scholars in the area of alpine grazing; and my own observations of user meetings and of the grazing areas themselves. The majority of my secondary sources are academic works, mainly books and dissertations, written by Swiss, German, and Austrian scholars. I also have used government publications and a few popular or journalistic sources. The government publications were written by experts in alpine agriculture, men who, in the course of compiling a land registry for the mountain area of Switzerland, each spent up to a decade visiting alpine grazing areas. The *Schweizerischer Alpkataster* that they wrote (e.g., Bäbler 1962, 1965; Indergand 1963; Marti 1966; Werthemann 1969; Imboden 1972; and Aeschlimann 1978) are distillations of their knowledge in this field. The popular or journalistic sources,

Introduction to Alpine Grazing

The alpine grazing areas of Switzerland exist either as pastures hewn centuries ago from the mountain forests or as natural grasslands lying above the timberline. The mountainous topography makes the areas unsuitable for virtually all other agricultural uses besides grazing and gathering "wild hay." They are subject to a climate that buries them under winter snow, yet warms enough in spring and summer to melt the snow and bring forth forage.

The climate results in a pattern of seasonal usage, in which farmers and their cattle change altitudes to take advantage of new forage as it appears. There are three general levels of pastures: the village-level fields, the "May fields,"[2] and the alpine grazing areas. After spending the winter protected in barns in the permanent settlements of the mountain valleys, the cows and other ruminants may be driven to the grazing areas at the village level first. Sometimes, however, no village-level fields are used and the animals go directly to the May fields just above the permanent settlements. In either event, the animals spend their time on these May fields for two to four weeks in the spring and for a similar period in the fall.

After the snow melts from the higher mountainsides and sufficient time has elapsed to allow the alpine grasses to grow, the animals are driven up to the true alpine grasslands. Most often this occurs anywhere from late May through mid-June. In some cases, the alpine grazing areas are contiguous units, on which the animals are rotated from one part to another all summer. In other cases, the grazing areas are divided into pastures at varying altitudes, each of which is called a *Stafel*. The lowest-altitude pasture is grazed first and the higher-altitude areas are grazed later as the grass appears. In such cases, each separate pasture often has its own set of buildings: a barn, a combined living quarters and milk-processing structure, and a pig stall. A complete relocation of the alpine grazing operation occurs when a move is made from one level to another. A return down the mountainside, grazing areas in an order that depends on each area's size and location, occurs later in the summer. Thus, an alpine grazing operation

---

of which there are six (Camenisch 1924; Imboden, Schohaus, and Schmid 1951; Schuler 1951; Thürer 1978; Rubi 1979; and Neff n.d.), are the work of academic or government experts in the field who used a popular publication (a newspaper, magazine, school book, or farmer's almanac) as an outlet. Because of who the authors are, we can have as much confidence in these sources as in the more conventional, academic works.

[2] Variously called *Vorsässe* (literally, "fore-seats"), *Maiensässe* (literally, "May seats"), or *Voralpen* ("forealps").

may traverse one or two and sometimes even three or four levels of mountain pastures in a summer. Final return to the May fields usually occurs in middle or late September.

This system has a simple economic rationale. More animals can be supported by using the mountain grasslands than if the farmers utilized only the pastures that are more easily accessible in the valleys. While the animals are feeding on the alpine flora, the farmers have an opportunity to harvest hay from their fields in the valleys and from second growth in the May fields. This feed is used to get the animals through the next winter. Estimates indicate that this system allows the Swiss mountain farmer to support approximately 30 percent more animals than could be supported if the alpine grazing areas were not used (Wohlfarter 1965: 8; Marti 1966: 108).

I emphasize that the village-level fields and the May fields are distinct from the alpine grazing areas. The village-level fields and the May fields are most often privately owned[3] and occur at altitudes that give them a more luxuriant grass growth. The alpine grazing areas can be either private or commons and are at altitudes that give them a rawer character. Farmers may work the village fields and the May fields by commuting to them daily from the valley settlement, whereas, in most cases, permanent residence is taken up for the summer on the alpine grazing areas. Swiss agriculturalists clearly distinguish between the true alpine grazing lands and other pastures, and they even have formal definitions of alpine grazing areas. The definition provided by Imboden, Schohaus, and Schmid (1951) is as follows:

An alpine grazing area is that mountain land that serves the summer grazing of cattle exclusively, and that, owing to the extent of its land area, makes a separate, self-contained operation possible. Land that can be used from the home farm on a daily basis or at similarly short intervals is to be considered [home] pasture. (My translation)

This book concentrates on the true alpine grazing areas. With the exception of a short account of village-level commons, I exclude the village-level fields and the May fields. The empirical work of Chapter 6 also includes only observations on the true alpine grazing areas.

An alpine grazing area has an interesting name in Swiss German. It is called an *Alp*. When the Swiss refer to an *Alp*, they do *not* mean the mountain itself, as an English speaker would when using the word "alp." The two words are related, of course: The European mountain

---

[3] There are exceptions to this rule. Some communities have "community commons" (*Allmenden*) at the village level. All community residents own and use these together, and thus they are not private. Where they exist, these commons substitute for private, village-level fields.

chain, the Alps, took its name from the alpine pastures found in it.
Subsequently, the word came to mean "mountain" in English, whereas
in German *Alp* has retained the meaning "grazing area in the mountains." After two years in Switzerland, calling the mountain grazing
areas "alps" has become second nature to me. For this reason, as well
as the economy that the single word "alp" provides over the phrase
"alpine grazing area," I will use the word "alp" in referring to the
mountain grazing areas.

Figure 4.1 is a map of Switzerland indicating the locations of the
cantons. This map is included for the reader's convenience, because I
will refer to the cantons often.

Summary of Swiss Common Property

Rights Systems

Swiss farmers use three primary rights systems to limit entry to the
alpine grazing areas. These three rights systems are used on what I
call the share rights alps, the community alps, and the *Korporation*
alps. Property alps constitute a fourth system found only in a small
number of instances.

Figure 4.1. The Cantons of Switzerland. Reproduced by permission of the
Swiss Federal Office of Topography, May 24, 1989 (Bundesamt für Landestopographie 1986)

The share rights alps limit entry by requiring users to possess grazing rights. In the archetypical case, a right allows its owner to graze one animal unit, usually equal to one cow. Instead of a cow, however, the owner may graze other animals with his rights, the number of rights required for each animal type depending on the grazing pressure that that animal type exerts. For instance, a two-year-old heifer may require two-thirds of a right, a one-year-old heifer one-half of a right, and a calf one-third of a right. The rights are perpetual (i.e., they do not extinguish annually or at any other interval), and they are transferable by rental or sale. Prices are most often determined by the market. The total number of rights is set at carrying capacity, which the group of users has determined from experience. When the carrying capacity changes for one reason or another, the total number of rights for the grazing area remains the same, but the users alter the number of rights required to graze one animal unit. For instance, to reduce grazing pressure, they may require one and a quarter units for a cow. In summary, the share rights system both limits access to parties who may want to enter from outside the group and defines grazing pressure rights clearly among users within the group.

The second major common rights system is found in the community alps, which are alpine grazing areas owned by communities or townships. In most cases, the primary requirement for use is residency in the townships. In some cases, "citizenship" in the community is required, a more stringent requirement based on the citizenship that every Swiss national has in the particular township from which his or her ancestors came. Although these requirements loosely limit the number of users, further restrictions became necessary long ago to limit the number of animals. The primary limitation on many community alps is that users must winter the animals that they send to the alp on hay harvested from within the township. Given that township lands can only grow a certain amount of hay, this rule often effectively limits the number of animals on the alp. If the wintering restriction is insufficient, however, then some further allocation rule is used to limit the number of animals to carrying capacity. Apportionment may proceed by equal division among applicants; division among applicants in the ratio of available capacity to total demand; division based on land ownership in the valley (measured by estimated hay productivity, area, or value); priority systems among township citizens, residents, and nonresidents; and allocation by rotation or lot. By whatever method, those without rights to the commons are excluded, and for those included, entry is limited to what the commons will bear.

Korporation alps represent the third major rights system, where *Korporation* means "corporate body of citizens." The *Korporation*s are ancient institutions surviving from a period between the tenth and thirteenth centuries when villagers in the inner cantons of Switzerland claimed rights to dozens of alps at a time. The *Korporation*s continue to be umbrella organizations that each own many alps. The "citizens" of the *Korporation*s are members of families with certain surnames—the old families of the districts in which the *Korporation*s were founded. Rights to use the *Korporation*s' alps are limited to these families. As with the community alps, such a restriction is inadequate, so further restrictions based on residency, wintering of animals in the district, and possession of "hut rights" are imposed. Hut rights are granted by a *Korporation* administration, and they allow the user to build or use an existing alp stall and to stock the commons with a certain number of animal units. Thus, entry is limited either by a wintering requirement or directly by hut rights.

Property alps represent a fourth system of limiting entry based on land ownership in the valley, a form of rights determination rather rare in Switzerland. The number of commons use rights is tied to ownership of particular parcels near the village or very occasionally particular tenements. If ownership of the valley land is transferred, the alp rights automatically transfer with it. If the land is divided by sale or inheritance, the number of rights transferred to each new owner is proportional to the number of hectares that each new owner receives. In this way, entry to common use of the alp is limited to those who have correspondent property interests in the valley, and overall use is limited at carrying capacity.

The alps of the canton of Glarus represent a final model of alp regulation. In Glarus, central government plays a major role in alp access. A cantonal law requires that the carrying capacity of all alps, whether commons or private, be reassessed every ten years. Every alp must possess a set of alp regulations, establishing the number and types of animals to be grazed.

Across rights types, limited entry by seasons is used. Regulations prohibit any user from ascending to the alp before a date set annually by a meeting of the users.[4] Annual adjustment of this date is impor-

---

[4] Occasionally, the day of the alp ascent is set by rights holders rather than by the users, if the two groups are not the same because of rental of rights. In most cases, however, users set the day of the alp ascent, whether the two groups coincide or not. Further explanation is given in the section entitled "Governance and Decision Making," later in this chapter.

tant for the resource, because the grass grows at different rates each year. Regulations also set the total number of weeks that users are allowed to graze the alp. Thus, regulations on seasons limit the duration of use, and the rights systems restrict the intensity of use.

Investment in Common Improvements

The Swiss have taken steps to combat the tendency of individuals to underinvest in maintenance and improvements of common property resources. They have done so through regulations, work duties, and fees.

Most commons alps have a set of written alp regulations, which some earlier group of alp rights holders composed and to which current rights holders subscribe. Current rights holders also have the power to alter these regulations. The alp regulations actually cover a variety of topics beyond simple investment in the commons—including the rights system and the number of animal units allowed on the alp. In connection with alp maintenance, however, the regulations require commoners to perform weed clearing, manuring, and stone and debris removal, and to stall their animals a certain number of hours per day during the critical early season to foster initial grass growth.

The alp regulations also frequently stipulate a work duty, which may be used to accomplish some of the tasks just mentioned (weed clearing, manuring, debris removal, and so forth). The work requirement also may be used to accomplish such tasks as fence erection at the beginning of the season or dismantling at the end, path maintenance, and building repairs. The work duty may be a requirement for users to do common work for a particular number of hours on the alp for each animal unit grazed. This is particularly often the case on commons that have a centralized herding operation, with the animal owners coming to the alp from the valley on particular days to perform alp maintenance and improvements. On decentralized commons, the work duty may not stipulate that users work a certain number of hours but rather require them to keep certain items under control, such as weed removal, manuring, and so on. Sometimes the work duty can be discharged by a monetary payment. Occasionally workers are paid for fulfilling the work obligation.

Fees are required for grazing on almost all alps, even though one holds rights to use. The fees are considered "grass money," but they are generally so low that they are not a deterrence to entry. For this reason, I include them here under means to provide for common improvements. The money goes into a common treasury used for alp administration and improvements.

Enforcement

Enforcement is necessary to ensure adherence to the rights systems, the seasons, the regulations, the work duties, the fees, and so forth. Swiss commoners have used compensation fees, fines, and the office of the alp overseer to provide the requisite compulsion.

Most alp regulations list fines for infractions, or they designate who has the power to set fines (commonly the meeting of the rights holders or their executive body). Thus, fines are imposed for stocking the alp beyond one's rights, not spreading manure, grazing before or after the season, not stalling animals at prescribed times, and so on. Not performing the work duty may also elicit a fine.

On a few alps, the number of animals a user drives to the commons may exceed the number of rights that the user holds if he pays a compensation fee. These fees are costly and often climb in marginal cost as users add more animal units beyond their limits. Indeed, the financial impact soon becomes so great that a user would not, for example, stock more than two animal units beyond an initial limit of twenty-four or twenty-five units.

The job of the alp overseer, who commonly presides over the users in the performance of their duties, is as diverse as the alp grazing systems are. On the one hand, the alp overseer may actively direct the users in the work of commons improvements. On the other hand, the alp overseer may only inspect the alp to make sure that duties such as weed clearing and manure spreading have been performed. If a user neglects a duty, the overseer often has the power to levy a fine. The alp overseer also often has the duty of checking each user's stock of animals against his rights.

In summary, the Swiss have devised a variety of tools to limit the number of animals on their commons and to encourage individual participation in the group enterprise. The remainder of this chapter elaborates what has been quickly described here. Other topics not summarized here, because they relate only indirectly to limited entry, are also discussed, including descriptions of the operating systems, the rights systems' histories, and the meetings and governance of the alps. I invite the reader to sample where he or she has interest, or read all of this story of the Swiss commons.

Agricultural Aspects of Alp Enterprises

An explanation of how both commons and most private alps operate, including what types of animals are kept, how they are husbanded, the products that result, and how pastures are tended, will serve as a background to understanding the rights systems, operating structures, history, and other aspects of the story.

Types of Animals and Types of Alps

By far the most important animals, in sheer numbers and in economic value, are the cows, heifers, and immature male cattle. The cows are kept for their milk production; the immature cattle are raised either for later use in milk production or for meat. In addition, calves, sheep, goats, pigs, and a few bulls are kept on the alps.

The Swiss characterize their alps by the kinds of animals that graze them. Thus, there are cow alps, immature cattle alps, sheep and goat alps, a few bull alps, and mixed alps. The most prevalent type is the mixed alp, where animals of different ages and kinds graze simultaneously, although different kinds of animals generally do not graze the same area of the alp together.

Whether on separate alps or within the confines of the same alp, the cows are allocated the better grazing areas. In a mixed alp, these are the areas around the buildings, which are more level, less rocky, and better fertilized, and require the cows to trek less distance to reach grass. The immature cattle are relegated to the slopes and less accessible grazing locations. These areas may have poorer grasses, and the immature animals can better traverse the steeper slopes because of their lighter weight and greater agility. The very steepest, remotest, highest, and rockiest areas are grazed by the sheep and goats.

Tending

The cows receive the most attention in any alp enterprise, whether commons or private. Similar daily routines are followed throughout Switzerland, centered around milking twice a day—once in the early morning and once at 4:00 to 5:00 P.M. The major difference in routines involves how much time the cows spend in the stalls and when the time in the stalls occurs. In the canton of Bern, for example, the cows are stalled for twelve to thirteen hours during the day. They are let out on the grazing area only at night. In the canton of St. Gallen, however, the animals are left stalled at night and let out on the grazing area during the day.[5] The cows generally receive all of their nourishment from the pasture and are not fed while in the stalls. Both of the stalling systems require that the alp workers bring the cows in for the two milkings only once per day, since the cows remain in the stalls between milkings. Twelve hours in the stalls also allows enough time for a good amount of manure to be collected for fertilizer. On some alps, in contrast, cows are kept in the stalls for only a few hours during the two milking periods. They are let out on a night pasture near the buildings and driven to a day pasture farther away. The disadvantages to this system are that the cows must be collected into the stalls twice a day, much manure is essentially lost because the cows do not distribute it well on the grazing area, and the night pasture tends to become trampled and overfertilized.

There are several systems of guiding—or not guiding—the animals on the grazing areas. The most liberal system allows the animals free run (*Freilauf*) on the alp. This leads to poor forage utilization, because the cows favor certain plants and the "lead cow" will favor certain areas. This results in some areas' being underutilized while others are overutilized.

Another traditional system has been herding, centered around one of the jobs on commons alps, that of the herder (*Hirt*). This person would take the animals to certain pastures and watch them through the day, keeping them within certain loosely defined boundaries. The pasture used would be rotated after a week or two to get better grass utilization. This system has fallen into rare use, because it is difficult to find alp personnel at reasonable cost in twentieth-century Switzerland.

Finally, a grazing rotation system has been used on some alps. This system entails dividing each pasture into sections using fences. The animals graze each section for a week or two before they move to a new section, and thus they are forced to crop preferred *and* disfavored plants in one section before they are allowed new grass. This system has the same effect as the herder system of former times, except that the fences do the herding. In past times, labor was less expensive and the capital investment in fences was relatively high, since wood fences and stone walls were the only alternatives. Today, the electric fence, a wire strung across the grazing area and hooked to a low-voltage battery, facilitates the task of grazing area subdivision and the rotation system of grazing.

---

[5] The most common reason given in Bern for stalling the animals at night is that the flies would afflict the cows during the day. I could discover no particular reason for the opposite practice in St. Gallen.

The immature cattle receive much less attention than the cows. In some cases, they graze virtually untended throughout the summer, although they are moved from one grazing area to another at certain times during the season. In other cases, a herder of immature cattle (*Rinderhirt*) has the duty of tending them. Not only does he guide their grazing, but he may be required to stall the animals in inclement weather.

The sheep, on alps where they are grazed, are even more likely to be left completely on their own throughout the summer, although there are exceptional cases in which shepherds tend large herds. The sheep graze the remote areas. In times past, goats were often tended in large herds on commons alps also. The goat herder would sometimes even bring the goats all the way back to the village for milking each day. Today, with a vast decline in the number of goats kept, they either graze untended with the sheep or stay near the alp buildings where they can be milked.

Finally, the pigs stay near the alp buildings. Sometimes they are allowed free run and sometimes they are kept stalled constantly. The latter practice keeps them from rooting up the grazing area and also, farmers believe, gives them a more sanitary food supply. In either case, the pigs are principally kept to feed on the waste milk products, primarily whey. They are slaughtered in the fall for meat.

Products

The primary traditional product from the alpine grazing areas is cheese. Even as the topography dictated a grazing agriculture, the remoteness of the areas necessitated a milk product that could be stored and one from which much of the water had been removed so that it could be transported back to the valleys.

In the traditional cheese production system, which is falling ever further into disuse, the "evening milk" is saved and combined with the "morning milk" to produce cheese once a day. The cheesemaker (*Senn*) heats the milk in large, copper-lined kettles over an open, indoor fire. He stirs it by hand as it heats, coagulating it with rennet. Again by hand, he removes the curds with cheesecloth and presses them into circular wooden molds. A salt bath the next day adds flavor. He produces scores of these cheeses in a summer, storing them, in most cases, in a cool room on the alp. The whey goes to the pigs. The cream, if some is separated before the cheese is made, is churned into butter.

On alps with a primary focus on meat production, the milk is used chiefly for calf and steer raising. The milk may be centrifuged to remove the cream for butter production first.

Technological innovation has altered the mix of products issuing from the alps. Transportation to and from the grazing areas has become considerably easier with the advent of motor vehicles, the building of better roads, and the construction of cable lifts. Another innovation has been the milk pipeline. This is a plastic pipeline laid in the ground through which milk flows by gravity from the mountain grazing area to the valley below. All of these transportation methods allow delivery of more fresh milk and cream to modern valley processing plants. These plants produce the whole range of milk products from milk and cream to cheese, butter, and yogurt. The alpine cattle owners are simply credited with the amount of milk or cream delivered and paid by check.

Care of the Pastures

Alp users employ a variety of practices to improve the productivity of the alpine pastures, whose intensity of application may differentiate the productivities of private property and common property.

The most important effort is fertilization. Historically, this has meant collecting the manure from the stalls and applying it evenly to the grazing area. Special concrete manure receptacles represent the model method for storage, since these prevent seepage of nutrients downhill from the buildings and consequent overfertilization of some of the land. However, even just collecting the manure in a pile for later distribution is superior to letting it wash away. Yet where interest in alp improvement is low, such waste of manure occurs. Where interest in alp productivity is especially high, users supplement manure with artificial phosphorous and nitrogenous fertilizers.

Other practices for pasture improvement include clearance of stones and debris. Because the grazing areas lie in the mountains, where avalanches and landslides may descend regularly on them, this is especially important. Cutting or uprooting weeds, which compete with the plants that the animals consume, are common practices to enhance grazing area productivity. Draining swampy areas can also improve the flora from an inedible variety to a useful forage base. If insufficient natural watering places are present, the construction of troughs can foster milk production. Finally, planning a good building location can affect milk output. A building placed too low in the grazing area makes the cows walk farther to get to most of the forage, and it also hampers rational distribution of fertilizer.

Private and Commons Operating Structures

More than a simple dichotomy between private property and common property is found in the Swiss alpine grazing systems. Many variations on both of these property forms exist. In considering the different systems, one must pay attention to two characteristics: (1) who owns the land or has rights to its use, and (2) the system by which the animals are tended and the milk is processed. The first of these characteristics can be labeled the *rights system*. The second might be called the *operating structure*. Although the rights system and operating structure are closely intertwined, I separate them initially in order to make their functions clear. Once I have explained them, I will recombine the various rights systems with the different operating structures to demonstrate the great variety of alpine grazing management schemes.

Before focusing on operating structures, I want to point out that both the rights system and the operating structure can be either individual or cooperative. However, the rights system (land ownership), not the operating structure, differentiates private property from common property. If land ownership is individual, the system is private property. If rights to use the land are vested in a group and separate cattle owners graze their herds together, the system is common property. The operating structure (or dairying system) may vary under each rights system. Individual herding and dairying on individually held land is the purest form of private property. Yet cows from different owners are tended together under certain private property operations to be described. Similarly, common property has two different operating structures: individual herding and dairying, and centralized herding and dairying. To clarify this distinction, let us turn first to the types of operating structures.

Operating Structures under Private Property

The private alps in their purest form are run by a family member. In most areas of Switzerland, this is the male head of the household. Depending on the size of the operation, a son or a hired boy helps. The private owner in this case leaves the family in the valley for the summer and ascends to the alp. Nowadays, with better roads and transportation, a private owner may commute back and forth—although generally not on a daily basis. The family in the valley, as well as the alp worker when he descends to the valley, harvests hay for the next winter.

Another method of running the private alp involves the whole family's moving from the valley to the alp, and possibly from one level (*Stafel*) on the alp to another. In this case, family members, including the children, divide duties on the alp—herding, milking, cheese making, cooking, tending the goats, splitting fire wood, fertilizing, and so forth.

Cooperative Commons

The cooperative commons (*genossenschaftliche Alpung*) is one of two main operating structures for common property. In this system, both use of the land and the dairy operation are conducted cooperatively. Jointly owned buildings (barn, milk-processing rooms, and living quarters) stand on the commons. Often a group of two to five hired alp workers conducts the animal herding, milking, and cheese and butter making.[6] This system is common in Graubünden, the St. Gallen Overland, and Over Valais. The farmers send their cows to the alp, handing their care over to those working on the alp for the summer. This provides one of the major advantages to cooperative commons. Delegating to others the animals' care for the summer, the farmers themselves can stay in the valley to harvest the hay that will carry their animals through the coming winter.

Several variations on the cooperative commons exist, particularly in the canton of Bern. In one variation, instead of there being hired alp personnel, a man or a family who has animals on the alp runs the operation. A second variation on the cooperative commons is that more than one cooperative operation exists on the alp. Users from the alp as a whole still own all buildings on the alp cooperatively, but a subset of cooperating farmers owns animals in each building. The farmers who have animals in each operation hire the alp workers for that operation.

Cooperative commons undertake milk processing cooperatively, working the milk from all owners' cows in one large, daily batch. Measurements on the milk production from individual owners' cows are taken at varying intervals over the summer: on some alps only twice, on others every two weeks, and in rare cases daily. At the end of the season, division of the product is based upon the average fraction of production that each owner's cows provided on measurement

---

[6] Traditionally, the make-up of the alp personnel has been the cheese maker (*Senn*), who is in charge of the whole operation, an assistant cheese maker (*Zusenn*), one or two herders (*Hirt*), and a boy who performs any and all odd jobs (*Bub*).

days. Traditionally, a celebration on the alp occurred around the dividing of the cheese, and the procedure for dividing it, in some cases, was elaborate. It might involve, for instance, calculation of equivalency between a number of "masses" of milk and "portions" of cheese, impartial officials assembling portions of cheese with similar amounts of new and old cheese,[7] and owners drawing lots for the awarding of each successive portion (Stebler 1901). Some alps follow similar procedures today. On the other hand, many commons alps simply sell the products and divide the revenues.

Even as commons farmers share the revenues, so do they divide the costs of operation. In times past, when less of a cash economy existed, in-kind contributions, turn systems, and cash payments all helped supply provisions and support to the alp. Each user furnished a certain amount of bread, flour, and other home-produced staples, according to the number of animals sent to the alp (Weiss 1941: 311). The turn system involved supplying meals and lodging on a rotational basis to the herders when they visited the village: the goatherd or shepherd on a daily basis and one of the cattle herders on a weekly basis (Stebler 1903; Messmer 1976: 49). Today, cash payments cover these costs and others, including wages and operating expenses for alp equipment. They are still divided on an animal-unit basis.

Dispersed Operating Unit Commons

The second major commons operating system is the individual or dispersed operating unit commons (*Einzelalpung*). In this system, the land is still under common use. However, the users have their own huts and stalls, often privately owned, built on the commons land. Accordingly, although the cows from different owners graze the same land, they are gathered into private stalls at night. Individuals pursue milking and milk processing on their own. Traditionally, this meant that the hut owner or renter would work the milk into cheese, butter, and other products on the alp. Although this arrangement still occurs, in many cases users truck or pipe the milk to processing plants in the valleys instead. In any event, the milk is privately collected and processed or sold, but land use remains common.

In some areas, the general shortage of manpower in farm families has forced a commuting system on users of dispersed operating unit commons. This is common in the Toggenburg Valley in the canton of

---

[7] The old cheese has a higher value per kilogram because it has already ripened and will lose less weight in the future than the newer cheese that was made later in the summer.

St. Gallen and in some parts of the canton of Graubünden. The user goes to the alp in the late afternoon, stalls and milks the cows, remains on the alp overnight, milks in the morning, and then returns to the valley to hay. Better transportation systems have allowed this pattern to arise. It is a disadvantageous system, however, because the demands of commuting and the user's diurnal sojourn in the valley result in poor care of the grazing area. As a result, a tendency is developing to convert dispersed operating unit commons into cooperative commons (Werthemann 1969: 132).

Private Property Rights Systems

The second feature that characterizes an alp operation is its rights system. Chapters 2 and 3 made clear that the primary purpose of a rights system is to confine resource exploitation to a definable set of people and to define rights within the set of users. Thus, a main aspect of concern here is how each rights system limits entry—both to new users and to additional inputs by current users. The current section handles variations on private property; the next describes common property in alpine grazing.

The purest form of private property occurs when the same person owns the land and operates the alp. By definition, entry of users is limited to the sole owner, and limitation of inputs is regulated by the private owner's optimizing decision. Although there are some poorly treated private alps, expert opinion holds that the private alpine grazing areas are generally well run (Werthemann 1969: 134; Aeschlimann 1978: 213; Imboden 1978).

The first major variation on private tenure is rental or leased alps. I distinguish between rental and leasehold on the basis of contract duration. Some rental arrangements are made on an annual basis for private alps, although seldom does an alp really change users this frequently. Still, short or insecure tenure may affect land use decisions differently than longer tenure. Some alp contracts are concluded with durations of ten years and include automatic renewal for specified periods beyond that.[8] There are even some leasehold alps that

---

[8] For example, a lease agreement between Mrs. Rosalie Meyer-Mayor and Mr. Fritz Früh for the alp Bütz in the township of Kappel, St. Gallen, states: "*Lease Duration:* 10 years fast, with the provisos that rent [be paid] punctually, at the latest one month after the date due, and the alp hut and grazing area [be] properly maintained. . . . *Contract Notice:* The contract runs as stated above until Martini [November 11] 1970. . . . If the same is not canceled by either side, it runs from Martini 1970 for a further three years until Martini 1973 and so forth until 1976, 1979, etc." (Meyer-Mayor and Früh 1961, my translation).

have remained in the same family for two or three generations.[9] In such cases, alp use may resemble private, owner-operated management. Under either rental or leasehold arrangements, the contract may specify the maximum number of animal units.[10]

Another variation on private property in the alps is private joint tenancy (*Gemeinerschaft*), found in the canton of Bern. Under this form of tenure, several individuals who do not constitute a cooperative own an alp. Most often, the joint owners are from the same immediate family or descend from a common ancestor. Aeschlimann (1978) puts the limits of such joint tenancy arrangements at two to six owners.[11]

There are some variations on private property that are actually diversifications on the operating structure rather than variations on who has control of the land. One is the private owner who not only summers his own cattle but accepts animals from others, tending them for a fee. The renter of an alp may also run such an enterprise. Another variation is the private owner who hires a herder to perform the alp work.

Finally, some alps owned by a community are rented to a private user. Although the community as a whole holds the rights to use, and historically the alp was probably a commons, today this can be considered merely another variation on private rental. The contracting parties are community administrators on the one hand and the private user on the other.

Common Property Rights Systems

There are many common property rights systems in the Swiss alpine grazing areas. They combine in various ways with the two commons operating structures to produce a multiplicity of commons types. In this section, I describe some of the major rights systems and then sort out some of the variations on them.

---

[9] The alp Rämisgummen in the township of Eggiwil, Bern, had been rented to the family Fankhauser for over 120 years when Aeschlimann wrote (Aeschlimann 1978: 324).

[10] The contract between Meyer-Mayor and Früh also states the following: "*Rental Item*: alp Bütz, township of Kappel, including alp hut and grazing area for the summering of 28 animal units" (Meyer-Mayor and Früh 1961, my translation).

[11] In the empirical analysis of Chapter 6, I have been more conservative and put the upper limit on such private joint tenancy alps at four owners or users. This does not correspond to the legal definition given in Aeschlimann (1978). However, the divergence between the joint tenancy alps in my sample and the official definition is small because there were few joint tenancy alps with five or six users in my sample.

Share Rights Alps

Limited entry on both cooperative commons and dispersed operating unit commons is often accomplished through a system of grazing rights. Although all basically the same idea, they have different names on different alps, including "cow rights" (*Kuhrechte*), "share rights" (*Anteilrechte*), "alp rights" (*Alprechte*), or "grazing rights" (*Weidrechte*). Generally, the ownership of one right permits the grazing of one cow, considered the basic animal unit, during the normal grazing period of the alp. Rights ownership also permits users to graze other types of animals. Systems vary, but Table 4.1 illustrates the numbers of rights needed for different animals in a typical case. The grazing rights can be broken up into fractions of a right. Occasionally, these fractions also have names: one-fourth of a right is a "foot" (*Fuss*), and one-eighth of a right is a "hoof" (*Klaue*). Even smaller divisions sometimes occur.

Grazing rights are salable and rentable. In most cases, the rental or sale price is governed by the market. The quality of the alp is the main determinant of the market price, where contributing factors include the quality of the grass; the proximity to the village; the climate, slope, and other natural conditions; and the capital improvements. Although the market determines prices in the vast ma-

Table 4.1. *Example of Number of Rights Required to Graze Animals on an Alp*

Type of Animal	Number of Grazing Rights
Cow	1
Pregnant heifer over two years	⅔
One- to two-year-heifer or steer	½
Calf	⅓
Sheep or goat	⅙
Horse over three years	2
Two- to three-year-old horse	1½
One- to two-year-old horse	1
Foal less than one year	½

Source: From the Korporation Kerns cited in Indergand (1963: 35). Other examples of the number of rights required to graze various animal types on other alps are cited in Frödin (1941: 70), Weiss (1941: 207), Indergand (1963: 35), and Aeschlimann (1978: 13).

jority of cases, the cantonal government regulates prices in some areas.[12]

The grazing rights are also inheritable. Typically, ownership of a fraction of a right results from inheritance, although fractional rights may result from market transactions as well.

Generally, there are no stipulations attached to the ownership of grazing rights. One need not be a resident of any particular community, own land in the valley, or have any particular family lineage. Generally, no restrictions apply to the selling of rights either. Occasionally a stipulation of preemption exists, whereby the member must give the cooperative a chance to purchase or rent the rights, possibly so that they can be retired, before selling or renting them to nonmembers (Frödin 1941: 70–71; Messmer 1976: 39).

The total number of rights owned by all users represents the carrying capacity of the alp. Because the rights are perpetual rather than annual, the users generally expect this carrying capacity to remain constant over the years. However, carrying capacity may change for several reasons. Overgrazing or poor pasture care can permanently reduce the alp's productive capacity. More important in recent years has been the larger, more voracious cow that has resulted from selective breeding and good animal health care. A grazing area can have a lower carrying capacity in today's animal units than in the animal units of past centuries, even though the grazing area's grass yield may have remained constant. A third way that carrying capacity may have shrunk is that a part of the grazing area can be permanently destroyed, for instance by an avalanche or a landslide. Finally, the shortage of alp herders today means that the animals stay closer to the buildings or in favored grazing areas, and the carrying capacity is reduced because the animals will not graze efficiently on their own.

If it becomes apparent with time that the carrying capacity of an alp has changed, the users adjust the allowable number of animal units. They make such adjustments in one of several ways. Most frequently, the members of the commons vote to require the ownership of more rights for each animal unit grazed (Weiss 1941: 207; Messmer 1976: 39; Aeschlimann 1978: 12). For instance, they may increase the number of rights necessary to graze a cow from one to one and a quarter. They raise the number of rights necessary for other types of animals accordingly. It is fairly common in Switzerland now to see more than

---

[12] Such is the case with the rights on the Schwägalp in the canton of Appenzell Ausserrhoden, according to the alp treasurer, Mr. Hannes Menet (1979). I did not confirm this assertion independently.

one grazing right required per cow. A second method of reducing grazing pressure is for the cooperative to buy its own rights and retire them (Messmer 1976: 39).

On some commons, holders of unused rights receive compensation. Those who drive cattle to the alp pay, via the commons treasury, those who own rights but did not use them or rent them (Werthemann 1969: 131). Compensation is a set amount per unused right. In earlier times, nonusers with rights demanded this practice by saying that animal owners who used the alp had more grass available to them. This was extra grass that presumably belonged to the nonusers, and users were called upon to compensate them for its consumption. This practice is followed less often today, because grazing plays a less central role in the economy; from both a financial and a fairness standpoint, users find it unreasonable to compensate nonparticipants.

On some alps another type of right exists alongside grazing rights. This is the "hut right" (*Hüttenrecht*). The hut right in theory gives the right holder the right to build on the commons, although more often it gives access to existing stalls. When hut rights exist, they are sometimes tied to a certain number of grazing rights. If a hut right changes hands, use of the hut and a block of say twenty-three, twenty-four, or twenty-five cow rights changes hands, depending on which hut on the alp is sold (this practice occurs in cantons Appenzell Innerrhoden and Appenzell Ausserrhoden). Where the hut rights and grazing rights are not bound together, they are bought and sold independently. In such cases, it is possible for an owner of many cow rights to have no hut right. This farmer might give his animals, along with due compensation for their care, to an owner of a hut right who has fewer animals and grazing rights than his building will accommodate (Frödin 1941: 73). The hut right system is most commonly found on dispersed operating unit commons.

The grazing right represents an effective limitation on entry. The group is limited to those who hold grazing rights, and their individual input levels are restricted to the number of rights held. A question that remains is how close to the optimal level of exploitation the total number of rights is set, which I discuss in Chapter 7.

Community Alps

The second commons alp rights system is the "community alp" (*Gemeindealp*). To understand this system, one must comprehend the concept of "community" (*Gemeinde*). Switzerland is divided up into 3,042 administrative districts that are like townships. Basically, within the borders of each "township" or "community" is one village, town, or city. In some cases, however, one township may include two or three villages, one or two hamlets in addition to a village, and so forth. The borders of a township include surrounding countryside and wild lands. One township borders directly on the next, there being no expanses of land in Switzerland that do not fall within the boundaries of some township.

Every Swiss person is a citizen of one of these communities, which determines his or her cantonal and, ultimately, national citizenship. Community citizenship does not change with change of residence to another community. A person inherits community, and therefore cantonal, citizenship from his or her father. This system arose in earlier times, when few people moved from their home communities and they enjoyed certain rights in their home communities that they did not enjoy elsewhere. It gave them claim to use of community goods, such as community lands and woods, as well as subsistence support if they became destitute. Most often, only citizens who resided in the township could claim these advantages (Gruner and Junker 1972). The citizenship system is an anachronism, since it can lead to a person's being a citizen of a community in which neither he nor his ancestors have lived for generations. Still, it has not been dismantled, and the system continues to have implications for alp use.

In some parts of Switzerland, communities own alps.[13] In the archetypical case, a community alp is within the boundaries of the township that owns it. Exceptions are numerous, however. Community alps lying outside the boundaries of the communities that own them arose when, at some point in the history of these communities, the number of animals grazing their valley and May field lands outstripped the grazing capacity of immediately surrounding alpine lands. Such communities went in search of alpine grazing opportunities around other communities that had excesses of alpine grazing land, and purchased territory from them (Weiss 1941: 176).

Because the people of the community own a community alp, it is primarily the people who live in the community who are entitled to its use. However, there are three groups of people with various rights respecting community alp use—citizens, residents, and nonresidents of the community—and their rights also differ from township to township. Before the late nineteenth century, only community citi-

[13] Community alps are found especially in the canton of Graubünden, but also in the cantons of Valais, Bern, and St. Gallen. The canton of Glarus also has a special type of community alp described in the section of this chapter entitled "Other Rights Systems."

zens had rights to most community alps. New settlers entering the community were excluded. However, access to any community resident, whether a citizen or not, has been the rule since the last century (Frödin 1941: 52; Weiss 1941: 197).[14] In addition, if there is excess capacity on an alp, some communities allow nonresidents to use the alp (Werthemann 1969: 129; Donau 1979). Nonetheless, the most prevalent requirement is that one be a resident of the community to have the privilege of alp use. This limits alp use by people from outside the community, but it is not effective against population growth. Other restrictions must help avoid overuse.

The first of these is that only animals that a farmer has supported through the winter can be grazed on the alp. Historically, this stipulation often put an effective limit on the number of animals going to the alp. A farmer could mow only a certain amount of hay from his private land during a summer, and most farmers had no means of purchasing hay from elsewhere. Nevertheless, to avoid the possibility of purchased hay swelling the animal population, some communities have expanded the stipulation. They require that the farmer send to the alp only animals that the farmer has wintered on hay won from land within the township's boundaries. The restriction that the farmer has to winter animals himself also protects against any person's buying animals in the spring, summering them on the alp at the expense of the community, and then reselling them.

Although the general rule is that only self-wintered cattle may go to the alp, some communities have a less stringent rule. These communities give preference to cattle wintered in the community, but cattle bought or rented in the spring may be taken to the alp if there is room.

If these two main restrictions on use for community alps—(1) residence in the community and (2) self-wintered cattle—are insufficient to restrict the number of animals, one of several additional methods is used. These other methods all involve estimating the carrying capacity of the alp and dividing this capacity among the farmers in the community. Frödin (1941: 54–55) presents five of these methods, the first five in the following list from several authors.

1. The carrying capacity is divided equally; that is, each resident may graze the same number of animal units whether the animals have been self-wintered or not (canton St. Gallen).

2. Each user may graze the fraction of his animal units from a self-wintered herd equal to the ratio of carrying capacity to total de-

---

[14] In Graubünden, a law to this effect was passed in 1874. Nonresidents still may receive lower priority or have to pay higher fees.

mand. For instance, if the alp's carrying capacity is 120 animal units and there are 240 animal units of self-wintered cattle in the community, each user may drive one-half of his self-wintered cattle to the alp.

3. The hay-producing capacity of land owned in the valley is used to apportion use rights. The capability of each user's valley and May field lands to produce hay is estimated. The proportion of the total estimated hay production in a community that an individual's land is capable of producing (according to the estimate) dictates the proportion of the alp's carrying capacity he may engage. Generally, the number of animal units he may drive to the alp is expressed as a certain number of animal units per hundredweight of hay that his lands can produce. The amount of hay that the valley lands and the May fields can yield is reappraised periodically—every five to ten years (Frödin 1941) or simply when deemed necessary (Rubi 1979). Because hay yield is so closely related to ownership of valley and May field land, alp use rights sometimes become conceptually tied to land ownership, and they notionally pass from one owner to another when land is sold. The use rights, however, are not personal use rights, as in the share rights system. Rental or sale of the rights themselves is forbidden.[15]

4. The number of animal units allowed to each user is allotted in accordance with the *area* of land owned in the valley. A certain number of animal units is permitted per hectare of valley land.

5. Very occasionally, the number of animal units allowed to each user is allotted according to the *value* of land owned in the valley.

6. Werthemann (1969: 129) gives a sixth method by which priorities are set for sending animals to the alp. Self-wintered cattle are given precedence over cattle newly bought or rented in the spring, *and* citizens of a community are given priority over residents who are not citizens. Combining these two precepts, priorities for sending cattle to the alp are: (1) self-wintered cattle from community citizens; (2) self-wintered cattle from noncitizen residents; (3) bought or rented cattle from community citizens; and (4) bought or rented cattle from noncitizen residents.

7 and 8. On some community alps, limited alp grazing opportunities are allocated by rotation and by lot. Many communities in Valais possess more than one alp, and because some are better than others, their use is reallocated periodically for the sake of fairness. Reallocation may take place once every one to twelve years, depending on the

---

[15] Besides Frödin (1941: 54–55), both Weiss (1941: 199–200) and Rubi (1979) discuss this system of restricting use on community alps at length. Of the five methods that Frödin recounts, it is probably the most widely used for apportioning limited grazing capacity on community alps.

community (Stebler 1903). Reallocation also occurs in other cantons. In an allocation system using lots, users indicate their preferences and then are reallocated by lot from an alp in excess demand to an alp with insufficient demand. A turn system may be used in a community that possesses multiple alps, some more desirable than others. When a family's turn comes up in a reallocation year, it gives the number of animals it wants to graze on the good alps, and the turn passes to the next family. This continues until the sum of the animal units that families have given equals the carrying capacity of the good alps. The family whose turn comes next but who was not allowed to send animals to any of the good alps becomes the first family in the next reallocation year.[16] Those who did not receive rights on the good alps according to the turn have rights on the less desirable alps. If one of these becomes overburdened through individual choices, a decision is made by lot on who must move animals to an alp in less demand. Lot and turn systems were more prevalent in earlier centuries than they are now.

In most of these systems, the users have the duty to report the number of animals that they desire to send to the alp by a certain date. This date may be as early as January or February or as late as the day of the meeting for deciding when to ascend to the alp. This allows time for allocating rights according to the rules for the particular alp.

Until now, I have introduced only the political unit of "the community" as an owner of "community alps." This is a simplification, because other similar groupings own alps. Use of the alps predates the current political subdivision of Switzerland into "communities," which took place in the nineteenth century. Consequently, other political groupings also hold exclusionary alp rights. Some of these groups are simple geographic subdivisions of the current-day community, such as the *Bäuert* of Bern and the *Ortsgemeinde* of St. Gallen. For these jurisdictions, residency is the only requirement for alp use. More often, the subdivision is a sociopolitical one in which citizenship based on family lineage gives one certain advantages, if not exclusive rights. These include the *Burgergemeinde* of Bern and Over Valais, the *Genossame* of Schwyz, and the *Tagwen* of Glarus. Finally, even old church parishes (*Kirchgemeinden*) serve as a basis for defining groups of people who own alps in scattered cases. These other types of community alps have much the same characteristics as those already described.

---

[16] In earlier times, the reallocation occurred according to a "turn board," a wooden board with family insignias carved into it in a particular order. During a reallocation year, names from the turn board would be read consecutively (Stebler 1903).

Korporation Alps

The third major alp rights system is embodied in the *Korporation*. A *Korporation* in Switzerland is not a business corporation as has arisen under modern capitalism. *Korporation* means "corporate body of citizens." In the three original Swiss cantons of Schwyz, Uri, and Unterwalden, certain family lineages are banded together into *Korporations* that own land in common. The precursors of the *Korporations* in these cantons were the state governments (See "A History of the Rights Systems," later in this chapter). In forming political-economic units as long as a thousand years ago, the people joined together and declared all land not privately owned as belonging to all in common. The result is that today the *Korporations* in Schwyz and Uri own all land, surface water, and groundwater that cannot be documented to be held by a private person, a township, a church, or the government (Korporation Uri 1916: art. 26).

As a consequence, these *Korporations* are superstructures built on top of the cooperatives that husband individual alps. That is, the *Korporation* is an umbrella organization that owns the land of many alps. In the canton of Uri, for example, two *Korporations* own 94 percent of the total land area used for alpine grazing. This encompasses seventy-six separate alps (Marti 1970: 97). Being a member or a "citizen" of a *Korporation* entitles one, under certain further restrictions, to use any of the alps owned by the *Korporation*.[17]

The largest *Korporation* in Switzerland is the Oberallmeind-Korporation in Schwyz. A citizen (rights holder) in the Oberallmeind-Korporation is a descendant of one of the ninety-six families that constituted the "old citizens of the district of Schwyz" (Oberallmeind-Korporation Schwyz 1974: sec. 1). These were families that originally settled Schwyz and banded together to claim the open lands in the thirteenth century, plus later immigrants arriving up through the sixteenth century. The latter had to purchase citizenship (Schuler 1951). Because certain families hold the rights, the rights are not transferable. Besides having appropriate family lineage, a member must reside in the canton of Schwyz to claim citizenship rights. A user

---

[17] Some share rights alps in Bern and St. Gallen call their ownership group a *Korporation* or a *Privatkorporation*. Although the name is identical or similar to that of the *Korporations* of Schwyz, Uri, and Unterwalden, the systems are completely different. Because the *Korporationsalp* of St. Gallen and Bern has a share rights system, access to it may be obtained simply by purchasing or renting grazing rights. In addition, it comprises only a single alp. In contrast, the basic right to use in the *Korporations* of Schwyz, Uri, and Unterwalden is ascertained by family lineage, and a *Korporation* owns many alps.

also must rent land from the Oberallmeind-Korporation upon which a hut exists or may be built. Huts are usually privately owned. Beyond these restrictions the number of animals allowed to each user is not strictly controlled (Frödin 1941: 60; Linggi 1979). However, the animals must have been kept in the district of Schwyz, a subdivision of the canton of Schwyz, from March 15 until ascension to the alp (Oberallmeind-Korporation Schwyz 1940: sec. 1)—in effect a requirement that cattle be wintered in the district of Schwyz (Schuler 1951). With special authorization, a rights holder may accept the animals of noncitizens, but the fees are one and a half to three times as high as for a citizen (Oberallmeind-Korporation Schwyz 1974: sec. 14).

There are two *Korporations* in the canton of Uri: Korporation Uri and Korporation Urseren. The former is by far the larger and also has more demand for its land. Although citizenship in the Korporation Uri was once as restricted as in Schwyz's Oberallmeind-Korporation, it was updated to include any citizen of one of the seventeen communities (*Gemeinden*) in Korporation Uri territory in 1889 (Korporation Uri 1916: art. 1; Marti 1970: 19). Descendants of these people who reside in the *Korporation*'s territory are current rights holders. Besides the rather loose limit on the user population, the *Korporation* controls the number of animals by requiring users to own a hut right that only it can grant. Unlike the rule in the Oberallmeind-Korporation in Schwyz, this hut right limits the user to twenty-five animal units (Korporation Uri 1961: art. 170). The hut right may be rented or sold, but only to other Korporation Uri citizens. The Korporation Urseren uses a slightly different rule, allowing noncitizens to graze animals on alps if special authorization of the *Korporation* council is obtained (Marti 1970: 100–102).

In Obwalden, one of the two "half-cantons" of Unterwalden, the *Korporations* are much smaller, lying more or less within the boundaries of single townships. Most often, citizens band together to draw a right to use from the *Korporation*. Their right, however, is limited to four to ten years, during which time they must purchase the building or rent it. Control of the number of animals is maintained through a rule similar to that used by many community alps: Users may take to the alp only cattle that have been wintered on hay harvested within the township (Frödin 1941: 64; Indergand 1963: 62–63).

Property Alps

Property alps (*Güteralpen*) represent the final rights system for commons. Only a limited number of these alps exist, occurring in the cantons of Graubünden, Valais, and Bern (Frödin 1941: 53; Imboden 1972: 184; Aeschlimann 1978: 209). For these alps, rights to use are irrevocably tied to ownership of land in the valley. When valley land changes hands, a corresponding number of alp rights transfers to the new owner automatically. The archetype of this rights system is represented by the alps of Grindelwald in the canton of Bern. These seven alps have a common set of regulations, which state in part:

Article 3. The right to the alps . . . is inseparably tied to the winter properties in the valley, and it may in no way be alienated from these properties. With property acquisition, the appertaining alp right is simultaneously acquired, regardless of whether this came into the discussion during closing of the transaction or not. Properties without their alp right or an alp right without the property to which it is tied may never and in no form transfer ownership.

Art. 5. With the division of properties, each parcel shall retain the part of the alp right that pertains to it. However, in the future, the division of an alp right . . . may not be extended farther than one-fourth of a cow right. Furthermore, the division of cow rights may occur into one-half and one-fourth units only; other fractions are now allowed. . . . (Quoted in Aeschlimann 1973: 5–6; art. 3 also quoted in Aeschlimann 1978: 210; my translations)

The Vorholzallmend in the canton of Bern is another example of a property alp (Aeschlimann 1978: 211). It has separate rights for spring and summer grazing, and both are tied to property ownership. For example, the spring grazing rights are tied to a certain amount of land in the valley or use rights on another alp according to the following schedule:

1 *Jucharte* of pasture land allows 4 "feet" of spring commons;[18]
1 *Jucharte* of good reed land allows 2 "feet";
1 *Jucharte* of fair reed land allows 1 "foot";
6 *Jucharte*s of poor reed land allow 4 "feet";
1 cow right on another alp allows ½ "foot."

Sometimes the alp right is tied not to the amount of land owned, but rather to the ownership of a particular house. Purchase of the dwelling imparts use rights. Should the building burn to the ground, the use rights would remain bound to the site.

The property alp system limits the number of animals grazing the alp through association with the limited amount of land tied to it in the valley. As the example of the Vorholzallmend shows, the basis of the tie between alp use and ownership of valley land really lies in the amount of fodder the valley land can produce. Therefore, the evo-

[18] A *Jucharte* is an antiquated measure of land area equal to 0.89 acre. Four "feet" equal one grazing right.

lution of the property alps may have begun with the same principle as found in both the community alps and some *Korporation* alps: One may take to the alp the number of cattle that one can winter. As limits needed to be put on alp use, users may have decided to permit on the alp only certain proportions of the animals that a piece of valley land could support through the winter. Then, with time, the right became inseparably tied to the land.

Other Rights Systems

Other rights systems exist, as well as variations on the ones described. For example, in some cases in Graubünden and Valais, two or more communities or several factions within one community own several alps (*Wechselalpen, Talschaftsalpen*). When the alps are not of equal quality, the communities or factions trade alps among themselves periodically. This exchange occurs every five to thirty years, and it may be determined by lot or rotation. Because the trading of user groups leads to lower interest in investing in the grazing land and structures, this system fell into disuse in many areas by the nineteenth century, although it still persists in some places (Weiss 1941: 202; Imboden 1972: 184).

Another type of rights system consists of a mixture of the share rights system with other systems. On some share rights alps, legal persons, most often communities or their factions, have bought grazing rights. In this case, citizens or residents of the community have claim to grazing rights on a share rights alp alongside private persons holding rights (Camenisch 1924). This situation often has arisen in communities that wish to keep use rights in local hands and available to local farmers (Werthemann 1969: 128). Other legal persons, such as breeding cooperatives, also sometimes buy into share rights alps (Bigler et al. 1969).

In yet another rights system, private decision making is mixed with community ownership and use. Some communities in the canton of St. Gallen (Buchs, for example) rent their alps to an individual, who in turn offers his services as a manager of the alp to community users. This departs from former practice in these communities, since the animal owners previously formed a commons group and hired alp personnel. The manager has a freer hand in running the alp, and simultaneously, the burden of many decisions is taken away from the commons group. To cover his costs and provide himself a return for his services, the manager charges each cattle owner for each animal unit that the owner grazes (Rhyner 1980).

Some *Korporation* alps have taken on private character in a different manner. As described in a previous section, *Korporation* members in some cantons must rent *Korporation* land on which they may construct a building or rent a previously constructed building. Formerly, such rented sites were scattered about an alp without boundaries between them. Although one user might have a sphere of primary use around his buildings, it was still possible for animals to range over the whole alp. In Nidwalden, the other half-canton of Unterwalden, hut right owners on many of these alps have erected fences between the scattered buildings, creating a situation similar to private property (Bäbler 1965: 65). In Schwyz, the same practice has been undertaken on Oberallmeind land within the last quarter century (Linggi 1979). The one difference between private land and these divided *Korporation* lands is that *Korporation* regulations regarding fertilization, clearing of debris, day of ascension, building maintenance, and so on must continue to be observed on *Korporation* land.

Finally, the canton of Glarus is special in two ways. First, it has a cantonal law governing alpine grazing for all alps, regardless of whether they are community, share rights, or private alps. The carrying capacity must be reestimated every ten years. Each alp must have a set of regulations governing number of animal units, what types of animals may be grazed and in what amounts, and the day of the descent from the alp. It must also have a description of required alp maintenance and improvements. Each voting district in Glarus has an alp overseer who makes sure alp users fulfill all duties. Glarus's alp ordinances regulate many other aspects of alp use, but this summary gives the flavor of how complete Glarus's alp regulations are (Wilckens 1874; Bäbler 1962: 42–43). Secondly, Glarus is unlike any other canton in that entire community alps are rented to private persons for their own use. Although "citizen communities" (*Tagwen*), composed of descendants of earlier residents of a village and its surrounding area, own 71 percent of the alps in Glarus, they rent 73 percent of these alps to individual farmers. The Glarners settle these rental decisions by auction. Thus, use here is closer to private than to commons, although the users must follow the cantonal law (Bäbler 1962: 42–43).[19]

---

[19] The Glarus alps also provide the unusual example of a switch from private to commons use. Wealthy private persons owned them until the seventeenth and eighteenth centuries. At that time, the private owners sold the alps to the communities in order to raise capital to invest in the blossoming industrial revolution (Bäbler 1962: 89–91).

Rental of Rights

A final, important note is necessary to understand alpine rights systems fully. In both the share rights and *Korporation* alps, one finds not only owners of grazing rights and hut rights but also renters of these rights using the commons. In the case of the *Korporation* alps, the renter of a hut right is merely a *Korporation* citizen renting the use of another's building. The *Korporation* administration must still approve him as a user. For the share rights alps, the division between owners and renters of rights can have much greater significance. The number of people who farm has changed greatly over the last century, and the rental of grazing rights has become quite prevalent. Many who leave agriculture do not want to give up their family heritage, so they rent the rights but retain family ownership of the rights through the generations. The result is two groups with different types of control over the alp: the users and the rights holders. Often these groups overlap, because some users are also rights holders. Cases do exist, however, in which the users and rights holders are completely distinct sets of people (e.g., the Schwägalp in Appenzell Ausserrhoden). This situation will be discussed further under "Governance and Decision Making," later in this chapter.

Combining the Rights System and Operating Structure

Having probed the operating structure and the rights system separately, we now turn to an examination of the varied ways in which Swiss alpine grazing rights systems and operating structures combine.

First, the share rights system may have either dispersed operating units on the commons or a centralized cooperative. Examples of the former are the Toggenburg alps of St. Gallen, where individual users have their own private huts on the commons and must hold grazing rights to use the area. Bern also has share rights alps with dispersed operating units. However, on these Bernese alps individual families tend more than their own herds, taking on animals from several owners, unlike families on the Toggenburg alps of St. Gallen. At the same time, examples of share rights alps with a centralized operating unit also occur in the canton of Bern. The alps of the Justis Valley are prime examples.

Similarly, users may operate *Korporation* alps on either a dispersed operating unit or a cooperative commons basis. The majority of *Korporation* alps function as dispersed operating unit commons, because the basis for use on many *Korporation* alps is the rental or obtaining of a hut right from the *Korporation*. The Urner Boden of Uri, the largest alp in Switzerland (i.e., supporting the largest number of animal units), exemplifies a dispersed operating unit commons on *Korporation* land. In Uri, whole families move to the dispersed operating unit alps and tend their own animals. In Schwyz, a hut right holder (renter of land from the *Korporation*) will tend his own and others' animals on the dispersed operating unit commons. On the other hand, cooperative commons are found on *Korporation* lands in the Uri Overland and in the Urseren Valley. Here, a farmer obtains a hut right from the *Korporation* and bands together with others to form a cooperative. They hire alp personnel to perform the alp tasks (Marti 1970: 124).

Finally, community alps also display dispersed operating units as well as cooperative operating structures. By far the more prevalent form of community alp is the cooperative commons. This is found throughout Graubünden, in the St. Gallen Overland, and in the St. Gallen Werdenberg district. Community residents own the buildings jointly, and they delegate care of their animals and milk processing to hired personnel for the summer. Community commons with dispersed operating units are represented in a few alps owned by *Bäuerts* (community factions) in Bern. Citizens of the community faction operate separate units in privately owned buildings, generally taking on animals from other owners.

A History of the Rights Systems

To clarify forces that created the various forms of Swiss property rights in grazing, I provide a brief history of the commons and private rights systems in this section. All three major common property rights systems—share rights, community ownership, and *Korporation* ownership—have similar origins in the Middle Ages. Private property also has roots in this period.

The Mark

Although the Swiss alpine region was settled before the medieval era, the Alemanni, new immigrants from present-day France and Germany, colonized the region between A.D. 300 and 1000. These people settled scattered farmsteads, and the settlers of a region took collective possession of areas bordered by natural landmarks, such as lakes, streams, woods, and mountain ridges. Such a region was called a "mark." Although individual farmers cultivated land in their immediate vicinity and considered it their own, they construed all other land within the mark as open to anyone's use, in accordance with Germanic law (Frödin 1941: 42; Weiss 1941: 169). The mark often took in whole valleys, in which several villages would eventually emerge. Hence the name *Talmarkgenossenschaft* arose, meaning "valley-mark community." Part of the mark was the alpine grazing land.

The people of a mark not merely were mutual users of an unrestricted resource but during the seventh to tenth centuries gradually became cooperators in economic and political affairs. The mutual clearing and use of woods and grasslands, construction of roads, wells, avalanche fencing, and flood levees, and joint purchase of imports like metals and salt occurred through the mark group. Political cohesion also formed as the people of the mark defended themselves against outside control from the Lenzburg and Hapsburg lords (Neff n.d.) and as they conducted border wars with neighboring marks over the use of grazing land (Marti 1970: 14–16). The political cohesion that emerged from this economic and military cooperation led to the elections of political leaders and judges (Thürer 1978).

Korporation *Alps*

The mark community (*Markgenossenschaft*) was the precursor of both the *Korporation* and the community (*Gemeinde*). Let us examine its evolution into the *Korporation* first. As population and use of collectively held land increased, the residents of the valleys in which a mark existed found it necessary to begin excluding newcomers. They did so by declaring current residents "citizens" and those coming later precisely that, "late settlers" (*Hintersässen*).[20] In both Schwyz and Uri, the definite separation of citizens from late settlers occurred in the fourteenth century (Schuler 1951; Marti 1970: 17), although by the time this regulation was written into the community rules, it was clear who was a countryman from time out of mind and who was a late settler.

The late settlers were allowed no rights to the community goods. Among those who were entitled to them, rights were passed from father to children, and in this way the corporate body of citizens emerged. This group of rights holders or citizens formed a state that made both political resolutions and economic decisions, the latter having primarily to do with agricultural land use. Because the economic organization coincided with the political body, the term *Korporation* for the corporate body of citizens was not even used in some

---

[20] Late settlers were also called *Beisassen*, meaning "settlers who live among us."

cases until later.[21] Rather, one was simply a citizen of the land and had rights to its collective property.

Because the mark had encompassed the whole valley and surrounding mountains, so did the state's (the *Korporation*'s) boundaries.[22] The rule from the mark community that anyone could use land that was not under individual control became a rule that land not in exclusive use was property of the corporate body of citizens. Finally, because the mark community had started down the road of democratic political organization, the state (the *Korporation*) continued in its stead, with an electorate, a legislative, and an executive branch (see "Governance and Decision Making," later in this chapter).

The final step in the formation of *Korporations* as we know them occurred in the nineteenth century, as matters of state and matters of the *Korporation* began to diverge. In 1836, a definite separation of state-owned goods and *Korporation*-owned goods occurred in Schwyz (Schuler 1951). In 1848, a new Swiss federal constitution formalized the cantons, requiring the Urner *Korporations* to split from the state apparatus as well, although this did not actually occur until 1888 (Marti 1970: 18). After the break, the *Korporations* became purely economic, agricultural associations of people descended from the inhabitants of the mark, who collectively owned alpine grazing areas, woods, and other common lands.

Community Alps

The mark was also the precursor in those areas where community alps emerged. Again, growing populations and the unlimited mutual use of common lands in the mark put these lands in danger of overuse. The users determined to split the mark into smaller settlement groupings. Although the original mark settlers had established primarily scattered homesteads, some settlements had developed into villages. If the mark had grown to include several villages, each got its share of the formerly open land. If the mark included several hamlets, each of these community factions obtained some of the mark (Frödin 1941: 45–46). The split happened at different times in different parts of Switzerland. In the Oberengadin, an expansive valley

---

[21] This is true of Uri, where the name *Korporation* for the group of holders of rights in the common lands and forests became official only in the nineteenth century (Korporation Uri 1916: preface).

[22] In Obwalden and Nidwalden, the two half-cantons of Unterwalden, the mark was split into community-size *Korporations* rather than canton-size *Korporations* before any documents began appearing to chronicle the existence of larger economic units (Bäbler 1965).

in Graubünden all of which had been a single mark, the division into communities and their appurtenant lands took place in 1538. In the Calanca Valley in Graubünden the split did not occur until 1866 (Weiss 1941: 169). In some cases, the remains of the mark persist to this day, where communities trade off use of jointly owned alps, as we have seen (the *Wechselalpen*). After the mark was divided among smaller, better-defined groups, "citizenship" in the community or community faction quickly emerged as a prerequisite for use.

Share Rights Alps

The final major common property framework, the share rights system, also has its seed in the mark, but its development is more roundabout.

Late in the Middle Ages, the feudal system developed in Europe, and it influenced the evolution of alpine grazing rights in some areas of Switzerland. Affluent and powerful members of the mark and church functionaries such as bishops and abbots managed to obtain feudal rights to large regions, including unused alpine forest and grasslands, by offering fealty to those higher in the feudal hierarchy (Frödin 1941: 43). These feudal rights holders seldom developed the lands themselves but rather granted them in feudal holding to other former mark citizens and later immigrants. In return for tribute payments to the lord, the feudal tenant received protection from the outside world and use of the land. The feudal tenant could cultivate the land in whatever manner he desired, as long as he did not decrease the land's value. In the early part of the feudal period, contracts were for land rental, they had to be renewed, and they were not automatically passed to succeeding generations. These arrangements gave the feudal lord control over who worked the land, but the insecure tenure afforded to the user and his descendants led to poor land use. As a result, feudal contracts began to be fixed for the lifetime of the tenant, and eventually, through the lifetimes of his descendants. That is, feudal holding became inheritable.

In some areas, the lord granted the alpine lands to groups of people rather than to individuals. There were several reasons for this. These areas were often farther from permanent settlements and sometimes covered with vast forests that required clearing. Under these conditions, a group of people could develop the land more easily than an individual. Also, if a group held the feudal rights, the lord was better assured of his tributary payment (Odermatt 1926).

The granting of feudal tenure to a group gave the participants the incentive to assure that distribution of benefits from the land was equitable. To realize the goal of serving all interests, they needed to cooperate. Moreover, the group effort required to clear the land, pay the feudal tribute, and possibly dissolve the tribute through a lump sum payment made group members believe that the land was their mutual, hard-won property when feudal duties later gradually disappeared. In this way, the cooperatives that would lead to the share rights system materialized (Frödin 1941: 43–45; Weiss 1941: 172; Anderegg 1976: 32–34).

The precise manner in which grazing rights in these cooperatives first emerged is unclear, because most systems date from between A.D. 1100 and 1400, and documents that give clues to the process are sparse or nonexistent. The development of grazing rights, however, may have transpired as follows (Wagner 1924). After the group had cleared the land, members had an unlimited privilege to graze cattle on it. Because feudal rights had become inheritable, this privilege was passed to members' children. With growth in the number of heirs through several generations, the number of users soon grew too large to allow discretionary use of the land. At this point, the group imposed limits by one of two methods. These methods are documentable in the Obertoggenburg alps of St. Gallen, and events there are probably representative of what happened elsewhere (Wagner 1924: 46–51).

The first method involved limiting the number of animals that a rights holder could send to the alp to that which he could support through the winter on hay from his own land in the valley. This limited the number of animals because valley land was fixed, and no animal could be taken to the alp that had been kept on hay purchased from elsewhere. Fairly quickly, the tie to land ownership was transformed into a personal right to use. That is, it was not tied to ownership of the valley land, but rather it became the personal right of the landowner to keep, even if he sold the land. Grazing rights as we know them had emerged, their number equaling the number of animals that a farmer's valley land originally had supported.

In the second process, a holder's general privilege to use the alp was passed on to all children, but at some point the group began limiting the *total* number of animals on the alp. This total, however, was not fixed, but rather reevaluated after the death of each rights holder. After being reset each time, the limit was divided equally among all new rights holders, that is, all former rights holders plus the deceased's heirs. With time the descendants of those who had originally cleared the land began receiving unreasonably small portions of the total quota. At this point, the group decided that a user's rights would not multiply when given to all of his children. Rather, rights would be split among children. At the same juncture, they fixed the total number of rights for the alp permanently. The number set was an estimate of the alp's carrying capacity, based on the years of experience of grazing the alp that had gone before. It was only one more step to the trading of rights between families, and again grazing rights had emerged.

Private Alps

Private property for the May fields and the alps did not arise out of the mark, but rather emerged in two other ways from later historical conditions.

First, some private alps grew from feudal tenure (Frödin 1941: 47). While groups obtained feudal rights to some areas, individuals obtained rights to others. These areas may have been closer to the permanent settlements, so that an individual could work them along with valley lands. The annual tribute was a fixed sum, and indeed, it became fixed for all time once feudal tenure became inheritable. Because it was fixed, the tribute payment often became relatively small as production from the land increased and inflation occurred. With time, farmers were able to dissolve the annual tribute through lump sum payments, or, in some cases, the payments were simply forgotten during the decline of the feudal system. With feudal tribute absent, inheritability established, and complete freedom of land management prevailing, the farmer came to view the land as his own. What the farmer formerly saw as land to which he had only use rights became land that he considered held in fee simple (Büchi 1972: 103–10).

Secondly, alps became private property through private purchases of former common property alps. Sometimes one of the participants in a share rights alp bought all of the grazing rights, bringing the entire alp under his ownership. This occurred in the Emmen Valley alps of Bern in the sixteenth to eighteenth centuries, as well as more widely in Bern in the decades around 1900. Individuals also purchased community alps in the seventeenth century in the canton of Graubünden (Frödin 1941: 47).

Common Property in Village Pastures, Meadows, and Woods

Other common property resources exist in Switzerland besides the alpine pastures, including the village pastures, meadows, and woods. They came under common property use for the most part, because they too were once part of the mark.

Some communities have a village-level commons (*Allmende*). This community-owned field serves for spring grazing and as a place for each household to keep a "home cow" to provide milk over the summer. Villagers may also keep work animals such as horses and oxen here. The animals graze the village commons by day and return to private stalls at night. As with the community alps, citizenship or residence in the community is required to use the area. Sometimes, if a user wants to keep more than one animal on the village commons for the summer, he must pay extra for the additional animal units. *Korporations* also sometimes possess these "home cow" pastures (Korporation Uri 1916: art. 112; Frödin 1941: 169–72).

Another practice still followed in some Swiss communities opens all village lands to common grazing for a certain period in the spring and in the fall. During these periods, the animals may graze anywhere— on fields as well as pasture land, on private as well as public land (Büchi 1972). Naturally these times occur before planting in the spring and after harvest in the fall. On the one hand, this system is advantageous where private parcels are so scattered that private grazing in the early spring and late fall is difficult. It also helps the small landowner, who would be hard pressed to support animals at these times in any other manner. On the other hand, the practice has been stopped in many areas because it harms the land and interferes with sound land management by the private owner (Frödin 1941: 172–75; Werthemann 1969: 113).

Another common property resource is "wild hay" (*Wildheu*), which consists of naturally growing grasses that lie higher even than the alpine grazing areas or else on slopes too steep for even the sheep and goats. These areas often belong to a community, *Korporation*, or share rights commons. The harvesting of wild hay has declined tremendously, because labor has become expensive and farmers can purchase winter feed. It once provided a significant addition to winter feed supplies, however, and was eagerly sought. Given these demands, the villagers set up common property rules for exploitation. Generally, they permitted harvesting only after a certain date in late July or early August. The most common form of dividing the wild hay areas was to draw borders around parcels of equal quality and allocate them by lot. Auctioning of the areas also occurred in some areas. Finally, a simple way to allot the supply was to allow each family as much wild hay as one person could harvest in one day—but no more than this— where a member from each family met with others and harvested on the same day (Waldmeier-Brockmann 1941).

In addition to grazing land and wild hay areas, the communities,

*Korporation*s, and share rights cooperatives own vast areas of forest. Switzerland now has a national forestry law, passed in the early twentieth century, that regulates all public and private forests. Before the enactment of this law, however, local citizens had established common property rules regarding the use of commonly held forest. For the most part, these involved quotas on how much wood a rights holder might withdraw annually, and for what purpose. For instance, in Visperterminen, a community in Valais, each citizen has the right to two and a half cubic meters of wood gratis each year. For the purposes of constructing a new building, each citizen is allowed fifteen cubic meters at a nominal cost (in 1969 it was SFr. 9 to SFr. 15 per cubic meter), and for building maintenance fifteen to twenty cubic meters are allowed (Imboden 1969).

Finally, individuals traditionally had the privilege of seeking and harvesting in the grasslands and woodlands berries, hazelnuts, medicinal herbs, small animals, plants for cult practices, flowers for decoration, and so forth. Limits on such resources were never really enforced (Waldmeier-Brockmann 1941).

Management Tools for Commons Alps

Certain management methods to regulate use and protect the resource—namely, alp regulations, fees, fines, work duties, and alp overseers—are practiced for virtually all commons alps.

Alp Regulations

For most alps, written alp regulations cover all aspects of alp use, including not only items discussed here but also the subjects upon which I expand shortly: fees, fines, work duties, alp overseers, and decision making. Following is an enumeration of points that one may find in any given set of regulations. No single set contains all of the points given, but any particular set is likely to include a number of them. Alp regulations vary in certain respects among *Korporation*, community, and share rights alps, as I note in particular cases. A set of alp regulations may include:

1. A description of the alp organization: who owns the alp, who has power to make decisions, what officers there are, their terms of office, their duties, and their salaries. This is discussed further in the next section ("Governance and Decision Making").

2. An explanation of who has rights to use the alp. On a community alp this regulation would determine whether citizens, residents, and/

or nonresidents have rights, the order of preference, and any allocation scheme. For share rights alps, owners or renters of grazing rights
may graze animals. For *Korporation* alps, citizenship and a hut right
are required. (See "Common Property Rights Systems," earlier in this
chapter.)

3. A statement of how often meetings of the rights holders takes
place.

4. The maximum number of animal units that may be grazed on the
alp.

5. A pronouncement of what types of animals are allowed, or on
which part of the grazing area each type of animal may graze. (See
"Agricultural Aspects of Alp Enterprises," earlier in the chapter.)

6. A description of the fees for alp use by animal type, or who will
set the fees—for example, the meeting of rights holders.

7. The date by which users must report the animals that they intend
to send to the alp.

8. An explanation of who determines the day of the alp ascent and
by what process. (See "Governance and Decision Making.")

9. The requirement that no one ascend to the alp early. Usually, this
is a stipulation that no animals cross the border of the alp before
sunrise or 4:00 A.M. on the day of the alp ascent.

10. A stipulation of a day after the alp ascent on which each owner's
animals will be counted and verified against his grazing rights or the
intentions he reported earlier in the year to send animals to the alp.

11. A requirement that a user remove any cattle driven to the alp
without rights, often stipulating a fine for the violator.

12. Occasionally, a regulation that animals be stalled during certain
hours for a certain number of days after the alp ascent to protect the
spring grass growth, for example, during the night and/or certain
daylight hours for the first seven, ten, or fourteen days.

13. On dispersed operating unit commons, a prohibition of driving
cattle, either the user's own cattle to certain areas or other owners'
cattle from areas that they are grazing. This rule exists for the sake of
fairness (although poor grass utilization results).

14. A requirement that an owner remove ill or infectious animals
from the alp.

15. A directive requiring prorated compensation or a replacement
allowance for animals that an owner must remove from the alp on
account of sickness or death.

16. A stipulation of the maximum number of weeks that users may
graze the alp or, occasionally, the last day on which they may occupy
the alp.

17. A work duty required of each user, usually based on the number of animal units driven to the alp. (See "Work Duty," later in this section.)

18. Rules regarding fertilization, which take various forms. They may require that each user apply the manure from his collection containers to appropriate areas by a certain date. They may stipulate that the user must gather manure from the heavily used areas to be spread elsewhere. In some cases, the alp overseer designates the ground to be fertilized. If the work is not done, the alp user group may have the right to perform it at the user's expense. On some alps, the users collectively hire a worker to carry out the fertilization. Some alps have prohibitions against transporting manure from the alp.

19. The requirement that each user keep a certain amount of hay in reserve on the alp to serve as insurance against bad weather.

20. A prohibition against removing hay or straw from the alp; alternatively, rules regarding the gathering of wild hay for personal use.

21. Rules regarding the felling of timber for firewood and building repairs. Generally, an overseer must approve wood removal.

22. Fines for violating any of the regulations. (See "Fines," later in this section.)

23. A declaration of who owns the buildings on the alp (i.e., whether there is private, community, or cooperative ownership), and of the people who have responsibility for building maintenance.

24. Regulations regarding the construction of new private buildings. Generally, the meeting of rights holders or their executive body must approve location and construction plans.

25. A stipulation on whether the users or the owners of the alp bear the operating costs (equipment, repairs, taxes, personnel wages, supplies, etc.).

The preceding provisions pertain more or less to any type of commons alp. The following alp regulations are found only on share rights alps:

26. A description of how voting occurs, that is, whether a one-person–one-vote rule applies, or whether users have votes according to the number of rights owned. (See "Governance and Decision Making.")

27. A statement of the number of grazing rights necessary to drive each animal type (cow, heifer, sheep or goat, etc.) to the alp.

28. Possible rules about compensation for driving extra animal units to the alp over and above one's rights. (See "Fines.")

29. Possible provision for using funds from the commons treasury

to compensate rights holders who do not use their rights. Usually, this is a set stipend per right.

These, then, are general contents of commons alp regulations. Let us turn to topics in these regulations and the ordinances based upon them of particular importance for regulating common property use.

Fees

Annual use fees exist for most alps, even for those where owners possess grazing rights. All commons alps need to raise funds to maintain certain common undertakings. If the buildings are jointly owned, then the group must finance building maintenance. There are roads or paths to maintain, perhaps wages for performance of the work duty to be paid (see "Work Duty"), and possibly compensation for elected alp officers. The fees are generally a set amount per animal unit or grazing right.

The fees on the community and *Korporation* alps are not merely regarded as a levy to cover maintenance and administrative costs but rather are considered payment for use of the grass. The grass, after all, belongs to the citizens, not just to the particular users of an alp. Because of this, some alp organizations call the fee "grass money" (*Grasgeld*).

Where fees exist, one might ask whether they cause the individual user to take into account the external effects of adding animals to the commons. Indeed, the Korporation Uri has a two-step, increasing fee schedule for animals driven to *Korporation* alps:

For the first eight animal units	SFr. 8.00/animal unit
For animal units over eight	SFr. 10.00/animal unit

The *Korporation* also charges an "improvement fee," which it uses for care and upkeep of the grazing area for which the fee is levied:

Per cow or two-year-old heifer	SFr. 2.00
Per one-year-old heifer	SFr. 1.20
Per calf	SFr. 0.80
Per sheep, goat, pig, etc.	SFr. 0.80

These fees also correspond in a proportional sense to the pressure on the pasture of an additional animal of each type. Therefore, in theory, both of these types of fees reflect an increasing marginal cost of more animal units or of larger animals. The fees, however, are very modest. In fact, the Oberallmeind-Korporation in Schwyz prides itself on providing grazing opportunities at cheap rates to the mountain farmer, who has a difficult time wrenching an existence from the land

(Schuler 1951). Given their low rate, the fees on *Korporation* alps probably do not cause the farmer to take into account the external effects of his alp use.

On community alps, user fees are seldom more than SFr. 20.00 to SFr. 30.00 per animal unit, although noncitizen residents may pay one-third more than these amounts. Such fees are also moderate. They are not an accurate reflection of the value of the alp to the users and are hardly a deterrent to adding more animals. To limit use, communities generally must depend on the quota methods explained in the section on the rights systems. Some scattered communities, however, have substantial alp fees. In the canton of St. Gallen, the community of Grabs charges SFr. 90.00 and the community of Buchs charges SFr. 75.00 per animal unit. In these cases, a farmer is more likely to take into account the impact he has on other farmers when he adds more animals to the herd.

Work Duty

Another practice to protect and improve the common grazing lands is a work duty, incumbent on users of many share rights and community alps.[23] The alp regulations often prescribe the work duty exactly, such as three hours, four hours, eight hours, ten hours, or rarely, more than a full day of work per animal unit grazed. Occasionally, the work duty is set as a certain number of hours for each user, regardless of the number of animal units grazed. Finally, in some cases, the work requirement is general: A user must perform it at the direction of the alp overseer.

The duties generally pertain to maintenance or improvements of the grazing area or its facilities—weed control, stone and debris clearing, fertilizing, path maintenance, building maintenance, erecting fences at the beginning of the season or dismantling them at the end, and so forth. Sometimes the users carry out the work as a group on a day that the alp overseer determines with the general consent of the users (Weiss 1941: 251). Other times, individuals perform a duty to destroy weeds for a certain number of hours or to spread manure on their own schedule (Genossenschaft Grosse Schwägalp 1976a). The alp overseer has the duty to make sure the work is done, and the user may have to report to him before and after working.

Sometimes work performed in fulfilling the requirement is unpaid.

---

[23] The *Korporations* tend to have improvement fees rather than work duties imposed on users. I believe that these fees go to hired workers who are paid to perform the tasks that are described in this section.

Failing to fulfill the obligation results in a fine. Other times, the worker receives a small hourly wage even though the work is required. In some cases, the user can discharge the work duty by paying a compensation fee.

The work requirement can provide important additions of labor to alp maintenance and improvement. Historically, it was not difficult to get the users to furnish their part of the common effort, and this spirit continues on some alps today. On many alps, however, lack of interest in the work requirement has arisen. Several developments in this century have hastened the process. The first is the rise of a cash economy. At one time, it was easier to provide the work than to pay the cash. Today, with the greater availability of cash and the many demands on a farmer's time, a commons user is quite likely to opt for the cash settlement. The second trend weakening the work duty is the proliferation of the part-time farmer. Much more prevalent in Switzerland today than in former times, part-time farmers often have less time for and interest in fulfilling an alp work duty.

Fines

Two enforcement tools to protect common property in grazing are compensation fees and fines. Compensation fees, which exist on some share rights alps, are imposed for driving more animal units to the alp than the user has grazing rights. Most share rights alps do not allow a user to stock more animals than the number of rights he holds. Some, however, allow a little flexibility, exacting compensation fees to discourage the practice. Fines are slightly different in that they are imposed for violations of the regulations.

The Schwägalp in canton Appenzell Ausserrhoden has an elaborate system of compensation fees and fines. It is run on the hut right system, with blocks of twenty to thirty-five grazing rights per user. Compensation fees for driving animals to the alp beyond one's hut right are as follows:

First extra animal unit	SFr. 60.00
Second extra animal unit	SFr. 120.00
Third extra animal unit	SFr. 180.00

These fees are additive. That is, for two animal units overstocked, the user pays SFr. 60.00 *plus* SFr. 120.00; a third animal unit beyond one's hut right would mean a total fee of SFr. 360.00. Theoretically, the fees keep climbing in the same fashion. The president of the Schwägalp cooperative, however, knew of no case in which more than three animal units too many were driven to the alp. It just becomes too expensive (Solenthaler 1979).[24]

Fines are a very widely used tool to enforce alp regulations. They are found on community and *Korporation* alps as well as share rights alps. To illustrate a system of fines, I once again turn first to the Schwägalp in canton Appenzell Ausserrhoden. It fines users for a variety of violations, including not spreading manure or controlling weeds, taking too many goats or sheep to the alp, leaving less than the required amount of straw for emergency purposes when departing the alp, being absent from any of the various herders' meetings, making false declarations at the cattle count, grazing the alp before daybreak on the day of the alp ascent, driving cattle on the commons,[25] and not stalling one's animals the first twelve nights. Other alps illustrate other types of fines. On Sellamatt in the canton of St. Gallen, driving more cattle to the alp than one has rights incurs a fine of SFr. 5.00 to SFr. 20.000. On Geilskummi in Bern, taking manure or straw from the alp or not descending from the alp on the same day as the others results in a fine (see Table 4.2).

Although fines are exacted for other offenses, such as not taking care of alp equipment or not cleaning up after building repairs, most of the fines are designed to protect the grazing land, as the examples just given illustrate. More accurately, the *alp regulations* were designed to protect the grazing land, for each fine results from the failure to meet a regulation.

Table 4.2 also indicates that alp rights holders have set some fines within ranges; a violation causes a penalty in proportion to its severity. In some cases the alp overseer and in other cases the alp administra-

---

[24] On the alp Krinnen in the canton of Bern, compensation fees become expensive even more quickly. They are paid for stocking combinations of cows and heifers slightly in excess of rights or stocking an extra goat or two. In theory, the compensation fees, described by Schallenberg (1980), are as follows:

First ⅙th of an animal unit	SFr. 5.00
Second ⅙th of an animal unit	SFr. 10.00
Third ⅙th of an animal unit	SFr. 20.00
Fourth ⅙th of an animal unit	SFr. 40.00
Fifth ⅙th of an animal unit	SFr. 80.00
Sixth ⅙th of an animal unit	SFr. 160.00

In practice, during the five years 1975 to 1979, only one person stocked as much as four-sixths of an animal unit over his rights, and he paid SFr. 20.00 (not SFr. 40.00) for this privilege (Alp Krinnen 1975–79).

[25] Cf. item 13 in the discussion of alp regulations.

Table 4.2. *Fines for Violation of Alp Regulations*

Alp and Offense	Fine (SFr.)
Schwägalp	
Taking more than six goats or sheep to the alp	20.00
Overdue spreading of manure	50.00
Failure to control weeds	100.00
Leaving less than eight cubic meters of straw when departing the alp	50.00
Absence from the herders' meeting to determine the date of alp ascent, from the cattle count on the alp, or from the day of paying fees	5.00
False declarations at the cattle count	20.00
Grazing the alp before daybreak on the day of the alp ascent	20.00
Cattle driving on the common	20.00
Failure to stall animals the first twelve nights	20.00
Sellamatt	
Driving more cattle to the alp than the user has rights	5.00–200.00
Geilskummi	
Taking manure or straw from the alp	5.00–50.00
Not descending from the alp on the same day as the others	5.00–50.00

Sources: Alp Geilskummi (1936: art. 13, art. 27), Alpkorporation Sellamatt (1958: art. 5, art. 29), Genossenschaft Grosse Schwägalp (1976b). Although the references for Sellamatt and Geilskummi are dated, these are the alp regulations that were still in force at the time of my research.

tion has the power to set the fine. On some alps, the meeting of all rights holders must establish the fine. Proceeds from fines go into the commons, community, or *Korporation* treasury.

Fines are not the final word on enforcement. If a violation involves neglected work, the alp overseer or executive officers might order that a third party perform it at the violator's expense. The ultimate penalty for repeated breaches of the regulations is expulsion from the alp.

Alp Overseer

The person who enforces the regulations, often imposes the fines, and performs many other duties to ensure an orderly running of the commons is the alp overseer (*Alpvogt* or *Alpmeister*). This position is as different as the alp systems are different. The job of alp overseer may be an office of the commons to which the rights holders elect someone from among themselves. This is often the case on share rights alps. In Valais, where one finds community alps, the job of alp master is rotated among the users. On community alps in Graubünden, the job may fall to the person who, during the term of the prior officeholder, had the most animals on the alp. Alternatively, the duties may be incumbent upon the community work master, who has duties for all community property—in the valley as well as on the alp. In Schwyz, the *Korporation*'s executive council appoints alp overseers. In Uri, six members of the *Korporation*'s executive council are elected by district, and they have oversight duties for the alps as well as for the other *Korporation* lands in their districts. On the Schwägalp, the commons cooperative hires a person to live on the alp, perform handiwork, and watch for infractions of the regulations. In all cases except the last, the job of alp overseer is a nonprofessional, sideline occupation that the holder practices in addition to his primary job.

The duties of alp overseer also vary greatly. In most cases, this person has the duties of counting the animals that each owner has taken to the alp and of checking the total against the owner's rights to graze animals or the owner's report of how many animals he planned to send to the alp. He may also have to figure the fee to charge the owner and collect it. It is the overseer's duty to make sure that no user drives cattle to the alp too early and that a grazier removes any animals that he has driven to the alp in excess of his rights. It is sometimes the alp overseer's job to keep the records of who has how many rights. The alp overseer directs the users in their work duty and must keep an account of who has fulfilled it. Erecting fences at the beginning of the season and dismantling them at the end of the season are under his direction. Further, the alp overseer ensures that manure is spread according to regulations, sometimes directing where to put it. He makes sure that weeds are controlled. He initiates and directs stone and debris cleanups. It may be his job to bring provisions or straw for fertilization to the alp and make sure operating equipment is in order. He may either have to check that personnel maintain the alp buildings or supervise alp users in building improvements. He inspects and directs maintenance of watering troughs and paths. In Schwyz, the alp masters have the obligation to inform the *Korporation* when a building needs repair or other major improvements are needed on the alp. Thus, the alp overseer is a key person in maintaining the quality of Swiss commons grazing areas.

Governance and Decision Making

In order to make the alpine commons run in Switzerland, users and rights holders have built formal decision-making and administrative structures. The structures have similarities across the three major types of alps: share rights, community, and *Korporation* alps. In each, the major organs consist of the alp owners or rights holders, an administrative or executive council, and the users. I list the rights holders and the users separately, because these two groups diverge on some alps. Whether the two coincide depends in part on the individual alp in question and in part on the rights type, as I clarify below. Let us proceed to examine governance, decision making, and meetings in the three major rights systems.

Share Rights Alps

The organs of a share rights alp are (1) the rights holders, (2) the executive committee, and (3) the users. The rights holders represent the original body politic of the alp. In the beginning, they constituted the reason for the whole alp organization, because they were the users. Regardless of whether they continue to be users today, they remain the ultimate source of authority in a share rights alp. The powers and prerogatives of the rights holders are to (1) elect executive officers, (2) amend alp regulations, (3) approve the financial statement, (4) set the maximum number of animal units on the alp, (5) determine alp use fees, (6) set fines, and occasionally approve each fine imposed, (7) establish a work duty, (8) set the amount of compensation for sick or injured animals removed from the alp, (9) make decisions about the construction of new buildings, or whether to allow users to build them, (10) make decisions about other major alp improvements (roads, bridges, drainage projects, etc.), (11) apply for loans, (12) resolve conflicts between members or between members and the alp group as a whole, and (13) handle all matters that the regulations do not treat or that are not delegated to other organs of the alp cooperative.

The rights holders usually meet annually sometime during the winter, although for some alps, rights holders meetings are held only every two to four years. Routinely, officers are elected and the financial statement is approved. The rights holders, however, may also discuss any changes in the alp regulations or other major matters affecting the alp's use—road improvements, forest use, perhaps a proposal by a ski company to build a lift, fines for violators, or other items already mentioned.

Voting on most alps occurs by one of two methods, the one used being anchored in the alp regulations. The first is one person–one vote. The second is that each person casts as many votes as he or she holds rights. By giving less weight to the holders of few rights, the second method can give a great deal of power to a few people. Alps that use the one-person–one-vote rule consider the second approach antithetical to their ideal of a person's worth regardless of holdings. Other alp groups use the proportional-to-rights system because it is fairer to the holder of many rights, who shares more of the costs of operation and major improvements.

To handle the trade-offs between equity based on one vote per person and equity based on financial holding, rights holders groups have reached various compromises in voting rules. A variation that departs only slightly from one person–one vote is that anyone who holds at least one grazing right has one vote, whereas holders of less than one right have the corresponding fraction of a vote. A more complex mixed system exists on Geilskummi in the canton of Bern (Alp Geilskummi 1936: art. 4). Its rights are divided into tenths of a cow-unit, and votes are allocated as follows:

Holders of $\frac{2}{10}$ to $1\frac{6}{10}$ rights have 1 vote;
holders of $1\frac{7}{10}$ to 4 rights have 2 votes;
holders of $4\frac{1}{10}$ or more rights have 3 votes.

Sometimes an alp group uses the one-person–one-vote rule for certain questions and the proportional-to-rights rule for others. Elections may be decided by the proportional-to-rights system, with all other questions decided by one person–one vote. On other alps, just the opposite rule holds. In some cases, administrative matters are settled by one person–one vote, and financial authorizations are decided by the proportional-to-rights system. Another system is that the one-person–one-vote rule is used unless one or more rights holders demand the use of the proportional system (Frödin 1941: 82).

The executive committee of a share rights alp is elected by the rights holders and is composed of the president, secretary, treasurer, alp overseer(s), and auditors. For smaller alps, these offices may be combined. For instance, the secretary and treasurer positions are combined on the Grosser Mittelberg alp in the canton of Bern (Mittelberg-Genossenschaft 1931: art. 8); on Ober-Egerlen, also in the canton of Bern, the jobs of president, alp overseer, and treasurer are combined in one person (Alpschaft Ober-Egerlen 1950: art. 8). In contrast, large alps may require not only the full collection of officers but multiple alp overseers as well.

The president has many duties that are typical of a chief executive's office: calling and leading rights holders meetings, carrying out their resolutions, and representing the rights holders in dealings with third parties. In addition, the president plays the role of organizational utility man: assisting the treasurer with financial matters, helping the alp overseer hire alp personnel, obtaining cost estimates for alp improvements, and so on. The alp overseer, when the position is separate from that of the president, is in charge of the operation of the alp (see the section entitled "Management Tools for Commons Alps," earlier in this chapter). The secretary and treasurer, in addition to having the usual duties attached to these offices, complete the executive committee and help make executive-level decisions, along with the president and overseer(s). On some alps, for instance, it is the executive committee's duty to determine the date of the alp ascent or descent. Members of the executive committee must also be ready to act in emergencies: accidents or sickness of animals or personnel, snowfall on the alp during the grazing season, and so forth. Executive committee members may serve without pay, although sometimes small cash payments or extra grazing rights compensate those who hold office.

The final body of people participating in share rights alps is the users. Users and rights holders often correspond closely. Through rental of grazing rights, however, the two groups can diverge considerably. The Schwägalp in Appenzell Ausserrhoden, for example, is used entirely by renters of hut rights. When users and rights holders diverge, the users must obey the determinations of the rights holders, who are owners of the alp. These may include regulations on fertilization, building upkeep, pasture cleanups, and the like. Most often the executive committee is still filled through election by the rights holders. In some cases in Graubünden, however, the users have a separate set of officers who are concerned with the alp's operating system (Weiss 1941: 261). The user group officers might be elected, appointed in rotation, or selected by lot.

Whether the user group differs significantly from the rights holders or not, the decision on the date of the alp ascent is often left to the group of current graziers.[26] This decision must be made each year because the progress of grass growth on the alp depends on the weather. Usually in May, the group of users gathers in a restaurant or a schoolhouse to decide when to ascend, and these meetings can be as

---

[26] As stated earlier, this decision may be left to the executive committee, but generally this is the practice only on alps where users and rights holders correspond.

much social as business occasions.[27] The official part of the meeting may last only five to ten minutes, or it may carry on for as long as half an hour, but the periods before and after the meeting are occasions for eating and socializing. The official part of the meeting occurs when the president, after calling the meeting to order, pronounces it time to decide the day of the alp ascent and asks for suggestions. Two or three attendees call out dates, which usually differ only by a few days. Sometimes, each gives a two- to three-minute justification for a nominated date. This goes into the details of who has been to the alp to observe the grass, how far along the grass is, what the weather has been like, and what days are allowed and what days are not, according to folk legend.[28] Sometimes no discussion ensues at all. In any event, the vote occurs by hand, and the one-person–one-vote rule applies.

After the decision is made, traditionally one of the officers reads the alp regulations in their entirety. Nowadays, the president may simply ask if each user has a copy of the regulations and if there are any questions. Renters of rights may be required, sometime before the alp ascent, to sign a statement that they understand the alp regulations. The president announces the date for the meeting to pay fees, which he sets according to the date just decided for the alp ascent. Other matters regarding the alp operation are discussed, and the meeting is adjourned to socializing and, in some cases, a banquet.

As just mentioned, a payments meeting is still held on some alps. On the Schwägalp, for example, the president and the secretary count the animals in each hut on the day of the alp ascent. Several days later, once fees have been calculated, the officers and all herders hold the payments meeting in the open air on the alp. The number and type of animals and the number of overstocked cattle—which again are allowed on the Schwägalp if the user pays a compensation fee—are read to the whole group for each of the twenty huts. One purpose for reading the whole list is so that all know who drove excess cattle to the alp and some peer pressure may be exerted on the worst offenders (Solenthaler 1979). The herders pay the treasurer on the spot.

Community Alps

I turn now to a description of governance and decision making on the community alps, where the groups of interest are (1) community

---

[27] The account in this paragraph is based on my attendance at several alp ascent meetings.

[28] In some regions, certain days of the week are considered lucky or blessed and some are considered unlucky or even accursed as days on which to make the alp ascent.

citizens and residents, (2) the executive council, and (3) the alp users.

Because a community alp is on land owned by the community and community taxes finance the physical plant, community citizens constitute the ultimate authority for alp decisions. Community ordinances may have a section that regulates alp use, the community may approve a separate set of regulations for the alp, or in less formal cases, the minutes of the community meeting may serve as legally binding stipulations for alp use.

Practically speaking, the meeting of community citizens plays only a limited role in alp governance. Still, it can have a large impact on alp operations, because major alp improvements such as construction of a new building or road must go through the community meeting. Any citizen may participate. Thus, nonusers as well as users may have a voice in matters affecting the alp, and all have a chance to express opinions. In most cases, the traditional method of voting by hand is used. In relatively recent times (the coming of this century), community meetings have begun to use a secret ballot for important or controversial matters, or, indeed, anytime that a member requests one. At the community meeting that I attended, the president and the secretary participated in all votes, even those taken by hand. Although attendance was small, the meeting authorized a large sum of money to construct a new alp building. (This decision was nevertheless based on extensive studies of cost, construction design, site geologic stability, etc.)

The executive council (*Verwaltungsrat*) for a community alp consists of the community president, the secretary, the treasurer, the work master, and sometimes the alp master. These are, with the possible exception of the alp master, general community officers, whom the community elects. They are usually unsalaried offices. Again, with the exception of the alp master, they all have general duties with respect to administering community matters. The alp, however, was, and in many places still is, an important part of community affairs. This is how community officers came to have duties of alp oversight.

With respect to the alp, the community president's job begins with presiding at community meetings where alp matters are decided. In some communities, he has a further tie to the alp operation, actually working with other community executive committee members in finalizing the alp accounts and in other matters. In other communities, the alp master takes on most of the detailed work. The community treasurer has the duty of collecting the use fees that the community ordinances impose on the alp users. The alp master may be a community officer (elected by the community meeting), an appointee of

136   Common Property Economics

the community executive council, or one of the alp users, elected by them from among their ranks.[29]

The last community functionary who can have duties affecting the alp is the community work master, found in Graubünden. The community of Peist provides an interesting example of the division of duties between the community work master and the community alp master. The work master has responsibility for the physical plant of the entire community: roads, fences, buildings, and public lands. As a subset, this includes alp roads, fences, and buildings and care of the pasture itself. The alp master, who is also elected by the community meeting, has duties that are restricted to the operation of the alp. He must hire alp personnel, arrange the day of the alp ascent, and make sure that the herding, milking, and cheese-making operations function. Counting the animals is also his domain. The distinction between work master and alp master represents an attempt to separate the duties and costs that fall to the community arising from its ownership of the alp from those that fall to the farmers who use the alp (Donau 1979).

The last group to consider in the community alp structure is the users themselves. Users diverge from owners of a community alp to the extent that nonfarmers reside in the community. In times past, there were few nonfarm families, and therefore virtually all families in a village had some direct interest in the alp. Today, the alp users are often in the minority. The users on a community alp with centralized dairying, which is the most common form of community alp, constitute the "alp cooperative." With the alp overseer as their leader, they care for the operating system, including performing the work duty and paying for alp personnel, utensils, supplies, and other variable costs.

On community alps, the user group often decides the day of the alp ascent. They may do so in a meeting like the one already described for share rights alp users. Alternatively, the alp overseer may collect votes by posting a list of several suggested days at a central point and assembling signatures in favor of different days (this is the procedure in Peist, canton of Graubünden). Or representatives of the owner group, namely the community executive council, may set the day of the alp ascent (this is the way it happens in Grabs, canton of St. Gallen).

---

[29] An example of the alp master's being a community officer is found in Peist, Graubünden (Donau 1979). In the communities of Sargans and Grabs, canton of St. Gallen, the executive council appoints the alp overseers (Rhyner 1980). In Buchs, canton of St. Gallen, as well as on many community alps in Graubünden, the users elect the alp overseer (Weiss 1941: 257).

Korporation Alps

Finally, we turn to governance and decision making in the *Korporation* alps.[30] The *Korporations* are much larger organizations than those that govern the share rights or community alps. The latter structures administer only single alps—or at most several alps in a community—whereas the *Korporations* manage dozens of alps. To handle this size problem, the *Korporations* are built like representative democracies.[31] The corporate body of citizens is the ultimate source of authority for *Korporation* governance. Next in line of authority is a legislative body of representatives elected by *Korporation* citizens from various districts. Finally, in some cases, there is an executive council consisting of such officers as president, secretary, treasurer, and councillors at large. The final two organs of the *Korporation* are the alp overseers and the users.

The corporate body of citizens has the powers to (1) elect officers, (2) act as the highest instance in the disposition of *Korporation* property, (3) determine use rights for *Korporation* lands, (4) set grazing fees, (5) set *Korporation* taxes (which are no longer levied), (6) award *Korporation* "citizenship," (7) approve new charity undertakings by the *Korporation* or change existing ones, and (8) change *Korporation* regulations (Korporation Uri 1952: 147–48).[32] To decide on questions relating to these powers, the corporate body of citizens meets once every two years in an open-air ring or town square. The body of citizens consists of several thousand people with certain family lineages. Yet attendance at the general meeting of citizens numbers in the low hundreds, because many people with *Korporation* rights are no longer farmers and they have little interest in the proceedings.

Although the meeting of citizens might discuss matters relating to any of the powers just listed, the most prevalent affairs handled are

---

[30] Material on user group meetings of *Korporation* alps, where not otherwise documented, is based on my attendance at meetings of the bodies of the *Korporations*. These include the Korporation Uri *Korporationsgemeinde* (meeting of the corporate body of citizens) on May 27, 1979, the Korporation Uri *Korporationsrat* (legislative body) meeting on July 3, 1979, both in Altdorf, Switzerland, and the Oberallmeind-Korporation *Verwaltungsrat* (executive council) meeting on June 6, 1979, in Schwyz, Switzerland.

[31] This is not surprising, for as the section in this chapter entitled "A History of the Rights Systems" indicates, the state and the *Korporation* were identical for centuries, and this single politico-economic entity arose around democratic principles. When the functions of the state and the *Korporation* split in the nineteenth century, both structures inherited a representative-democratic form.

[32] Point 8 comes not from the reference cited but rather from my personal observation of a change in the *Korporation* regulations at the meeting of the corporate body of citizens in Altdorf, Switzerland, on May 27, 1979.

the election of officers and changes in the regulations. Many of the proceedings occur on the podium, guided by the president and other officers, rather than involving extensive attendee participation. Both nominations for office and discussion on other points of business may be scarce. Discussion from citizens is not completely absent, however. To voice an opinion, a citizen steps into the middle of the ring to talk. Votes are by show of hands, and the one-person–one-vote rule applies.

The legislative body in Uri (*Korporationsrat*) consists of the president, the vice-president, the administrator, and approximately thirty-five people elected from districts within the seventeen communities of the *Korporation*. It normally meets four times a year, with the *Korporation* president presiding. The legislative council makes decisions on proposals that have been worked out by the executive council, which I describe momentarily. The more important powers of the legislative council are administering *Korporation* property, which includes approving hut rights to alp users. The council must approve the rental or sale of any *Korporation* land. The legislative council also makes operational decisions regarding improvements on particular alps— new buildings, building improvements, drainage projects, and the like. After discussion, votes are held by hand and the majority prevails. A member has the right to demand a roll call vote.

In Uri, the executive council (*Engerer Rat*) is the next most exclusive group, consisting of the president, vice-president, administrator, and six executive council members. The legislative council elects these officers from among its own membership, and they remain members of the legislature. The executive council meets twice and sometimes three times per month. It implements the decisions of the legislative council and prepares reports and proposals for it. It deals with governmental authorities, prepares the budget and *Korporation* accounts, performs contract negotiations with third parties, and imposes fines for violation of *Korporation* regulations. It is, one might say, the body that keeps the *Korporation*'s administration running.

In the Oberallmeind-Korporation (OAK) in Schwyz, the functions of the legislative and executive councils are combined in a single body called the executive council (*Verwaltungsrat*). This body is composed of twelve councillors, elected to four-year terms by the general meeting of *Korporation* citizens. From these twelve, the president and treasurer were originally chosen at the meeting of all *Korporation* citizens every two years. It now appears that the president's job is rotated among councillors every year. Although it is a taxing position, the president's post is nonprofessional, carried out in addition to another full-time job. The treasurer and secretary are full-time, paid workers. These three members carry out the greater part of the administrative work.

Technically, the executive council of the OAK is the executive organ for the corporate body of citizens. In a formal sense, it carries out the resolutions of the general meeting of citizens, represents these citizens in administering *Korporation* property, and handles dealings with third parties. In order to fulfill these duties, the executive council of the OAK functions like the legislative council of Uri in meetings held once per month. Interestingly, these meetings employ no voting but rather reach decisions by consensus. After extensive discussion, the president formulates a proposal based on his reading of the group and asks if everyone is in agreement. Generally, no one objects and that settles the matter. The president is virtually equal to the others in the discussion, participating with a bit more authority owing to his current office and knowledge. The executive council decides on capital improvements to particular alps, on some alp personnel matters (including wages), on sales of *Korporation* land, and on regional conservation and development plans, such as a forestry plan for a particular area. Executive council members also have duties as members of special committees. Finally, each councillor must visit a certain number of alps each spring to inspect the condition of the land and physical plant.

In the *Korporation* alps, a fourth group of people, the alp overseers, stands somewhere between the alp administrations and the alp users. On the alps of Korporation Uri, the alp overseers are rather close to the users, because the users of each alp elect them from among their own number. They have the primary duty of making sure the pasture is protected and grazed according to all of the regulations of the *Korporation*. In Schwyz, on the other hand, all alp overseers are appointed by the executive council. Each tends to be a grazier on alp land, but he has the duties of making sure that other hut right holders do not ascend to the alp too early and do properly spread their manure, maintain fences, keep the proper emergency hay supply, and clear the grazing area of debris.

Again, the final class of people with decision-making power in the *Korporation* structure is the users. This class subdivides functionally into a number of user groups, each one of which utilizes a single *Korporation* alp. In the Korporation Uri, each such group meets every year in the spring to vote on the day of the alp ascent, as Korporation Uri regulations prescribe. On the other hand, the day of the alp ascent in Schwyz is technically set by the *Korporation* executive council for all alps on which meat animals graze, that is, for the greater part of the alps in Schwyz. Practically speaking, this means that the alp overseer determines the ascent date, since he makes the recommendation to the executive council. The overseer may consult with other hut right owners on the alp, but he is not obliged to do so. On the few cow alps in Schwyz, the users determine the alp ascent by majority vote.

In some ways, owners and users diverge less in the *Korporation* structure than in the other two systems. All primary users must be citizens of the *Korporation*, although with special permission citizens may take on animals from noncitizens. In contrast to the practice in the community alps, in the *Korporations* nonparticipating citizens have no tax duties or interest in participating in the decision making. On the other hand, the influence that a user has on how the alp is run is attenuated by the large *Korporation* structure. Most of the important decisions are made in the legislative and executive councils. Thus, the primary gulf between decision making and use practices in the *Korporation* alps does not result from a divergence of users from owners. Rather it lies in the separation between control exercised by the administration and the actual use practices exercised by the graziers.

Summary

Swiss mountain farmers have developed elaborate, formal rights systems to protect their common property in grazing. Using tradable rights, residency requirements, or family lineage, as well as several different systems of allocation, they have limited entry and defined extraction rights among members of the resource user group. They have set up regulations and enforcement devices to protect the resource and to ensure individual contributions to investment in the common property resource. To implement all these things, they have created practical, democratic governing institutions.

The share rights alps use tradable rights (which are both salable and rentable) to perform both functions of limitation and allocation. Ownership of a right generally permits the grazing for the summer of one cow—or a combination of other animals whose grazing pressure equals that of a cow. The total number of rights limits total use. Allocation occurs through the holding, buying, and selling of rights. Because these are unregulated in most cases, the market allocates alp use.

Community alps combine the requirements of township residency and of wintering animals on self-harvested hay to limit use. In most cases, nonresidents may enjoy use privileges if space permits, albeit often at higher fees. Generally, communities do not allocate alp use by a market means. Where the alp resources are ample, rights are allocated on a first-come–first-served basis, with long-standing use lending an advantage. Where the alp resources are in shorter supply, most communities allocate rights directly or indirectly according to the amount of land users hold in the valley. Commonly, the amount of hay for winter feed that users' land produces determines their alp use rights; allocation is thus connected with landownership, although it is not exactly proportional to the number of hectares owned. Some communities also apportion alp use by lot or by rotation.

Family lineage as a prerequisite for use is the device of the *Korporation* in the inner cantons. Users in some *Korporation*s can elude this remnant from the Middle Ages by obtaining special permission from the *Korporation* to summer noncitizens' animals, if space on the alp permits. The *Korporation*s also sometimes supplement the family lineage criterion with requirements of residency and/or wintering animals on hay harvested within community or district boundaries. *Korporation*s allocate alp use among rights holders primarily by demanding application to the *Korporation* for hut rights. Secondarily, the market helps allocate use on some alps, because renters of hut rights may take on animals from users who have no rights.

Swiss common property graziers also define and enforce their use systems with formal regulations, fees, fines, work duties, and an alp overseer, who ensures that the alp regulations are observed. Fees are generally too low to curb alp grazing pressure effectively, but fines and compensation fees for overgrazing are substantial enough to do so. Work duties are still maintained, although to a lesser degree than in the past because of the greater time demands on today's part-time and full-time farmers and the frequent provision allowing discharge of the work duty by a cash payment.

Right holders and users of an alp may differ, depending on the alp's rights type. On share rights alps, rights holders are those who own units of grazing rights; users are owners or renters of rights. On community alps, rights holders are all community citizens and to a lesser extent noncitizen residents; users are the community's farmers, both citizens and noncitizen residents. On *Korporation* alps, rights holders are *Korporation* citizens, people with certain surnames; users include the farmers among these citizens and, indirectly, specially permitted people who contract with citizens to take their animals to the alp. In all rights systems, rights holders possess the fundamental decision-making powers for the alp, although users often make decisions affecting seasonal or daily operations.

Governance of the cooperative systems is almost universally democratic. Both rights holders and users make most decisions using a one person–one vote rule. Exceptions lie in some share rights alps where votes are proportional to the number of rights held, at least for some decisions, and in the large alp *Korporations*, where representatives of the rights holders make decisions in legislative and executive bodies.

This sophisticated system of commons use is testimony to the viability of common property. A similar system emerged in medieval England, and a study of it will help us understand how another people decided to manage a resource cooperatively. In the next chapter, I present a comparison of the English medieval commons with the Swiss system.

CHAPTER 5

Comparisons with the English Open Field System

The open field system that prevailed in England and much of the rest of Europe during the late Middle Ages provides a number of parallels to common grazing in Switzerland. Indeed, common alpine grazing probably emerged from a similar social system placed in a mountainous environment. In this chapter, I draw parallels in rights, origins of rights, regulations, fees and fines, and the meetings held to decide land use rules, as well as point out some contrasts. This will put the Swiss system in a wider context, both for those familiar with the English system and for those who are not.

The comparisons I make are to a large extent between a historical system in England and a current system in Switzerland. The common property of England has mostly died out, whereas most of the discussion of Switzerland concerns practices that continue to this day. Therefore, where contrasts exist, it is not always possible to tell whether they indicate that the Swiss system is more mature or that the difference between environments is responsible. This is the case in part because thorough historical research was not one of my main objectives in Switzerland.

One sharp contrast between the two systems should be kept in mind. The British open field system centered around growing crops, whereas the Swiss system is dominantly pastoral. Grazing did occur as a significant component of the English system, but it was secondary. In the Swiss Alps, the environment favors grazing and arable land is limited. Some of the differences in grazing practices arose for this reason.

Characteristics of the Open Field System

The distinguishing characteristics of the English open field system were (1) open field arable, (2) community control of cropping, and (3) common pasture of stubble, fallow, meadow, waste, and balks in the open fields (Thirsk 1964; Ault 1965: 5; Hoffman 1975: 24). Generally, each village had two or three large fields, each of which was divided into numerous narrow, long strips. Each strip was held by a peasant in feudal tenancy, but the tenants left their strips unfenced—hence the name "open fields." Some aspects of the farming were cooperative and some were individual. The peasants plowed the strips using cooperatively formed teams of oxen, and crop rotation of entire open fields followed community rules, but the farmers sowed and harvested their own strips. The origins of the strips and common cropping patterns have been widely debated, but I will leave the description of the cropping patterns at this, because my primary focus is on grazing.[1]

As just indicated, the third distinguishing characteristic of the open field system was that much of a township's land underwent common grazing during one season or another. The waste, which was land beyond the arable fields, was grazed in common during the summer. The meadows, which were land reserved to grow hay in spring, were thrown open to common grazing after hay harvest. The arable land was subject to common grazing of the stubble after harvest and during the year it lay fallow, and by tethered animals on any balks or common ways while it was in crop. Let us turn to these practices of common grazing, as well as community control of hay land, for parallels and contrasts with Switzerland.

Rights Comparisons

Common grazing rights in the English open field system varied geographically and temporally, even as we have seen in Swiss common grazing systems. The comparisons made here are based on a mature English open field system such as was prevalent in the Midlands of England in the late Middle Ages, unless otherwise stated.

The Swiss have allocated and used their grazing land in ways very similar to those of the medieval English. The waste beyond the English village arable could easily be compared to the alps themselves. The English meadows could be likened to the Swiss May fields, because both provide or provided hay as well as grazing. Finally, both systems include or included arable that was grazed during certain seasons.

Common rights to grazing for tenants and freeholders in the English system arose from several precedents: (1) the right appendant to

---

[1] The interested reader may pursue the debate on the origins of the strips and the common cropping pattern in Slater ([1907] 1968), Orwin and Orwin (1954), Thirsk (1964, 1973), Baker and Butlin (1973), Hoffman (1975), McCloskey (1975), Dodgshon (1980), and other citations on the English open field system given in this chapter.

the standard peasant holding of a virgate (ten to thirty acres) of land, (2) the right to common pasture associated with ownership of certain tenements ("tofts") in the village, (3) the right to common appurtenant to land as a result of long use, and (4) personal grants of common rights by the lord.[2] The last of these was far less frequent than the others (Slater [1907] 1968: 10–11; Vinogradoff [1923] 1967: 263–64; Roberts 1973: 199; Thirsk 1973: 267). Thus, the majority of claims to common pasture in England were praedial. In contrast, the majority of rights to common in Switzerland have long since become personal in some way or another—through residency, citizenship, family lineage, or the holding of share rights. Only rights on property alps in isolated spots in Switzerland developed praedial relationships, and it is likely that they evolved as the alps became stinted, not as a result of the original granting of rights to the alps.

Like early practice on the Swiss alps, original commons privileges on the English wastes allowed a user an unlimited number of animals (Slater [1907] 1968: 9–10; Orwin and Orwin 1954: 57). So much waste lay between villages early in their history that intercommoning of animals from different manors occurred. As population grew, however, more waste was converted to arable, and the amount of waste declined in most Midland townships to the point where it was a limited, valuable commodity. As a result, the first major response to growing population was the drawing of definite borders and the splitting of the waste between townships (Dodgshon 1980: 84–85). With the disappearance of intercommoning, the English system reached the point that one witnesses in Switzerland today: very clear borders drawn between the alps.

As population increased further and the number of animals grazing the English common multiplied, a second and a third major response developed to expand and allocate available grazing resources. The second response was the opening of the arable to common grazing after harvest and during the year when a field lay fallow (Thirsk 1964: 16, 1973: 279; Ault 1965: 5; Baker and Butlin 1973: 645;

---

[2] During the enclosure movement, as the open field system declined, rights to common were defended in court. Legal rights to common were categorized slightly differently. Legally, peasants were held to have rights to the commons by one of four means: *common appendant*, the right of a freehold tenant of a manor to pasture commonable cattle on his arable, the wastes, and other common pasture; *common appurtenant*, the right that had become appurtenant to land either by long use or by express or implied grant; *common in gross*, a personal right to common and not a right arising in connection with land; and *common par cause de vicinage*, a vague right to common waste that arose from intercommoning between people of neighboring villages (Vinogradoff [1923] 1967: 265–71).

McCloskey 1975: 83). A very similar practice is still followed in some Swiss communities, in which all village land—both private and common, both fields and pasture—is opened to grazing early in the spring and after harvest in the fall. The practices seem to differ in that, in England, the animals grazed only the open field strips when they were in stubble or in fallow. Closes held in severalty were not opened. In Switzerland, all land in a village that practices open arable grazing becomes fair ground for the roaming cattle.

The third major response to increased grazing pressure in England was stinting of the commons (Ault 1965: 10). Communities accomplished this goal using rules similar to the ones that they had used in the original granting of common rights. Arable land held or a tenement owned determined a user's stint (Vinogradoff [1923] 1967: 261; Thirsk 1973: 248, 267). In the first case, not only the number but the types of animals allowed depended on the size of the user's arable holdings. In the second case, each toft (household) that had rights was allocated a certain number of animals by type.[3] Seventeenth-century Coleby in Kesteven Heath provides an example of both systems. Landholders were allowed two beasts, one follower, and five sheep per household, plus two oxen or horses per oxgang (twenty to thirty acres) in the "Oxpasture" and two cows, two young beasts, and thirty sheep per oxgang in the "Cowpasture" (Thirsk 1973: 248–49).

Although Swiss farmers used the same methods of stinting in isolated situations, most often they limited access differently than the English. To be sure, the two forms of property alps parallel the major forms of stinting in England closely, since either the amount of property held in the valley or ownership of a particular dwelling determines rights for these alps. These, however, are unusual forms of rights in Switzerland. Stinting is accomplished far more often by limiting the number of animals per individual or by requiring the ownership of grazing rights. Again, these are personal rather than property-related forms of stinting. Moreover, regardless of whether the limitation is property related or personally related, Swiss practice does not specify the types of animals to be grazed, but rather a certain number of animal units. More prevalent in England was the exact specification of types and numbers of animals.

The divergence between the English property-related rights and the Swiss personally related rights was bridged somewhat in a few situations in England where grazing rights were transferable. Slater

---

[3] Differences in stints for the lord, for freeholders and copyholders, and for feudal tenants complicated the system, but because most people fell in the last class, land or tenement holding determined most stints.

([1907] 1968: 12) and Ault (1965: 27) cite situations in England in which a tenant who had a right to pasture but who owned fewer sheep than he was allowed could offer pasture rights to other township residents at a price. "Gates" (rights to tether cattle on grass breaks in the open field) were also transferable in Laxton, Nottinghamshire (Orwin and Orwin 1954: 136). These practices, however, do not seem to have been widespread. In contrast, transferable rights in Switzerland are quite prevalent.

In both Switzerland and Britain, stints were changed as the need arose. Swiss farmers, for example, sometimes increase the number of rights required to graze an animal unit, thereby shrinking the number of animal units on the commons. In Britain, the peasants regularly revised the stints, changing both the numbers of and the allocation among types of animals and generally making them more restrictive over time (Vinogradoff [1923] 1967: 261; Ault 1965: 10; Thirsk 1973: 255–56).

One form of stinting seems to have been commonplace in both countries. This is the requirement that no one keep more animals on the commons in summer than he could winter (Vinogradoff [1923] 1967: 262; Orwin and Orwin 1954: 133; Ault 1965: 26–27; Thirsk 1973: 249). This requirement appears to have become prevalent in Britain by the fourteenth century. Closely related to this is the restriction, which began emerging in the sixteenth century, that no one could graze strangers' cattle on the commons (Vinogradoff [1923] 1967: 262; Thirsk 1973: 251–56). Switzerland has its parallels to the latter restriction in the residency requirement for community alps and the requirement that all animals on *Korporation* alps belong to *Korporation* citizens.

The medieval bylaws of Pinchbeck and Spalding indicate a typical example of rights that emerged in the fens of Britain, areas whose soils were wetter than those of the Midlands and were more suited to pasture than to arable (Thirsk 1973: 250–51). To ensure all commoners a fair share of the common fen, even though it was relatively extensive, they applied the restriction that every man have a fixed place for grazing on the fen. When he died, his wife inherited his place (his "labour"), or if she did not claim it, the first man who "manured" it—that is, put forth effort to improve it—could claim the labour. No one could sell his labour although exchanges were allowed. This situation is similar to, and may be the precursor of, the hut right system in Switzerland. Hut rights lead to a situation in which individuals have a particular station on the commons. Add to this the prohibition of driving animals on the commons and one emerges with

a situation similar to the labour of the British fens. The main difference, of course, is that hut rights in Switzerland have become transferable.

Meadows, May Fields, and Wild Hay Areas

In medieval England, most townships reserved certain grasslands,
usually on the wetter soils, to produce hay for winter feed. These
meadows have their parallels in two resources in Switzerland, the May
fields and the wild hay areas. Ownership and allocation practices compare interestingly between England and Switzerland in these three
resources.

In England, the meadows were common in the same sense as the
arable fields. Community rules governed their use; yet like the arable,
the meadow was divided into strips, and an individual reaped the
produce of each. The meadows were closed for certain dates in the
spring to grow hay but, like the arable, were thrown open to common
grazing again after hay harvest (Ault 1965: 5, 34; Elliott 1973: 62;
Thirsk 1973: 248). Typically, haying had to be completed by Mid-
summer Day or by July 1. Bylaws often indicated that townspeople
could not let animals out on the meadow until August 1, which implies
that there was a need for time to let the grasses regrow. Once open,
the meadow was pastured for three to six months. As in other forms
of pasture, stints on the number and type of animals on the meadow
became prevalent in the sixteenth and seventeenth centuries (Vinogradoff [1923] 1967: 260; Ault 1965: 34–35; Thirsk 1973: 248).

Rights to the meadow were divided between the lord of the manor
and his tenants. The strips were generally allocated among tenants by
one of three methods. First, each tenant sometimes had fixed strips in
the meadow, as did the lord. Second, it was very common practice to
reallocate the strips annually by lot. Third, the strips might be reallocated in a set rotation. The farmers also sometimes performed the
haying communally, proceeding from one strip to the next as they
finished each (Vinogradoff [1923] 1967: 259; Orwin and Orwin 1954:
59–60; Ault 1965: 34; Baker and Butlin 1973: 651; Thirsk 1973:
248).

The Swiss May fields are comparable to the English meadows in
that farmers also alternate them between grazing and hay growing.
The timing is different, however. In Switzerland, grazing occurs before hay growing in the spring, possibly because the mountainous
climate requires the farmer to wait longer for the grass on the alp to
be ready than the English peasant had to wait for the waste. As a

consequence of this early spring grazing, the Swiss farmer must allow his May field hay to grow longer into the summer than the English peasant did, cutting in July or August rather than before July 1. As in the English practice, however, the May fields are grazed again in the fall after hay harvest and after the animals have returned from the alps. Despite similarities in use, a major difference between the May fields and the English meadows lies in the former's being largely private. Generally speaking, lands as close to the settlements in Switzerland as the May fields are private.

The wild hay areas of Switzerland, when they were used more prevalently, did not alternate between hay growing and pasture use. Yet here the land tenure and allocation practices were similar to those for the common property of English meadows. Swiss villagers allocated the wild hay areas by lot, by auction, or by first come–first served on the appointed day. As on the English meadows, harvesting was allowed only after a certain day, although it was later in the summer than it was in Britain. August 1 was most popular; "Jacob's Day" (July 25) and August 13 (August 1 in the old Julian calendar) were also popular dates (Waldmeier-Brockmann 1941). The Swiss, however, did not harvest their wild hay communally, as some English townships did.

Historical Roots

The origins of common rights to pasture in England and Switzerland are probably quite similar. They both apparently lie in the new in-migration of Germanic peoples to the respective regions in the early Middle Ages and subsequent population growth. Let us briefly review the English history as current scholars understand it and compare it to the history in Switzerland related in Chapter 4.

Common pasture rights in Great Britain appear to go back to a period before the Anglo-Saxon invasions, when inhabitants claimed rights over vast expanses of moor and forest, the sizes of current English counties (Thirsk 1973: 245–46). When the Anglo-Saxons invaded and settled Britain in the fifth and sixth centuries, they built settlements similar to those they had left on the Continent, namely, isolated farmsteads or small hamlets of two to three families. They practiced a primarily extensive, pastoral economy in the wastes and forests along with primitive agriculture in rectangular fields. Their custom of intercommoning on the wastes extended the practice of common pasture started before them (Ault 1965: 5; Hoffman 1975: 36–41). We can draw a functional parallel between the customs of those times, both before and after the Anglo-Saxon invasion, and the situation under the German mark in Switzerland. Land was so extensive beyond the farmstead plots held in severalty that settlers claimed and used it in common. Indeed, virtual open access was the rule, except that men outside the county or outside the mark had no rights.

Between the seventh and eighth centuries and the Norman Conquest, Anglo-Saxon villages underwent nucleation, possibly under the pressure of lords who saw the political advantage of concentrated settlements (Hoffman 1975: 42–45). At the time of the Norman Conquest, there still existed a great deal of common waste beyond the villages, and intercommoning continued for some time thereafter. This system parallels the period in the history of the alpine grazing areas when, researchers believe, whole valleys claimed and shared alpine grasslands without much clear division of the grazing areas. Then, in the twelfth and thirteenth centuries, intercommoning in England declined as the country's population doubled (Ault 1965: 6). Townships drew fast boundaries between themselves, and areas of common waste became the possession of individual communities. This period parallels the breakup of the mark in Switzerland, when individual communities claimed rights to particular alps and other common property resources.

Cooperative land reclamation in England followed a somewhat different course from that in Switzerland, where many share rights alps arose from collective land clearing. In the Domesday of St. Paul (1222), we can read of villagers bringing new land under cultivation cooperatively, then dividing it in proportion to amounts of land already held (Ault 1965: 6). Such activity continued in northwest England as late as the sixteenth and seventeenth centuries (Elliott 1973: 45). In the fens, the building of dikes and drainage called for large, intervillage cooperative efforts, but after the land was reclaimed it was divided first among hundreds, then among villages, and finally among individuals. Because the participants in this process were freeholders, they held the land in severalty (Thirsk 1973: 269). Thus, the land was divided in England after cooperative clearing, whereas in Switzerland it was held in undivided common. Cooperative clearing, however, did not lead whimsically to different results in the two places. In all the English cases cited, the land was put to use as arable, where the system involved individually held strips under community rules for cropping. Undoubtedly, the use to which the land was put caused it to be divided rather than put to common use.

As we have seen, increased population pressure late in the Middle Ages—with the exception of the depopulation during the Black Death in the fourteenth century—led to further definition of pasture rights in England. The rights to graze stubble and fallow, as well as stinting in various forms, emerged. Those without claims to grazing rights based on land or tenement ownership were often excluded. In Switzerland, exclusion became based on family lineage, residency, possession of transferable rights, and occasionally land ownership.

A final parallel and a distinction between English and Swiss commons history arise in the evolution of feudal tenure in the two places. In Switzerland, the holders of land and common rights granted under feudal contracts gradually came to regard their land as held in fee simple. In England, this process also occurred for much of the arable (Cunningham, Stoebuck, and Whitman 1984: 17–20). Rights to the commons, however, became embroiled in a war between lords and tenants during the enclosure movement. For the most part, the lords prevailed, and common grazing had largely disappeared in England by the end of the nineteenth century. In contrast, common rights held either in fee simple (share rights) or as personal claims (based on citizenship, etc.) live on in Switzerland.

English Bylaws and Swiss Regulations

Regulations governing alp use in Switzerland have their parallel in the bylaws of the English village communities. The earliest bylaws still extant are from around 1270 (Thirsk 1973: 232). There is a basic difference in codification between the Swiss alp regulations, at least between those in existence since the eighteenth century, and the English community bylaws of medieval times. In England, basic agricultural rules were never codified but rather were generally accepted precepts based on use from time out of mind. The rules that began appearing in manorial court rolls in the thirteenth century were changes in, additions to, or presentments of fines for violations of the unwritten rules. Over time, a long list of bylaws collected in the manorial court rolls from the annual court meetings, without the original set of bylaws ever being written down (Thirsk 1973: 246–47). This contrasts with the situation in Switzerland, where complete sets of alp regulations have been kept at least since the eighteenth century (Medicus 1795).[4] The Swiss system, however, may have advanced farther than the English system ever did simply because the former system has lived longer.

---

[4] Besides the reference to alp regulations in Medicus (1795), sets of alp regulations from 1744 are still extant for the Schwägalp, canton of Appenzell-Ausserrhoden (Frehner 1925).

Bylaws in England controlled a variety of matters already discussed, including stints, dates of stocking pastures, proper tethering, and the like. Bylaws not yet examined included a requirement that certain animals be put in the care of a village herdsman (this commonly affected sheep and pigs, and sometimes held only for certain pastures), a stipulation that pigs be ringed to prevent them from rooting up the grazing areas, a provision that pigs be stied at night, a prohibition of geese on the commons, a stipulation that fences and hedges around the open fields be kept in good repair, a regulation that people cut thistles on the common before these weeds seeded, a requirement that watering places be scoured, specification of a date on which lambs became sheep, and a host of other rules that protected the community or its common property (Tawney 1912: 242; Orwin and Orwin 1954: 133, 153–54; Ault 1965: 26–30; Thirsk 1973: 247).

Swiss parallels to several of the bylaws just mentioned exist, although some of them are seldom found in alp regulations themselves. For example, sheep or goats are required to be in a common herd and be taken to the sheep or goat alp. Similarly, some alps sty their pigs, but ringing requirements are not common.[5] Some communities prohibit geese on the commons (Rubi 1979). Scouring watering places and keeping fences in repair correspond to work duties on the alps that require the erection of fences and caring for the grazing area. Cutting thistles on the English common corresponds directly to alp regulations that require destroying weeds on the alps. Finally, the setting of a date on which lambs become sheep is analogous to the dates set in some alp regulations on which calves are declared heifers and the practice in Switzerland of examining the number of teeth a heifer has to determine whether it will count as a one-year-old or a two-year-old.

Fees and Fines

Like the Swiss, the English used fines to enforce the bylaws. Indeed, we know of many of the bylaws of the open field system only because of the written records in manorial court rolls of fines imposed for their violation. The manor court imposed fines for exceeding one's stint, letting animals onto the stubble before it was opened, shirking

---

[5] However, the regulations for the Lombach alp in the canton of Bern state: "No unringed pigs will be suffered on the alp. Each herder is required to follow this directive, in the contrary case forfeiting a fine of SFr. 5 per head" (Bergschaft Lombach 1928: art. 19, my translation).

the duty of fence or hedge maintenance, not cutting hay in the meadow by the fixed date, leaving pigs unringed, not attending the manorial court itself, letting cattle stray, not scouring ditches, or encroaching on common grasslands by cropping them (Orwin and Orwin 1954: 127–37; Ault 1965: 29–30). Direct parallels in Switzerland include fines for grazing more animals than the user holds rights, grazing animals on the alp before daybreak on the day of the alp ascent, not attending meetings of the users, and not performing the work duty.

Before the fifteenth century, fines in England went to the lord of the manor. During the fifteenth century and afterward, manorial courts began designating that half the fines be paid to the parish church, the lord retaining the other half. Because the court consisted of town residents who were simultaneously parishioners of the local church, the peasants had found a way to pay half the fines to a community undertaking (Ault 1965: 50). Still, fines paid in Switzerland go into a coffer that more directly benefits the grazing undertaking for which the users have banded together: the treasury of an alp, *Korporation*, or a community.

The practice of charging grazing fees, which emerged in Switzerland, appears not to have arisen in England. English tenants considered the feudal fee that they paid to their lord to be, in part, compensation for their rights to the commons. As feudalism declined and feudal fees disappeared, however, English peasants apparently decided that fees for the unextinguished common rights would not be beneficial or perhaps not legal. In Switzerland, by contrast, fees for the common benefit became common course.

Meetings and Officers

Whether originally intended for the purpose or not, the English manor courts evolved into a forum in which residents of the village discussed, defined, and enforced the rules of the agricultural community. Freeholders and tenants alike participated in these annual meetings to settle disputes, delineate the rules of the open fields, and settle on common rights. The proceedings were often recorded on manor rolls, surviving examples of which date back as far as the fourteenth century (Vinogradoff [1923] 1967: 277; Orwin and Orwin 1954: 127–28; Ault 1965: 42–54; Thirsk 1973: 232). In communities where the manor and the village did not coincide, evidence exists that the village held its own meetings. The documentation is scarcer, because the peasants were uneducated and did not keep many records. It is clear, however, that villages as well as manorial courts held meetings (Ault 1965: 51–54).

The court was a flexible instrument for defining community bylaws, as the participants could and sometimes did adjust decisions from year to year. Some debate exists over how democratic the meetings were. On the one hand, some scholars emphasize the body's cooperative management of community resources (Tawney 1912: 244–45; Orwin and Orwin 1954: 146–47). Resolutions were generally prefaced or concluded with phrases like "[by] common consent," "[by] the assent of the community of the ville," "by the whole homage of the town," or "by all the lord's tenants free and villein" (Ault 1965: 41). On the other hand, Ault (1965: 42–46) argues that those who mattered in the decision making were those with more land, whether tenant or free. There was "no counting of heads," he says, and he claims that the lord of the manor also sometimes had a heavy hand in drafting bylaws. He points out that the officers elected were almost exclusively the more landed and hence more prominent of the village. In contrast, as we have seen, the Swiss peasants built institutions specifically to weight decisions either according to strict democracy or on a basis of proportional interest, depending upon the decision. (That is, sometimes one man–one vote applies, and sometimes the number of rights held is the basis for voting.) Although we cannot ignore the likelihood that more powerful or persuasive actors wield more political influence, Swiss user meetings definitely give the impression of democracy.

In England, the court steward, an agent of the lord, presided over manor court meetings. He called the suit roll, and all tenants were expected to attend on pain of a modest fine. The court meeting selected a jury and a foreman. The jury's jobs were to settle disputes, to inspect the fields, and to impose fines. The foreman issued notices to declare the opening of the fields on the proper dates, and so forth (Slater [1907] 1968: 11–12; Orwin and Orwin 1954: 127–29). Other officers elected by the court meeting included the bailiff, who was a liaison between the tenants and the court steward; constables; the pinder, who impounded stray cattle and released them again to their owners on payment of a fine; and wardens or burleymen, who enforced the agricultural bylaws of the community throughout the year. The wardens gave the presentments of fines at each manor court meeting. No pay accrued to any of the jobs, and duties were rotated regularly. The wardens, for instance, rarely held office in consecutive years. Although court rolls reveal that some wardens held office several times during their lives, it was generally in scattered years (Orwin and Orwin 1954: 127–28; Ault 1965: 49).

Swiss parallels to the court and village meetings and many of their offices indicate similar responses to like problems of community control. Annual meetings of rights holders and users are prevalent in Switzerland, as the previous chapter elaborated. Of course, the rights holders or users run these meetings themselves, the meetings neither now nor historically arising from a manor court in most cases.[6] Still, the difference is not great, because the English peasants learned to use the manor court for themselves and did not let it be simply an instrument of the lord of the manor. An imperfect parallel to the jury might be found in the executive councils of the *Korporations*, communities, and share rights cooperatives, since the executive councils sometimes inspect alps and impose fines. The wardens of England are most comparable to the alp overseers of Switzerland, although alp overseers often have duties of supervision wider than mere oversight.

Finally, the jobs of shepherds, hogherds, and goatherds were community positions in both England and Switzerland wherever community herds were kept. In both places, payment of the herders came from community collections or rotations of in-kind contributions. In England, we see shepherds being paid with sheaves in the fields (Ault 1965: 26); in Switzerland, there were turn systems by which households were required to provide bread, cheese, salt, and other staples to the herders (Carlen 1970: 119–20).

Forests and Other Resources

Like their counterparts in Switzerland, medieval Englishmen exploited their forests for building materials and firewood. Common rights in the forests accompanied rights in the arable (Roberts 1973: 199). Stints were eventually imposed under the same principle used for grazing, namely, restrictions according to the amount of arable owned (Vinogradoff [1923] 1967: 276). Timber and firewood stints in Switzerland also were defined as allowances per household. In both places, permission of a forest overseer was sometimes a precondition for harvest of wood resources.

Even as other wild products of the land were subject to common rights in Switzerland (berries, herbs, etc.), so were there common

---

[6] The *Korporation*s are perfect examples of this. The political basis for their founding lay in all families settled in a region and did not derive from the power of a lord. Likewise, most Swiss mountain villages did not coincide with a manor during medieval times, so that a manor court was not the instrument used for village meetings.

rights in England in fish, eels, reeds, down, and peat for fen communities (Thirsk 1973: 251) and acorns, beech mast, and hogs' "pannage" (miscellaneous feed) for forest communities (Orwin and Orwin 1954: 57). Bylaws strictly controlled use of these other resources, in contrast to the situation in Switzerland. For instance, fishing for eels was restricted to a certain season and certain days of the week in Pinchbeck and Spalding, Lincolnshire, in the fifteenth to eighteenth centuries. In another example, there was a strict prohibition on the selling of peat outside the community, and anyone who cut more peat than he could carry away between May Day and Martinmas (November 11) forfeited the excess to others in the township (Thirsk 1973: 251–52).

Conclusion

The English learned—as did the Swiss and other Europeans—to respond to resource limitations in a communal manner. As pressure on their grazing resources increased, both the English and the Swiss responded by excluding outsiders and placing stints on users. Both systems used fines and community officers to enforce the rules. Differences lie in that the English bound their use rights more to property tenancy than did the Swiss. Similarly, the English stints were more definite, specified in terms of numbers and types of animals, whereas the Swiss stinted in generic animal units (although the Swiss did specify which parts of a grazing area certain animal types might graze). The English did not codify their communal regulations formally, as the Swiss have done, but rather based them on practices accepted from time out of mind, altering and adding to them through the annual manor court.

The hay lands in the two countries also have contrasting elements of individual and communal tenancy and management. Individual tenancy prevailed over both English meadow strips and the Swiss May fields, but the former were more stringently subject to communal rules and more often underwent cooperative harvesting. From the standpoint of communal regulation, the Swiss wild hay areas more closely resemble the English meadows, both being strictly controlled as to harvesting dates and methods.

The question that remains is what we can learn from all this, and primarily from the Swiss system that I have highlighted. There are two areas that I wish to address in the remainder of this book. In Chapter 7, I will extend some of the resource management principles that lie hidden in Swiss common property grazing to other group resource use situations, discussing their practicality in these other situations. Before I do this, however, I wish to ask the economic question whether common property performs as well as private property. Rationalist models argue that in the context of the Middle Ages, peasants weighed the costs and benefits of holding property in severalty against those of holding it in common and, given their state of technology, decided on the latter regime for many resources. Although private property has become more prevalent in most areas of resource ownership, the survival of Swiss commons allows us to test the idea that private property is necessarily better. This is important in an age when new institutions are being designed for many group-used resources, sometimes where either a common property or a private property approach might be applied. Therefore, in Chapter 6, I compare common property with private property statistically, and the result gives a first cut at the efficiency of common property.

An Econometric Comparison of Commons and Private Grazing

Chapter 2 showed that a resource is not exploited optimally under open access, and Chapter 3 laid out the differences between open access and common property. This discussion has presented the possibility that common property, contrary to the faults attributed to it when it is thought of as open access, may allocate resources as well as private property. Unraveling the theoretical puzzle, however, does not answer the empirical question: Can common property perform as well as private property in the real world? Because it is a group solution, some of the incentives inherent in group use that one observes under open access will remain under common property. Once access has been limited to a certain number of users, one might well ask whether common property controls on individuals—such as stinting and regulations requiring contributions to joint welfare—can overcome the incentives to cheat on the group solution. This chapter explores the question empirically, comparing common property with private property in Swiss alpine grazing. I use private property as a benchmark in the empirical comparison because economists generally agree that private property leads to good resource allocation. If we are to know whether common property provides adequate resource management on more than just theoretical grounds, an empirical comparison with private property is a good place to start.

The Econometric Models

The comparison between common and private property proceeds through a number of econometric models. This section introduces these models, which begin with a simple formulation and progress to more complex models that reflect more sophisticated efforts to model natural and institutional relationships. Sections subsequent to this one present a theoretical discussion that justifies some of the econometric tests, a description of the data, and the results. The reader less interested in econometric details may want to skip the econometric theory.

Before proceeding to statements of the models, I wish to link the ideas of nonoptimal resource exploitation from previous chapters to

158

an empirical measure of such exploitation. This measure is used in all of the models that compare different management systems.

An Empirical Measure of Overgrazing

To contrast the management of grazing land used as commons with the management of land under private property, one might compare the grazed condition of a number of parcels exploited under the two systems. Whereas the models of Chapter 2 indicate that overgrazing ought to be defined in terms of dissipation of resource rent, I assume for the purposes of this chapter that overgrazing and mismanagement would be accompanied by a degraded grass condition, both because of overinvestment in animals and because of underinvestment in common improvements. Therefore, if common property suffers from some of the same faults as open access, those faults would turn up in the condition of the land.

Although range ecologists have the ability to judge the condition of grasslands, such data are not available for Swiss alpine grazing areas. An available proxy for grazed condition is milk productivity. This variable can serve as a substitute for grazed condition because, other things being equal, overgrazed areas or areas with a poor grass condition resulting from underinvestment in common improvements ought to exhibit lower productivity than grazing areas with a good grass stand. Of course, one must control for other factors that might affect the grass condition or the cows' productivity. But given that this can be done, milk productivity ought to be a good indication of grazed condition. Thus, milk productivity in the form of herd averages of liters of milk per cow per day is used here to compare commons with private property to see whether the two management systems perform equally well.

A Simple Model

First I introduce a simple model estimable by linear regression to compare the productivity of the two rights systems of common and private property. If we represent the rights systems as R, the simple model has the form[1]

$$y_1 = \gamma_1 R + \beta_1' x_1 + u_1, \tag{6.1}$$

---

[1] The variables in equation (6.1) have been subscripted with a 1 to differentiate them from other variables and vectors in more complicated models investigated below.

where

y_1 = average milk production (liters/cow/day);

$$R = \begin{cases} 1 \text{ if private} \\ 0 \text{ if commons;} \end{cases}$$

$\mathbf{x}_1$ = a vector of exogenous variables other than the rights system that might affect grass condition or the cows' productivity;

γ_1 = an unknown coefficient;

$\boldsymbol{\beta}_1$ = a vector of unknown coefficients, including a constant term;

u_1 = a stochastic disturbance, $E(u_1) = 0$.

In equation (6.1), the coefficient γ_1 acts as a shifter for milk productivity. If it is nonzero, the dummy variable R will shift milk productivity y_1 when the grazing area is private ($R = 1$) above or below the productivity of commons ($R = 0$). Whether the shift for private property is above or below the productivity for commons will depend on the sign of γ_1. In either event, a regression of average milk productivity on the rights system R and the other exogenous factors $\mathbf{x}_1$ would result in significance of the estimate of γ_1. If there is no significant difference between the performance of commons and private, then the estimate of γ_1 will be insignificant.

The vector $\mathbf{x}_1$ contains other independent variables that may affect milk productivity. These include such natural factors as elevation; exposure of the grazing area toward the north, south, east, or west; soil type; labor input; and so forth. Because most of these variables are natural conditions, I term them the natural factors. They are more completely characterized in the data description.

Equation (6.1) is a simple model from which to start. More sophisticated models can be introduced, however, to address concerns that this basic model cannot handle.

A Simultaneous Equation Model

The first complication that may make the simple, single-equation model an inadequate representation is that simultaneity may exist in the determination of average milk productivity and the rights system. This situation arises because not only may milk production depend on the natural factors $\mathbf{x}_1$, but so may the rights system. Casual observation indicates that commons alps are farther from permanent settlements, at higher altitudes, possibly on poorer soils, and otherwise under less favorable natural conditions than private grazing areas. If the natural factors determine both the rights system and average milk productivity, simultaneity bias may exist in an equation like (6.1); the right-hand side variables would not be independent. A simultaneous equation model is necessary to handle this case, which can be written as follows:

$$y_1 = \gamma_1 y_2 + \beta_1' x_1 - u_1 \tag{6.2a}$$
$$y_2^* = \beta_2' x_2 - u_2 \tag{6.2b}$$

where

$$y_2 = \begin{cases} 1 \text{ if } y_2^* > 0 \\ 0 \text{ otherwise,} \end{cases} \tag{6.2c}$$

and where

$y_1 =$ average milk production;

$y_2 = \begin{cases} 1 \text{ if private} \\ 0 \text{ if commons;} \end{cases}$

$y_2^* =$ a latent, continuous variable on $(-\infty, +\infty)$ representing the propensity to be private;

$x_1 =$ the same vector of exogenous variables that might affect grass condition or the cows' productivity as in equation (6.1);

$x_2 =$ a vector of exogenous natural factors that might determine the rights system;

$u_1, u_2 =$ stochastic disturbances, $E(u_1) = E(u_2) = 0$;

$\gamma_1, \beta_1, \beta_2 =$ unknown coefficient and coefficient vectors; β_1 and β_2 include constant terms.

The simultaneous equation model can be thought of as having two parts: equation (6.2a), which models milk productivity, and equations (6.2b) and (6.2c), which model the potential dependence of the rights system on the natural factors. To clarify the model, three issues must be addressed: (1) the relationship of equation (6.2a) to the simple model (6.1), (2) the way in which equations (6.2b) and (6.2c) model the influence of the natural factors on the rights system, and (3) the problem arising from endogeneity of the rights system y_2 in the model.

To begin, although the notation has changed, equation (6.2a) and the simple model (6.1) are identical. Equation (6.2a) models the idea that milk productivity depends on the natural factors x_1 and the rights system y_2, as did equation (6.1). Equation (6.2a) differs from equation (6.1) only symbolically in that y_2 has replaced R as the variable for the rights system—in order to indicate that the rights system is endogenous in equation (6.2a)—and the disturbance term u_1 has been negated. Whereas the change in sign of the disturbance is merely a definitional alteration in the model that makes some of the subsequent derivations simpler, the endogeneity of y_2 is a more fundamental econometric complication that is discussed after equations (6.2b) and (6.2c) have been explained.

Equations (6.2b) and (6.2c) model the idea that the rights system variable y_2 is dependent on certain natural factors x_2. Two equations are required, because the variable y_2 is dichotomous. To model dichotomous dependent variables, the literature on qualitative response defines an unobserved or latent dependent variable y_2^* that is continuous and lies on the interval $(-\infty, +\infty)$ (Maddala 1983: chap. 2). Defined in this way, (6.2b) is a normal, linear equation that could be estimated by ordinary least squares (OLS) if y_2^* could be observed. The variable y_2^* can be thought of as a propensity for a grazing area to be private ($y_2 = 1$). The propensity itself depends on a set of exogenous variables, the natural factors x_2, according to the relation (6.2b). The link between the latent variable y_2^* and the observable dichotomous variable y_2 is given by (6.2c). If the propensity y_2^* is great enough, that is, beyond some threshold value such as zero, then we observe $y_2 = 1$. That is, if the natural factors as a set are sufficiently favorable for private property, then we observe private property. If the exogenous variables have values such that the propensity y_2^* is not large, then we observe the other event, common property ($y_2 = 0$). Exceptions to these rules are allowed, because the random disturbance u_2 can be large enough—either positively or negatively—to cause y_2^* to change sign. Also, it should be noted that the natural factors x_2 may overlap with the natural factors x_1, but they need not be the identical set. Modeling dichotomous dependent variables as in (6.2b) and (6.2c) allows one, given the assumption that the error term u_2 is normally distributed with zero mean and unit variance, to apply probit analysis to estimate the unknown coefficient vector β_2 (Judge, Griffiths, Hill, and Lee 1980; Amemiya 1981; Maddala 1983).

Finally, the endogeneity of y_2 needs clarification. The variable y_2 is said to be endogenous in equation (6.2a) because, although an independent variable itself, it depends on some of the other independent variables on the right-hand side of the same equation. These other independent variables are the intersection of the variables found in x_2 and in x_1. The nature of y_2's dependence upon these other right-hand side variables is defined by equations (6.2b) and (6.2c). The endogeneity of y_2 presents a problem for OLS if the error terms u_1 and u_2 are correlated. The difficulty arises in this event because y_2 depends on y_2^*, which in turn depends on u_2. With y_2 dependent on u_2, if u_1 and

u_2 are correlated, the right-hand side variable y_2 in (6.2a) will be correlated with the error term u_1 in the same equation. This will cause OLS to be biased and inconsistent for the coefficients in (6.2a).

Equations (6.2), however, are recursive simultaneous equations because y_1 does not appear in the second equation, (6.2b). This means that if u_1 and u_2 are uncorrelated, y_2 is a predetermined variable in (6.2a) and the system can be estimated equation by equation using OLS or probit analysis (depending on whether the equation has a continuous or a dichotomous dependent variable). Otherwise, a two-stage least squares or some other simultaneous equation estimation method must be used to estimate (6.2a). The crucial question, then, is whether u_1 and u_2 are correlated.

Estimating the coefficients β_2 with probit analysis as just outlined will answer two questions. First, it is instrumental in testing whether u_1 and u_2 are correlated and hence whether simultaneity exists in the simple, single-equation model, equation (6.1) or, equivalently, equation (6.2a). The details of this test are given in the section on econometric theory, later in this chapter. Secondly, the estimation of the coefficients β_2 will indicate whether certain natural factors predispose a grazing area toward becoming private property.

The Expanded Rights Types Model

Another complication that may make the simple model (6.1) inadequate is that there is, as Chapter 4 showed, more diversity in rights systems than a simple dichotomy between commons and private property. There are two major types of common property, cooperative commons and dispersed operating unit commons, as well as some variations on these common property systems. Among private alps, there are many variations besides the pure, owner-operated private alp. These include rental private, long-lease private (leases of more than twenty years), private where the owner accepts most of the animals from others for a fee rather than grazing his own animals, and others. This complexity in both common and private rights, attributable in part to variations in the grazing areas' operating structures, can be investigated by an expanded rights types model. A dummy variable can be created for each variation of both private and commons rights types, and these rights dummies (except one)[2] can be included in an equation similar to equation (6.1). This model can be written:

---

[2] One dummy must be dropped to avoid singularity in the regressor matrix.

$$y_1 = \gamma_1' \mathbf{r} + \beta_1' \mathbf{x}_1 + u_1, \tag{6.3}$$

where

y_1 = average milk production (liters/cow/day);

$\mathbf{r}$ = a vector of rights dummies, r_j, where j = any rights type included in the equation; the equation includes all rights types in the model except one to avoid singularity; for any observation i, r_{ij} equals 1 if the observation is of rights type j; otherwise, it is zero;

$\mathbf{x}_1$ = a vector of exogenous variables other than the rights system that might affect grass condition or the cows' productivity;

γ_1 = a vector of unknown coefficients;

β_1 = a vector of unknown coefficients, including a constant term;

u_1 = a stochastic disturbance, $E(u_1) = 0$.

There are several reasons for differentiating the rights types more finely than into the simple dichotomy of private and common property. First, deviations in private management systems from pure, owner-operated private—such as rental, leased, herder-run, and other private types—might have different yields than owner-operated private grazing areas. If we bunch the divergences from pure, owner-operated private with owner-operated private, the differences between owner-operated private property and *common property* might be obscured. If lack of a differentiation between commons and private occurs in estimating equation (6.1), then estimation of equation (6.3) will indicate whether that may have occurred because of obscuration of the private rights type. Secondly, the different types of commons and private rights might perform with varying degrees of success. This hypothesis also can be tested by examining the estimated coefficients of equation (6.3).

Another method for testing the differences between private and common property is to include only observations on pure, owner-operated private and the two main types of common property. This would exclude all variations on the main private and commons forms—rental, leased, hired herders on private land, cooperative commons run by herders with their own animals on the alp, and so on. Of course, the natural factors $\mathbf{x}_1$ would still be included. This is a variant on model (6.3) with fewer observations and only two dummy variables in the $\mathbf{r}$ vector—say, the two commons rights types. (Again, one dummy variable must be dropped to avoid singularity.) This model will be tested also, with the null hypothesis being that there is no difference between the productivity of the various rights forms.

The Users and Rights Holders Models

Until now, models have represented different management and decision-making structures through the use of dummy variables. An alternative is to measure the structure of the grazing system according to either (1) how many users or (2) how many rights holders are involved. Recall from Chapter 4 that the set of users and the set of rights holders may not coincide and that each group may make different types of decisions. The users and rights holders models represent the postulate that the institutional structure is continuous, measurable on a scale of either users or rights holders. The idea is that the scale moves from pure private property with one user or rights holder into private property of several users or rights holders, which in turn melds into common property, which itself exhibits variously sized units. Given this concept, the question is whether the land's quality and the cows' milk productivity are affected as control is spread over larger groups.

To investigate this question, I estimate the model:

$$y_1 = \gamma_1 N + \beta_1' \mathbf{x}_1 + u_1, \tag{6.4}$$

where

N = the number of users or the number of rights holders;

γ_1 = an unknown coefficient that gives the relationship between number of users or rights holders and milk productivity; all other variables are as defined in model (6.1).

As before, the important coefficient in equation (6.4) is γ_1. Its sign and significance will indicate whether the number of users or rights holders affects milk productivity. If the rules of common property provide as tight a control on resource use as those of private property, an insignificant estimate of γ_1 will result.

A Model of Farmers' Adjustment to the Natural Factors

All of the models presented so far have included a set of natural factors $\mathbf{x}_1$ to control for their effects on milk productivity. These variables include elevation; precipitation; north, south, east, or west exposure of the grazing area; and similar natural conditions. The farmers, however, may take into account the natural circumstances of the grazing areas and adjust the number of animals to keep milk productivity at an acceptable level for their rights system. If so, they effectively control for the natural conditions so that the regression equations will not need to do so. This would cause the estimated coefficients β_1 on the natural factors to be insignificant.

A model to investigate whether the farmers adjust the number of animals to comply with the exigencies of the natural conditions can be tested. This model takes the form

$$U = \delta'x_1 + \tau'r + u, \tag{6.5}$$

where

U = normal animal units per hectare;

x_1 = a vector of natural factor variables that might affect the cows' productivity found in equations (6.1), (6.2a), and (6.3);

r = a vector of rights dummies defined for equation (6.3);

δ = a vector of unknown coefficients, including a constant term;

τ = a vector of unknown coefficients;

u = a stochastic disturbance, $E(u) = 0$.

The dependent variable U, or normal animal units per hectare, is a measure of grazing pressure. It indicates the number of animal units "loaded" on the grazing area per hectare per normal grazing season of one hundred days. If the farmers adjust grazing pressure to accommodate the natural conditions (i.e., if grazing pressure is dependent upon the natural conditions), then a regression of U on the natural factors x_1 will result in significant estimates of the natural factor coefficients δ. The rights dummies are also included as regressors in equation (6.5) to control for potential differences of grazing pressure across property types.

Some Econometric Theory to Support the Models

Whereas the simple model (6.1) is based upon standard econometric theory that requires no further discussion here, the simultaneous equation model (6.2a, b, and c) and the expanded rights types model (6.3) involve more advanced econometric theory and other nuances that warrant further elaboration. (The reader who is not inclined to understand the econometric details may wish to omit this section.)

The Simultaneous Equation Model

In the section on the models immediately preceding, the crucial question for estimating the simultaneous equation model was whether the disturbance terms u_1 and u_2 in equations (6.2a) and (6.2b) are correlated. To answer this question, the $\operatorname{cov}(u_1, u_2)$ can be estimated with two approaches based on work by Heckman (1979) on sample selection bias. The first of these approaches is a modification of Heckman's procedure made possible because I had a more complete data set available than Heckman assumes. The second approach is a direct application of Heckman's original procedure.

A modified Heckman procedure. Before looking statistically at the modified Heckman method, consider the intuitive parallel between Heckman's procedure and the present case. Heckman concerns himself with parameter estimation using samples formed through choices by the subjects on whether or not to participate. Although a grazing area does not have the capacity to select itself, it can be thought of as having been selected as a commons or a private area before the determination of milk productivity. Its individual, natural characteristics caused this "self-selection" into one subsample or the other. This parallels an individual's socioeconomic characteristics' determining whether he or she selects to be in Heckman's observed sample or not. The only difference in the grazing area case is that observations are available on both the "selected individuals" (say, private alps) and the "unselected individuals" (commons alps). If we were to eliminate observations on either one or the other, our problem would be identical to Heckman's. With this background, let us derive a method to estimate the $\operatorname{cov}(u_1, u_2)$.

OLS regression calculates the linear projection of the dependent variable on the independent variables. For equation (6.2a), this means finding the conditional expectation

$$E(y_1|y_2, \mathbf{x}_1) = \mathrm{E}(\gamma_1 y_2 + \boldsymbol{\beta}_1'\mathbf{x}_1 - u_1|y_2, \mathbf{x}_1). \tag{6.6}$$

Since the variables in $\mathbf{x}_1$ are assumed uncorrelated with u_1 and u_2, $E(u_1|\mathbf{x}_1) = E(u_2|\mathbf{x}_1) = 0$. Therefore, we may simplify the notation by suppressing the conditioning on $\mathbf{x}_1$, although it is always implicit. By finding the conditional expectation of (6.6), we have

$$E(y_1|y_2) = \gamma_1 y_2 + \boldsymbol{\beta}_1'\mathbf{x}_1 - \mathrm{E}(u_1|y_2). \tag{6.7}$$

Equation (6.7) shows that the conditional expectation inherent in regressing y_1 on y_2 and $\mathbf{x}_1$ depends on an expected error term $E(u_1|y_2)$ that may not be zero. This will be the case if u_1 and u_2 are correlated, because then u_1 and y_2 will be correlated. We can evaluate $E(u_1|y_2)$ by utilizing the fact that y_2 takes on only two values, $y_2 = 0$ and $y_2 = 1$. This will allow us to find out how the conditional expectation (6.7) is affected by different y_2 values. In fact, we can rewrite (6.7) to incorporate the $E(u_1|y_2)$ as a "weighted sum" of two terms, H_1 and H_0:

$$E(y_1|y_2) = \gamma_1 y_2 + \beta_1' \mathbf{x}_1 - [H_1 y_2 + H_0 (1 - y_2)], \tag{6.8}$$

where

$$H_1 = E(u_1|y_2 = 1);$$
$$H_0 = E(u_1|y_2 = 0).$$

When $y_2 = 1$ in (6.8), the H_1 term is included and the H_0 term drops; similarly, when $y_2 = 0$, H_0 is included and H_1 drops.

If we can find expressions for H_1 and H_0, they could be included in (6.8) and the conditional expectation function would be estimable. To do so, define the disturbances u_1 and u_2 to be bivariate normal:

$$\begin{pmatrix} u_1 \\ u_2 \end{pmatrix} \sim N \left[\begin{pmatrix} 0 \\ 0 \end{pmatrix}, \begin{pmatrix} \sigma_{11} & \sigma_{12} \\ \sigma_{12} & 1 \end{pmatrix} \right],$$

where $\sigma_{11} = V(u_1)$ and $\sigma_{12} = \text{cov}(u_1, u_2)$. Notice that u_2 is defined to have unit variance. This normalization is imposed because probit analysis estimates the parameters β_2 only up to a factor of proportionality in equation (6.2b). That is, if we defined $V(u_2)$ as equal to σ_{22}, only the ratios β_2/σ_{22} would be econometrically identified, so we might as well impose the restriction $\sigma_{22} = 1$ (Maddala 1983: 22–23).

With these definitions, we can find an expression for H_1:

$$
\begin{aligned}
H_1 &= E(u_1|y_2 = 1) \\
    &= E(u_1|y_2^* > 0) \text{ using (6.2c)} \\
    &= E(u_1|\beta_2' \mathbf{x}_2 - u_2 > 0) \text{ using (6.2b)};
\end{aligned}
$$
$$H_1 = E(u_1|u_2 < \beta_2' \mathbf{x}_2). \tag{6.9}$$

The right-hand side of (6.9) is the expected value of a random variable (u_1) from a truncated bivariate normal distribution. Standard statistical theory (see Johnson and Kotz 1972: 112–13) has shown that the expected value of u_1 given the truncation is

$$H_1 = -\sigma_{12} \frac{\phi(\beta_2' \mathbf{x}_2)}{\Phi(\beta_2' \mathbf{x}_2)}, \tag{6.10}$$

where $\phi(\cdot)$ is the standard normal probability density function (p.d.f.) and $\Phi(\cdot)$ is the standard normal cumulative density function.[3]

---

[3] Expression (6.10) differs from the expression given by Heckman (1979) for the expectation of a truncated normal random variable in two respects, but the differences are inconsequential. First, Heckman gives the negative of $\beta_2' \mathbf{x}_2$ in the parentheses in the numerator of (6.10). However, since $\phi(\cdot)$ is a normal p.d.f., $\phi(\beta_2' \mathbf{x}_2) = \phi(-\beta_2' \mathbf{x}_2)$. Secondly, H_1 is the negative of the expression given by Heckman. This difference results because I subtract the error term u_2 in the model (6.2), rather than adding an error term as Heckman does. This is an inessential difference since an error term may be defined as positive or negative as one wishes. If we use a negative error term, the sense of the inequality and the sign of $\beta_2' \mathbf{x}_2$ in (6.9) are altered. This alteration causes truncation at the "other end" of the bivariate normal distribution and changes the sign of the expected value of the nontruncated random variable. This

Similarly, we can derive an expression for H_0:

$$
\begin{aligned}
H_0 &= E(u_1|y_2 = 0) \\
&= E(u_1|y_2{}^* < 0) \\
&= E(u_1|\beta_2'\mathbf{x}_2 - u_2 < 0) \\
&= E(u_1|u_2 > \beta_2'\mathbf{x}_2); \\
H_0 &= \sigma_{12} \frac{\phi(\beta_2'\mathbf{x}_2)}{1 - \Phi(\beta_2'\mathbf{x}_2)}.
\end{aligned}
\tag{6.11}
$$

Finally, substituting (6.10) and (6.11) into (6.8), we get

$$
E(y_1|y_2) = \gamma_1 y_2 + \beta_1'\mathbf{x}_1 + \sigma_{12}\left[\frac{\phi(\beta_2'\mathbf{x}_2)}{\Phi(\beta_2'\mathbf{x}_2)}y_2 - \frac{\phi(\beta_2'\mathbf{x}_2)}{1 - \Phi(\beta_2'\mathbf{x}_2)}(1 - y_2)\right].
\tag{6.12}
$$

In equation (6.12), the $\text{cov}(u_1, u_2)$ appears as a multiplicative factor in the last term. In addition, the last term involves one ratio that appears only when $y_2 = 1$ and another ratio that appears only when $y_2 = 0$. If we could estimate a new variable h, known as the Heckman correction term, where

$$
h = \begin{cases}
\dfrac{\phi(\beta_2'\mathbf{x}_2)}{\Phi(\beta_2'\mathbf{x}_2)} & \text{for } y_2 = 1 \\[3ex]
-\dfrac{\phi(\beta_2'\mathbf{x}_2)}{1 - \Phi(\beta_2'\mathbf{x}_2)} & \text{for } y_2 = 0,
\end{cases}
\tag{6.13}
$$

the "observations" on h could be included as an independent variable along with y_2 and $\mathbf{x}_1$ in an OLS regression.[4] This would give consistent estimates of γ_1, β_1, and σ_{12}. Furthermore, the usual formula for the standard error of $\hat{\sigma}_{12}$ is appropriate for the null hypothesis $\sigma_{12} = 0$ (Heckman 1979).[5] Therefore, this regression would provide a valid

---

makes no difference in subsequent expressions, since we end up subtracting a positive term rather than adding a negative one as Heckman does (see equation 6.12).

[4] Heckman's (1979) article on sample selection bias describes calculating a correction term only for observations where, say, $y_2 = 1$. The reason for this is that Heckman deals with truncated or censored samples. That is, when $y_2 = 0$, he gets no observations on y_1. Since my data set includes observations on y_1 (average milk production) for all observations, it is possible to modify Heckman's procedure to include h whether $y_2 = 1$ or $y_2 = 0$. Indeed, it is essential to modify the procedure in this way, or γ_1 would not be identified in equation (6.2a)—it would collapse into the constant term, one of the regressors in $\mathbf{x}_1$. This case is more fully discussed later in the text.

[5] The usual formulas for the standard errors of the other coefficients γ_1 and β_1 do not give consistent estimates of the coefficients' population standard deviations. They are not appropriate for testing the null hypotheses $\gamma_1 = 0$ or $\beta_{1i} = 0$, where β_{1i} is any coefficient in β_1 (Heckman 1979).

test for whether the $\text{cov}(u_1, u_2)$ is significantly different from zero. Determining this was the original purpose of these calculations; we wanted to see if the recursive equation system (6.2) could be estimated equation by equation using OLS, and $\text{cov}(u_1, u_2) = 0$ would allow this.

The variable h cannot be observed because β_2 is unknown. However, estimates $\hat{\beta}_2$ of the parameters β_2 can be obtained by performing probit analysis on equation (6.2b). Using these estimated coefficients in place of β_2 in (6.13) yields observations on h. In turn, these estimates of h can be included in a simplified version of equation (6.12):

$$E(y_1|y_2) = \gamma_1 y_2 + \beta_1' \mathbf{x}_1 + \sigma_{12} h. \tag{6.14}$$

Equation (6.14), then, is the equation to estimate to determine whether the rights system y_2 is a predetermined or a correlated endogenous variable in the simultaneous equation model. Again, whether the estimate of σ_{12} is significantly different from zero will indicate this. This determination will indicate whether the coefficients from the simple model (6.1) or (6.2a) estimated by OLS accurately reflect the differences in rights systems' effects on milk productivity, or whether estimates of the coefficients β_1 in the simple model must be calculated by two-stage least squares.

Heckman's original procedure. One problem with the modified version of Heckman's procedure is that the estimated Heckman correction term h and the rights dummy y_2 in equation (6.14) can be highly correlated. This can inflate the estimated standard error on either $\hat{\gamma}_1$ or $\hat{\sigma}_{12}$, resulting in insignificance of one or the other of these estimated coefficients. It then may be possible that the collinearity between y_2 and h unduly drives the coefficient on h to insignificance. If so, the $\text{cov}(u_1, u_2)$ may not be zero, but we cannot detect this because of the collinearity. Of course, when collinearity is present, if both regressors must be included in the equation, then the statistical tests are valid; standard errors are unbiased and consistent, even though they may be large. Still, it would be more satisfying if the significance of the coefficient on h could be examined without the confounding effect of collinearity.

Fortunately, it is possible to estimate a modified version of equation (6.14) that eliminates the private dummy and hence the collinearity between y_2 and h. In fact, this estimation exactly parallels Heckman's original suggestion for correcting sample selection bias. In the estimation, only those observations for which $y_2 = 1$ (i.e., only private grazing areas) are used.

To understand this procedure, define h_1 as the values of h for which $y_2 = 1$. That is, from (6.13), we have

$$h_1 = \frac{\phi(\beta_2'x_2)}{\Phi(\beta_2'x_2)} \quad \text{for all } y_2 = 1. \tag{6.15}$$

Now consider the conditional expectation (6.7) only for observations where $y_2 = 1$:

$$E(y_1|y_2 = 1) = E(\gamma_1 y_2|y_2 = 1) + E(\beta_1'x_1|y_2 = 1) - E(u_1|y_2 = 1)$$

$$= \gamma_1 + \beta_1'x_1 + \sigma_{12}\frac{\phi(\beta_2'x_2)}{\Phi(\beta_2'x_2)} \quad \text{using (6.10)};$$

$$E(y_1|y_2 = 1) = \gamma_1 + \beta_1'x_1 + \sigma_{12}h_1 \quad \text{using (6.15).} \tag{6.16}$$

Because γ_1 is a constant in equation (6.16), it is not distinguishable from the constant term contained in the β_1 vector. That is, γ_1 and the intercept term for the regression are not econometrically identified, and we can only estimate their sum. Because γ_1 collapses into the constant term, we must drop y_2 as a regressor. But if we do this, there is no longer a problem of collinearity between y_2 and h. In summary, the regression to be performed includes h and all other regressors in x_1, and it is performed on the subset of observations for which $y_2 = 1$. This will give us an estimate of $\text{cov}(u_1, u_2)$ without the interference of potential collinearity between y_2 and h. This test will also be examined in the results section.

The Expanded Rights Types Model

When specifying the expanded rights types model (6.3), I noted that there were two practical reasons for preferring it over the simple model. First, mixing milk yields from owner-operated private grazing together with deviations from owner-operated private grazing (such as rental, leased, hired-herder private, etc.) might obscure the difference between the productivities of private and common property. Secondly, the different private and common property systems might have different productivities, which would be obscured if they were combined into respective, single dummy variables. Both of these possibilities exemplify a single principle: The simple model (6.1) may be an econometric misspecification.

Econometrically, the misspecification involved in lumping all of the rights systems into two categories can be conceptualized as follows. Entering a single, dichotomous variable that is the combination (i.e., the sum) of dummy variables representing a finer categorization is equivalent to entering all of the dummies while constraining the co-

efficients to be equal for all dummies in each of the two major subdivisions. For example, because the dummy variable R in equation
(6.1) takes the value one for any private rights type and zero for any
commons rights type, the coefficients on all private rights types are in
effect constrained to take on the same value, while the coefficients on
all commons rights types are constrained to be zero. Yet significant
differences may exist between the coefficients of the various rights
types, and such implicit constraints on the coefficients could be a
misspecification. Unfounded linear constraints can lead to bias in the
estimated coefficients of the remaining included variables. Perhaps
the most widely recognized example of this is coefficients wrongly
constrained to be zero, that is, variables improperly omitted from a
regression equation. The result is omitted variable bias for the coefficients of the included variables. An example of this may exist in
estimating equation (6.1). Constraining all commons rights types variables to have zero coefficients could result in omitted variable bias for
the private rights coefficient γ_1, as well as for the natural factor coefficients. Constraining all of the private rights types to have the same
estimated coefficient compounds the problem for a similar reason.
For all these reasons, the estimated coefficients in the simple model
may be biased, and the expanded model may be better. This eventu-
ality will be resolved when we examine the estimations of the simple
and the expanded rights types models.

The Data

Before examining the results of the statistical tests given in the
previous sections, I describe the data. The collection and preparation
of the data tell a story of their own that builds on the account of Swiss
grazing in Chapter 4.

The Population and the Sample

Whereas the description of alpine grazing in Chapter 4 dealt with
much of the German-speaking part of Switzerland, the statistical work
is restricted to the canton of Bern. In fact, only Bernese alps where
cows graze and milk is produced are part of the population. Those
alps where only heifers and meat animals graze may be different
enough to be outside the population. The sample from this population consisted of grazing areas for which milk production data were
available. Data on milk production are collected in order to provide a

Swiss federal subsidy to cheese producers in mountain areas.[6] Therefore, only alps where cheese was produced *and* users applied for the
subsidy are included in the sample.[7]

The unit of observation is an entire grazing area. Thus, values for
the dependent and independent variables were aggregated over all
cows, dairying operations, and land area for each grazing area used as
an observation. The number of alps with data on average milk production was 345. Missing observations on the independent variables
reduced this number considerably: The number of observations used
in the regression analyses was 245 or 244, depending on the analysis.
Attrition of observations owing to missing values on the independent
variables does not introduce any biases into econometric estimates
(Kmenta 1971: 336).

The Dependent Variable

For the purposes of the subsidy, data are collected on total milk
production in liters, number of cows, and number of days on the alp.
The dependent variable was formed by dividing total milk production
from the entire alp for the summer by the number of cows involved
and the number of days that grazing occurred. I call this variable
AVEMILK for average milk production. The dependent variable
measures average productivity rather than total production, and the
equations estimated are productivity equations rather than production functions. This is because the form of the dependent variable
implies that the regressions explain a variable that is independent of
the size of the grazing operation.

Data for purposes of the subsidy are collected for each operation on
an alp. For private alps and for cooperative commons, only one op-

---

[6] I used 1978 data provided by the Bernese Milk Producers' Association (Milchver-
band Bern). This association collects the data and serves as an intermediary between
the farmers and the federal government, which provides the subsidy.

[7] I did not test for differences between subsidized, cheese-producing alps and alps not
in this class. My qualitative observation is that cow alps are run similarly (except for
differences in rights forms), irrespective of the dairy products produced. Therefore,
I believe the sample is representative for all cow alps. One might imagine potential
differences, however, between subsidized, cheese-producing alps and other types of
cow alps. For example, cow alps where milk or cream is produced for transport to
valley creameries may lie closer to valley locations. Alternatively, the subpopulation
of cheese-producing alps from which no application for subsidy is received may be
worked by less careful users. If so, sample selection bias may exist for the population
defined as all cow alps. Although I present the results as representative of all cow
alps, the more conservative assumption would be to consider the population as including only cow alps that applied for the subsidy.

eration exists on each alp. On the dispersed operating unit commons, however, two or more operations may report milk production. For this type of commons, I aggregated the milk production over all operations and divided by the inner product of the number of cows and number of days grazed by all operations. This effectively gives a weighted average milk productivity figure for a dispersed operating unit commons, with the weights being the sizes of the operations and the number of days they grazed. Also, at times, only a subset of all operations on such an alp reported milk production, number of cows, and number of days grazed. In these cases, the data were aggregated only over the subset.

The Independent Variables

The variables used to explain milk productivity can be divided into four sets: the rights systems, the natural factors, labor input, and the lactation period. The rights system variables are those of interest for testing the differences between common and private property. The other three categories are control variables to ensure comparison of rights systems' performances while holding other influences constant, all of which are included in the x_1 vector in models (6.1) to (6.4). The data for these four categories of independent variables are described in what follows.

The rights system. There were 111 commons and 134 private alps included in the analyses. Whether the grazing area was managed under common property or private property was determined from the Swiss federal government reports entitled *Land- und Alpwirtschaft-licher Produktionskataster*, hereafter referred to as the Alp Assessments (Abteilung für Landwirtschaft 1961–73, 1978).[8]

These reports, one written for each township in the mountainous regions of Switzerland, contain extensive descriptions of each alpine grazing area, including ownership form, amount of labor employed, total number of animal units grazed, physical description, and other information. The reports for the Bernese alps were authored primarily between 1961 and 1973.[9] The fact that they were not written in a common year does not affect the use of their data gravely, because

---

[8] *Land- und Alpwirtschaftlicher Produktionskataster* translates approximately to Assessment of Agricultural and Alpine Production Capacity.
[9] Two of the township assessments used in this study were left unfinished in 1973 and completed in 1978.

Table 6.1. *Rights System Dummy Variables*

Variable	Description
P-OWNER	Private, owner-operated alp
P-RENTAL	Private or (occasionally) public alp rented to a user
P-LEASE	Private alp, leased to user for more than twenty years
P-ACCPAN	Private alp, owner accepts more than half of total animal units from others for a fee
P-ACCPRN	Private alp, renter accepts more than half of total animal units from others for a fee
P-MLTUSE	Private alp, multiple (two to four) users
P-FAMUSE	Private alp, multiple (two to four) users within same immediate family
P-HERDER	Private alp with landowner's cows on it, but run by a herdsman
P-ORGNZN	Alp owned and operated by a public body not concerned with farming as a primary means of livelihood, such as a prison, a charitable foundation, or an agricultural school
P-CRENT	Alp owned by a township or cooperative, but now run by a private renter who grazes his and others' animals
C-DISPER	Dispersed operating unit commons. In Bern, often an alp with a large number of users who hand care of cattle over to a smaller number of operators. Operators may also own cattle grazed on the alp.
C-COOP	Cooperative commons: centralized dairying by hired alp personnel who have no animals of their own on the alp
C-COOPHD	Cooperative commons: centralized dairying by shepherd–cheese maker who has own and others' cows on the alp
C-SMALL	A single, outlying commons observation with only three users and high milk productivity (see text)

rights relationships, labor employed, and total animal units grazed change only gradually over the years.

These reports made it possible to break down the rights systems into more than a simple dichotomy between commons and private, so that models of the form of equation (6.3) could be estimated. The two major types of common property, cooperative commons and dispersed operating unit commons, were distinguishable. Furthermore, a few observations among the cooperative commons were identified where the operator was not merely an employee of the cooperative but rather had some of his own animals on the alp. Ten variations on private property management were identified. Table 6.1 contains a list of rights types. I will report the number of observations on each rights type after explaining the attrition of observations that occurred from missing observations on other independent variables.

Creating a dummy variable for each of the fourteen management forms allowed for any level of breakdown in the rights systems, depending on the regression analysis performed. Thirteen dummies could be included in a regression for a complete breakdown.[10] A simple dichotomy between private and commons could be examined by creating two new dummies, PRIVATE and COMMONS, by adding all P- and all C-prefixed variables in Table 6.1. Other subdivisions were also possible, for instance, private, cooperative commons, and dispersed operating unit commons.

Some of the alps had "mixed" rights types. As described in Chapter 4, alpine grazing occurs in stages that move the herd up a mountainside through the summer. At times, a herd will move from private grazing areas at lower altitudes to a commons at higher altitudes. If the operation that applied for the subsidy on mountain cheese reported milk production for time spent on both the private area and the commons, then the observation was not suitable for this study. The effects of the different rights systems on total milk production were confounded and could not be separated. Of 345 observations reporting total milk production, 13 had this unusable mix of rights systems. In addition, 3 observations were eliminated because milk production occurred solely on a forealp, which is grazed earlier in the year and at a lower altitude, and thus may not have produced observations that were from the same population as milk production from the alps.

One observation on a commons alp was an outlier that altered results dramatically whenever it was included in a regression. It would change significances of coefficients remarkably, which is suspect in a data set of 245 observations. It had average milk production of 14.8 liters per cow per day, 2.7 standard deviations above the mean of 10.0 liters per cow per day. A closer look at the observation revealed that, although it was a commons alp, it had only seven rights holders and only three users. Because of its small number of users, it could almost be considered private. For this reason, the observation was given its own unique dummy variable C-SMALL and was not included in analyses when various commons rights types were combined.

The natural factors. Besides the rights systems, the natural environment in which the cows graze may affect milk productivity. For this reason, all of the productivity equations tested in this chapter include a set of natural factors as independent variables. Some natural factors

---

[10] Again, at least one of the fourteen dummy variables must be excluded to avoid singularity in the regressor matrix.

might affect the cows' productivity directly, such as slope, drinking water availability, and degree of protection from inclement weather provided by woods. Others might affect the cows' productivity indirectly by affecting the grass quality first and milk production in turn. Examples are ground quality (soil type), direction of exposure of the mountainside (north, south, east, or west), elevation, precipitation and wind conditions, potential for landslides and debris accumulation, and other special difficulties. One variable, building location, is included among the natural factors even though it is humanly determined, because building location can affect milk productivity by making the cows walk greater or lesser distances, expending greater or lesser amounts of energy that could go into milk production.

The data to represent the natural factors were index numbers. Cantonal authorities collect these data for property tax purposes. In Switzerland, agricultural and grazing lands are taxed on the basis of use value, as determined by grading systems in which points are given to the land on certain quality factors during on-site inspections. These quality factors and a summary of their meanings are contained in Table 6.2. An appendix to this chapter contains a translation of the section in the assessors' evaluation guide that describes the variables' meanings more thoroughly.

The range of points possible for each variable depends on how heavily the officials weight the variable in determining a grazing area's value. While some variables have a range of 1 to 5, others have a range of 2 to 10. The latter are judged more important in determining use value. A grade can take on integer and half-unit values, like 3.0, 3.5, and so on, a specificity that gives the variables some measure of continuity. The higher the numeric value of a grade, the higher is the quality of the grazing area on that variable (5.0 indicates higher quality than 1.0). Grading sheets were available for 275 alps in the sample, in comparison to my request for 329 grading sheets. The attrition of over 50 observations occurred because the original grading sheet could not be located in the township office.[11]

---

[11] The grading sheets are known as *Punktierungen*, or point sheets. They are page 1b of the *Bewertungsprotokol für landwirtschaftliche Betriebe*. I acquired them with the assistance of the Bernese Cantonal Tax Administration, Inspectorate for Agriculture (Kantonale Steuerverwaltung Bern, Inspektorat Landwirtschaft). The grading sheets actually reside in the township offices. With the assistance of a staff member at the Bernese Cantonal Tax Administration, I asked to have photocopies of the grading sheets from forty-four townships sent to the cantonal tax office by mail. Data from thirty-six townships were included in the analyses: Adelboden, Beatenberg, Boltigen, Brienz, Brienzwiler, Därstetten, Diemtigen, Erlenbach, Frutigen, Gadmen, Grindelwald, Gsteig, Gsteigwiler, Gündlischwand, Habkern, Hasliberg, Hofstetten,

Labor input. A further variable to include in the $\mathbf{x}_1$ vector in the econometric models is labor input. Labor input can affect the cows' productivity, but mainly indirectly: through time spent improving the grazing area by clearing the area of stones and debris, fertilizing, building suitable watering troughs, destroying weeds, and so forth.

Labor on the alps is composed of two main elements: (1) labor from full-time workers residing on the alp for the summer, and (2) in the case of commons alps, labor contributed by members of the community or cooperative who must fulfill a work duty. I found information for the two different labor components in the Alp Assessments (Abteilung für Landwirtschaft 1961–73, 1978).

For the first component of labor, the reports contained a census of the number of full-time workers—men, women, and children—on each alp. The first component of labor input combined these three types of workers using the weights of 1 for an adult male, 0.75 for an adult female, and 0.5 for children under fifteen years of age of either sex.[12] The result of finding a weighted sum of the three types of workers is a number representing person-equivalents working on the alp for the entire summer.

The second component of labor input arises from the work duty required of users of some commons. Although data on this component for most observations could be determined from the Alp Assessments, these data were more difficult to ascertain, because only at the discretion of the author of an assessment were they included. Fortunately, the author of the Bern assessments mentioned the work re-

Innertkirchen, Iseltwald, Kandergrund, Kandersteg, Krattigen, Lauenen, Lauterbrunnen, Lenk, Lütschental, Meiringen, Oberried, Oberwil im Simmental, Reichenbach, Saanen, Saxeten, Schattenhalb, Sigriswil, St. Stephan, and Zweisimmen. Grading sheet data from eight townships were requested but did not contribute to the statistical analyses. These townships were Aeschi, Blumenstein, Bönigen, Eggiwil, Guttannen, Leissigen, Reutigen, and Schangnau. From seven, the grading sheets were not available. For the eighth (Reutigen), I could not determine values for a variable unassociated with the grading sheet information (the amount of labor provided through the commons work requirement; see the next section in the text).

For some alp units, more than one grading sheet existed, because the grazing operation moved between geographically separated areas. In these cases, a weighted average of the grades from the separate grading sheets was found. The weights were the percentages of total alp time that were spent on each grazing subunit, which were found in the federal Alp Assessments (Abteilung für Landwirtschaft 1961–73, 1978).

[12] Swiss authorities use a weighting system of this type in calculating labor units employed in alpine grazing, although they give the same weight to the women as to children (Aeschlimann 1978: 259). Giving less weight to the women than the men is justified because some women on the alps do not participate in care of the animals or grazing areas directly. However, my personal observation is that women on alps contribute more to the alpine grazing operations than the children and should be so weighted.

Table 6.2. *The Natural Factor and Labor Measures Used as Independent Variables*

Variable	Description	Range[a]	Mean[b]	Std. Dev.[b]
GRDQUAL	Soil quality and grass condition	3–15	10.7	2.1
SFORM	Surface form (hilliness, slope)	2–10	6.4	1.6
ROAD	Condition of the road to the alp	2–10	5.3	2.2
WATER	Drinking water availability to the cows	2–10	6.9	1.5
EXPOSURE	Exposure (compass direction the mountainside faces)	2–10	6.9	1.3
ELEVATN	Elevation	1–5	4.4	0.8
PRCPWIND	Precipitation and wind conditions	1–5	3.6	0.9
WDSGRASS	Distribution between forest and grassland	1–5	3.5	1.2
SLIDEDGR	Potential for landslides and debris accumulation	1–5	3.1	1.1
BLDGLOC	Suitability of building location	1–5	4.0	0.9
MKTLOC[c]	Location relative to market	1–5	2.7	1.0
SPECIALD	Special difficulties	1–5	3.0	0.9
LABORPAU[d]	Labor in person-equivalents per animal unit month	—	0.069	0.026

[a]Range is the theoretical minimum and maximum of the variable according to the cantonal handbook *Bewertung der Landwirtschaftlichen Grundstücke und der Waldungen* (Valuation of Agricultural Lands and Woods) (Kanton Bern 1973; see the appendix to this chapter). Observed minimums or maximums may vary.
[b]Means and standard deviations are given for 245 observations.
[c]The range for MKTLOC of 1–5 given here differs from the range of 2–10 implied in the appendix to this chapter. The alp grading system was altered in 1973 to give more weight to an alp's location relative to market. Old grading assessments, however, remained in widespread use when I collected data. I standardized MKTLOC to a range of 1–5 for all observations.
[d]This variable was constructed from sources different from those for other variables in this table. See text.

quirement in most cases. Nevertheless, there were 30 commons for which the work requirement could not be deduced. Exclusion of these alps from the analyses reduced the number of observations to 245.

Generally, the work obligation for commons alps is stated as a number of hours or days required per animal unit that a user grazes. Such a measure had to be converted in order to combine it with the first component of labor input, which was in person-equivalents per summer. To perform the conversion, I assumed a ten-hour day, which is reasonable for the alps, and used the following formula:

$$\text{person-equivalents} = \frac{ha}{10d}, \tag{6.17}$$

where

h = the work duty for users in hours per animal unit;
a = the total number of animal units grazed on the alp (this information was also available from the Alp Assessments);
d = the length of the summer season in days.

The total amount of labor on the alp for the summer in person-equivalents is the sum of the first component of resident labor described above and the second component of part-time labor resulting from expression (6.17). In the case of private alps, the second component always equals zero.

Finally, the level of labor input on the alp should be measured not by the absolute number of person-equivalents but rather by the number of person-equivalents *per animal unit*. The reason is that a person-equivalent of labor will have a different effect on the productivity of the animals if the herd is small rather than large. However, if we normalize the number of person-equivalents by the number of animal units, we may assume that no matter what the herd size, an additional person-equivalent per animal unit will have the same effect on average milk production. It is this type of variable that should be included in an estimation in which the dependent variable, average milk production, has already been normalized to be independent of herd size. Thus, the final measure of labor input used in all regressions had the form of person-equivalents divided by number of animal units, called labor per animal unit (LABORPAU).

Lactation period. A cows' milk production varies greatly over her lactation period. After she gives birth to a calf, milk production is high and remains so for six to eight months, tapering off rapidly toward the end of this period. Most Swiss alpine graziers time the calving date of their cows so that peak milk production does not occur while the animal is in the mountains. Since data on calving dates were not available for individual cows, much less for whole herds, it must be

Table 6.3. *Numbers of Observations by Rights Type*

Variable	No. of Obs. on Avemilk	Grading Sheet Available	LABORPAU Calculable[a]	Obs. Used for Probit Anal.
P-OWNER	69	57	55	55
P-RENTAL	35	29	28	28
P-LEASE	9	6	6	6
P-ACCPAN	8	7	7	7
P-ACCPRN	12	10	9	9
P-MLTUSE	10	9	9	9
P-FAMUSE	12	9	9	9
P-HERDER	6	4	3	3
P-ORGNZN	3	3	3	3
P-CRENT	7	6	5	5
C-DISPER	101	91	76	76
C-COOP	39	31	27	27
C-COOPHD	17	12	7	7
C-SMALL	1	1	1	—
Mixed Rights[b]	13	—	—	—
Forealp[b]	3	—	—	—
Totals	345	275	245	244

[a]LABORPAU was not calculable when information on the work duty for a commons alp was not contained in the Alp Assessments (Abteilung für Landwirtschaft 1961–73, 1978). See text.
[b]Excluded from the analysis. See text.

assumed that the average calving dates across herds are fairly uniform, with one important exception.

In the Justis Valley (Justistal), a type of mountain cheese has been developed that is prized and commands a high market price. For this reason, users of the Justistal alps time the calving dates of their cows to get peak milk production and hence peak cheese production during the time on the alps. To control for this shift in the lactation period of Justistal cows, a dummy variable called LACTATN was created with the following definition:

$$\text{LACTATN} = \begin{cases} 1 \text{ if Justistal alp} \\ 0 \text{ otherwise.} \end{cases}$$

Summary. Table 6.3 gives an overview of the number of observations, broken down by rights type, and indicates where observations were lost because of missing values on the independent variables.

Genetic Uniformity Assumption

For the subsequent analyses to be valid, herds of cows must be considered genetically uniform across rights types in milk-producing capabilities. If, for example, the cows that go to commons are in general genetically inferior, this would depress the estimated coefficient on the commons dummy relative to private property. Indeed, if the cows are not on average genetically uniform, then genetic quality would be an omitted variable that could bias all estimated coefficients of variables included in the regression equations.[13]

Estimation of the Simple Model

To estimate model (6.1), all dummies prefixed by a P in Table 6.1 are summed to create a new dummy variable, PRIVATE. PRIVATE will equal one for any observation having a rights type with a P prefix, and it will equal zero otherwise, that is, for any observation having a C prefix in Table 6.1 (all commons rights types). The other independent variables described in the previous section are also included to control for natural factors and other forces that might affect milk productivity.

The hypothesized signs on the natural factor coefficients come from the manner in which these variables were generated. All of the index numbers for the natural factors and building location are constructed such that the higher the grade, the better the grazing area. The better the grazing area, the higher is the expected milk productivity, so I hypothesize positive coefficients on all natural factors and the building location. Similarly, because greater labor input and the shift in lactation period on Justistal alps should have positive effects on milk productivity, we can expect positive coefficients on LABORPAU and LACTATN.

Finally, if common property performs as well as private property, as argued in Chapter 3, there should be no significant difference between commons and private productivity and an insignificant coefficient on the PRIVATE dummy. The alternative hypothesis to insignificance is a positive coefficient on the PRIVATE dummy, because

[13] Data on genetic makeup of the herds were not readily available. Records of each cow's performance while in the valley during the winter, which would measure her genetic capacity to produce milk, are collected by a professional breeding association. However, given hundreds of alps, scores of cows per alp, and often many owners of cows per alp, determining which cows went to which alp was unmanageable. Missing-data problems also would have been severe, because many farmers do not participate in the breeders' association.

Table 6.4. *Estimation of the Simple Model*

Regressor	Coefficient	Std. Error	T-statistic
Constant	7.0420	1.0380	6.78[a]
PRIVATE	0.7497	0.2473	3.03[a]
GRDQUAL	0.0550	0.0579	0.95
SFORM	0.0025	0.0884	0.03
WATER	−0.0479	0.0805	−0.60
EXPOSURE	0.0149	0.0961	0.16
ELEVATN	0.1799	0.1820	0.99
PRCPWIND	0.0937	0.1696	0.55
WDSGRASS	0.0056	0.1464	0.04
SLIDEDGR	−0.0164	0.1647	−0.10
BLDGLOC	0.1247	0.1598	0.78
SPECIALD	0.0299	0.1453	0.21
LABORPAU	6.3680	4.5070	1.41[a]
LACTATN	1.2483	0.6685	1.87[a]

Dep. var.: AVEMILK $R^2 = 12.9\%$ Regression $F = 2.62^b$

[a]*T*-statistic significant at .10 level. One-tailed tests are used except for constant term.
[b]*F*-statistic significant at .01 level.

most economists would argue that private property will perform better than common property—and not vice versa. By this reasoning, a one-tailed test on the PRIVATE dummy's coefficient is appropriate.

The results of the simple model are continued in Table 6.4, where the regression was performed on 244 observations. (The C-SMALL observation was dropped.) The most prominent conclusion is that the coefficient on PRIVATE is highly significant and positive. With a *t*-statistic of 3.03, it is significant at the .002 level in a one-tailed test. This initial look seems to indicate that private property performs significantly better than common property on the basis of milk productivity. One also concludes from Table 6.4 that labor input and the shift in the lactation period of the Justistal alps have significant, positive effects on milk productivity, as expected.

Finally, none of the natural factors are significant. This seems surprising. Do none of the natural factors affect the cows or the grass condition sufficiently to affect the milk productivity? Although a full explanation will be postponed until the expanded rights types model (6.3) and the model of the farmers' adjustment to the natural factors are estimated, the abbreviated answer is twofold. The more complex models like equation (6.3) do show significance in some of the natural factors, and model (6.5) indicates some adjustment of the number of animal units to the natural factors to keep milk productivity up, which makes the natural factor coefficients insignificant.

The low R^2 for the estimation of the simple model (6.1) is troublesome, and it corresponds to the insignificance of many of the independent variables. The more complex, single-equation models to be discussed subsequently demonstrate higher R^2's, so we will not trouble ourselves further with the poor fit of this estimation.[14]

Estimation of the Simultaneous Equation Model

Before moving to the expanded rights types model (6.3), we need to examine whether the rights types and milk productivity are simultaneously determined by the natural factors. This examination will indicate whether estimation of single-equation models like (6.1) and (6.3) result in unbiased coefficients, or whether only simultaneous equation models such as (6.2) adequately represent the determination of milk productivity.

Testing for Simultaneity

Four separate tests of simultaneity are considered. Initially, I apply the modified Heckman procedure, which I can do because observations on both $y_2 = 0$ (commons) and $y_2 = 1$ (private) are available. Secondly, to eliminate a problem of collinearity between the Heckman correction term h and the dummy variable y_2, I apply Heckman's original procedure, which includes only observations on private grazing areas.

Both these tests are applied twice. First, the modified Heckman procedure is applied to the entire data set: All types of private alps contained in Table 6.1 (all P-prefixed rights types) are aggregated, and all types of commons (all C-prefixed rights types) are combined also.[15] Then, to eliminate the collinearity problem, the original Heckman procedure is applied to the subset of the data represented by observations on all private rights types. In the second set of applications (the third and fourth tests) of the modified and original Heck-

---

[14] Nevertheless, the regression F for the estimation of the simple model (6.1) is 2.62, which is significant at the .01 level [$2.62 > F_{.01} (13, 230) = 2.22$]. Therefore, the regression meets this minimal test of adequacy, and the predictors as a set are not completely irrelevant.

[15] The single C-SMALL observation, however, is not included. Because of its unusual characteristics, it could lead to unwarranted conclusions if combined with other cooperative rights types.

man procedures, only observations on pure, owner-operated private property (P-OWNER alps) and the two pure forms of common alps (C-DISPER and C-COOP alps) are included. This second set of simultaneity tests is to ensure that the mixing of owner-operated private alps with rental private alps, leased private alps, private alps where most animals are taken on from others, and so on, as well as the inclusion of some dispersed operating unit commons where the herder is hired, does not obscure a potentially nonzero $\text{cov}(u_1, u_2)$ that may exist when "pure" rights forms are examined. Therefore, the third test includes P-OWNER and C-COOP plus C-DISPER alps, and the fourth test, again to eliminate collinearity problems, applies Heckman's original procedure only to all P-OWNER observations.

The first step in determining whether endogeneity exists while using all observations is to estimate the relationship hypothesized by (6.2b) and (6.2c) using probit analysis. (Again, [6.2b] and [6.2c] represent the idea that the natural factors may create a tendency for the grazing area to be either private or commons.) This estimation yields a set of estimated coefficients $\hat{\beta}_2$ that can be substituted into (6.13) to produce observations on h, the Heckman correction term. The results of estimating β_2 are reported later in a discussion of the determinants of private property and common property, since the coefficients β_2 are precisely the hypothesized determinants of a grazing area's propensity to be private or commons. For the moment, we are interested in results from the OLS estimation of equation (6.14). Substituting the constructed h variable into (6.14) and estimating by OLS, I obtain the results contained in Table 6.5, where HECKCORR ("Heckman correction term") is the acronym for the constructed h variable.

The t-statistic on the Heckman correction term in Table 6.5 is only 0.10. Clearly, this is not significant. Thus, the first estimation would indicate that the $\text{cov}(u_1, u_2) = 0$ and that there is no simultaneity bias in estimating milk productivity using a single equation, were it not for the problem of collinearity between two of the regressors. The first clue to this problem is that the coefficient on the PRIVATE regressor in Table 6.5 is also insignificant, in contrast to a highly significant PRIVATE coefficient in the estimation of the simple model (Table 6.4). As mentioned before, this result may arise because of collinearity between the Heckman correction term (HECKCORR) and the PRIVATE regressor. The simple correlation coefficient between these two variables is 0.94. Without much doubt, a correlation this high makes it impossible for the regression to separate the effects of the two independent variables PRIVATE and HECKCORR, and thus drives PRIVATE into insignificance and possibly reduces the signifi-

Table 6.5. *Estimation of the Model with a Heckman Correction Term*

Regressor	Coefficient	Std. Error	T-statistic
Constant	6.9550	1.3500	5.15[a]
PRIVATE	0.5660	1.8390	0.31
GRDQUAL	0.0613	0.0857	0.72
SFORM	−0.0086	0.1410	−0.06
WATER	−0.0471	0.0811	−0.58
EXPOSURE	0.0216	0.1171	0.18
ELEVATN	0.1891	0.2039	0.93
PRCPWIND	0.1099	0.2339	0.47
WDSGRASS	0.0031	0.1488	0.02
SLIDEDGR	−0.0086	0.1821	−0.05
BLDGLOC	0.1244	0.1601	0.78
SPECIALD	0.0371	0.1619	0.23
LABORPAU	6.4160	4.5420	1.41[a]
LACTATN	1.2438	0.6715	1.85[a]
HECKCORR	0.1140	1.1300	0.10
Dep. var.: AVEMILK		$R^2 = 12.9\%$	Regression $F = 2.42$[b]

[a] T-statistic significant at .10 level. One-tailed tests are used except for the constant term.
[b] F-statistic significant at .01 level.

cance of HECKCORR. This suspicion is strengthened by comparing the standard error for PRIVATE of 0.2473 in the simple model (Table 6.4) with the standard error for PRIVATE of 1.8390 after HECK-CORR has been added (Table 6.5). The collinearity has driven the standard error on PRIVATE up and the coefficient on PRIVATE into insignificance.

Given these results, it is useful to apply Heckman's original procedure to the subset of observations in which $y_2 = 1$, but still including all types of private alps. This eliminates the PRIVATE dummy variable from the equation and the collinearity between PRIVATE and HECKCORR, as described in the theoretical section on the Heckman procedure. There are 134 observations for which $y_2 = 1$ in the data set, and these are used to estimate equation (6.16). Results of this regression are contained in Table 6.6.[16]

Again, the important statistic in Table 6.6 is the t-statistic for HECK-CORR. With a value of $t = 0.01$, the coefficient on HECKCORR is totally insignificant. The $cov(u_1, u_2)$ again appears to be zero.

[16] LACTATN is omitted because all observations for which LACTATN = 1 are commons alps. Because commons alps are excluded from this second test, LACTATN would be a meaningless vector of zeros if included, causing singularity in the regressor matrix.

Table 6.6. *Estimation of the Model with a Heckman Correction Term,*
Including Only PRIVATE Observations

Regressor	Coefficient	Std. Error	*T*-statistic
Constant + PRIVATE[a]	10.1300	4.5990	2.20[b]
GRDQUAL	0.0452	0.1419	0.32
SFORM	−0.0936	0.2179	−0.43
WATER	−0.1057	0.1135	−0.93
EXPOSURE	−0.0110	0.1803	−0.06
ELEVATN	0.1439	0.3274	0.44
PRCPWIND	0.0647	0.3619	0.18
WDSGRASS	0.1306	0.2340	0.56
SLIDEDGR	0.0436	0.2820	0.15
BLDGLOC	−0.1099	0.2900	−0.38
SPECIALD	0.1802	0.2459	0.73
LABORPAU	−6.0950	7.1230	−0.86
HECKCORR	0.0110	1.8300	0.01
Dep. var.: AVEMILK	R^2 = 4.6%	Regression F = 0.48[c]	

[a]The estimated constant term subsumes the PRIVATE dummy (see text).
[b]*T*-statistic significant at .05 level in a two-tailed test.
[c]*F*-statistic insignificant at .05 level.

Let us, however, also examine tests on the $cov(u_1, u_2)$ for "pure" rights types. To perform these tests, we must reestimate the probit analysis of equation (6.2b), because the sets of observations constituting $y_2 = 1$ and $y_2 = 0$ change to P-OWNER and C-DISPER plus C-COOP, respectively. Reestimating (6.2b) gives new estimates of β_2 and hence new values on the Heckman correction term h in relation (6.13).

For the third test, equation (6.14) is estimated much as it is in the first test, using the new values on h, the dummy y_2, and the independent variables x_1. Only observations on these variables from the 55 P-OWNER and the 103 C-DISPER and C-COOP alps are used. Results are in Table 6.7, which indicates a *t*-ratio for the Heckman correction term of 1.32. Although $t = 1.32$ is large relative to prior regressions, it is still not significant in a two-tailed test, even at the .10 level.[17] Moreover, not only is the coefficient on HECKCORR insignificant in Table 6.7, but the coefficient on P-OWNER is *negative*. In no other regression does the private dummy's coefficient show a negative sign. It is likely that collinearity is again confounding the regres-

---

[17] A two-tailed test is appropriate because there is no a priori reason to believe that σ_{12} is either positive or negative.

Table 6.7. *Estimation of the Model with a Heckman Correction Term on 158 P-OWNER, C-DISPER/C-COOP Observations*

Regressor	Coefficient	Std. Error	T-statistic
Constant	6.0340	1.2940	4.66[a]
P-OWNER	− 0.7330	1.5350	− 0.48
GRDQUAL	0.0996	0.0727	1.37[a]
SFORM	− 0.0228	0.2132	− 0.11
WATER	− 0.1337	0.1061	− 1.26
EXPOSURE	0.0579	0.1247	0.46
ELEVATN	0.3797	0.2112	1.80[a]
PRCPWIND	0.0592	0.2284	0.26
WDSGRASS	− 0.1436	0.1843	− 0.78
SLIDEDGR	0.0749	0.2094	0.36
BLDGLOC	0.2506	0.1710	1.47[a]
SPECIALD	0.0701	0.2202	0.32
LABORPAU	13.1300	4.9920	2.63[a]
LACTATN	1.2530	0.6591	1.90[a]
HECKCORR	1.2228	0.9250	1.32

Dep. var.: AVEMILK $R^2 = 27.1\%$ Regression $F = 3.79$[b]

[a]*T*-statistic significant at .10 level. One-tailed tests are used except for the constant term.
[b]*F*-statistic significant at .01 level.

sion's ability to estimate the coefficients accurately. The correlation between the private dummy P-OWNER and the new Heckman correction term HECKCORR (from the 158-observation probit analysis) is 0.90. With a correlation coefficient this high, it is likely that a negative coefficient on P-OWNER and a more strongly significant coefficient on HECKCORR are spurious. Indeed, it is possible that, in this sample, the positive variations that P-OWNER is expected to explain is better explained, although spuriously, by the collinear HECKCORR variable. This would give HECKCORR's coefficient an unduly high (although insignificant) *t*-statistic.

Given these ambiguous results from the data set containing "pure" rights types when both P-OWNER and HECKCORR are included, it is again advantageous to eliminate the collinearity between these two regressors. The fourth test can be done by using the method that was applied to the entire data set in the second test: performing OLS on the subset of private alps, in this case 55 P-OWNER grazing areas. The newly estimated Heckman correction term for these observations is included, but no P-OWNER or LACTATN dummies are. The results of this regression are in Table 6.8. The *t*-statistic on HECK-CORR's coefficient ($t = 1.01$) is insignificant by any commonly

Table 6.8. *Estimation of the Model with a Heckman Correction Term on 55 P-OWNER Observations*

Regressor	Coefficient	Std. Error	T-statistic
Constant + P-OWNER[a]	3.9080	4.7790	0.82
GRDQUAL	0.2170	0.1673	1.30[b]
SFORM	−0.1180	0.5644	−0.21
WATER	−0.4204	0.1985	−2.12
EXPOSURE	0.0770	0.2901	0.27
ELEVATN	0.8662	0.4933	1.76[b]
PRCPWIND	0.0516	0.5010	0.10
WDSGRASS	−0.0710	0.4385	−0.16
SLIDEDGR	0.4299	0.4944	0.87
BLDGLOC	0.0961	0.3968	0.24
SPECIALD	0.0329	0.5421	0.06
LABORPAU	1.5600	11.9200	0.13
HECKCORR	1.9710	1.9550	1.01
Dep. var.: AVEMILK	$R^2 = 20.8\%$	Regression $F = 0.92$[c]	

[a]The estimated constant term subsumes the P-OWNER dummy (see text).
[b]T-statistic significant at .10 level in a one-tailed test.
[c]F-statistic insignificant at .05 level.

accepted standard. The hypothesis that u_1 and u_2 are correlated is again rejected. In addition, the constant term, which is a mixture of the normal intercept term and the coefficient on P-OWNER because the two are not identified, is *smaller* than the intercept term when the CONSTANT and P-OWNER coefficients are identified (Table 6.7). This indicates that the P-OWNER part of Constant + P-OWNER is probably negative, again an unlikely event given other coefficient estimates for private property in this chapter.

In summary, little evidence from the four applications of the simultaneous equation model—in particular, the four estimations that included a Heckman correction term—supports the conclusion that there is correlation between the disturbances u_1 and u_2. This being the case, the model can be considered recursive and estimated equation by equation. For the first equation (6.2a), this would mean applying OLS without a Heckman correction term; that is, the model collapses to the simple model (6.1). Another way to view this is to say that σ_{12} has been shown to be insignificantly different from zero in equation (6.14), and the equation could be simplified by dropping the h regressor. Again, this collapses the model to the simple model (6.1). Thus, the results from the simple model, particularly that private performs significantly better than commons on the measure of average milk production, can continue to be trusted.

The Determinants of Private and Common Property

In addition to permitting the simultaneity tests, constructing the simultaneous equation model offers the opportunity to examine the conditions under which a grazing area is likely to become private property rather than common property. Taken alone, equations (6.2b) and (6.2c) constitute a simple dichotomous dependent variable model to explain the determination of the rights system (private or commons), and if the natural conditions affect the choice of the rights system, then probit estimation of equation (6.2b) should show this.

First, let us examine the independent variables and hypothesized signs on their coefficients. Observations on all of the variables in the x_2 vector of equation (6.2b) are index numbers for the natural attributes of the grazing areas, and these variables were constructed so that the higher the grade given on a natural factor, the more advantageous the property is for grazing. Hypothesizing that the more desirable grazing areas are more likely to be private, I expect positive signs on all of the coefficients β_2 in equation (6.2b)—except the constant term, which has an indeterminate presumed sign. It should be noted that a new regressor, location relative to market (MKTLOC) appears in the x_2 vector that did not appear in the x_1 vector of previous regressions. This is because location of the grazing area relative to a market may be important in whether the area becomes commons or private.[18]

Results from a probit analysis on the entire data set[19] are presented in Table 6.9. Besides the constant term, three of the ten coefficients have the hypothesized positive sign and are significant at the .10 level. These are ground quality, exposure, and precipitation and wind con-

---

[18] Location of the grazing area relative to market (MKTLOC) and another accessibility variable, the condition of the road connecting the grazing area to town (ROAD), were erroneously deleted in early regressions to explain milk productivity. Although these variables would not affect milk productivity by influencing the grass condition, as do the natural factors, they may operate on milk productivity through the output price (the price of milk, cheese, etc.). In a von Thünen model (see Katzman 1974; Samuelson 1983), farm gate (alp edge) prices for the product decreases as accessibility diminishes, and this causes land rent to decline going away from market. This could affect labor–land and capital–land ratios, which in turn affect milk productivity. I am indebted to Don Jones for this point. See note 23 to this chapter on the effect of including these accessibility variables in a regression.

[19] With the exception of the C-SMALL observation, which is again excluded because of its confusing effect when combined with other commons rights types.

Table 6.9. *The Determinants of Private Property:*
A Probit Estimation of Equation (6.2b)

Regressor	Max. Likelihood Estimated (MLE) Coefficient	Std. Error	Ratio of MLE to Std. Error
Constant	−2.7345	0.8309	−3.29[a]
GRDQUAL	0.0927	0.0452	2.05[b]
SFORM	−0.1723	0.0710	−2.43[a]
WATER	0.0282	0.0620	0.45
EXPOSURE	0.1103	0.0748	1.48[b]
ELEVATN	0.1802	0.1439	1.25
PRCPWIND	0.2864	0.1332	2.15[b]
WDSGRASS	−0.0097	0.1148	−0.08
SLIDEDGR	0.1434	0.1274	1.13
MKTLOC	−0.1803	0.1051	−1.72[a]
SPECIALD	0.0862	0.1132	0.76
Dep. var.: PRIVATE		psuedo-R^2 = 8.7%[c]	

[a]*T*-statistic significant at .10 level in a two-tailed test.
[b]*T*-statistic significant at .10 level in a one-tailed test.
[c]The pseudo-R^2 = $1 - (\ln L_\Omega)/(\ln L_\omega)$, where L_Ω = the maximum of the likelihood function when maximized with respect to all of the coefficients in the probit equation β_2, and L_ω = the maximum of the likelihood function when maximized with respect to the constant term β_{20} only (McFadden 1974; Maddala 1983: 39–40).

ditions. A fourth regressor, elevation, is just barely insignificant on this test.

On the basis of these significant variables and their description (see the appendix to this chapter), it can be concluded that areas favored by better soil, fewer swampy spots, and better grass condition as a result of the soil type are more likely to become private property. In addition, areas with poor exposure to the sun (on a north slope, in a ravine, in the shadow of surrounding mountains, or shaded by forest) are not favored for private use. Poor precipitation and wind conditions—including low precipitation amounts; the danger of snow, frost, and hail in the summer; the lack of natural protection against these weather events; and strong north and east prevailing winds with their negative effect on grass quality—also discourage private ownership. Elevation, one factor that my personal, nonquantitative observation indicated to be an important determinant of rights type, is not significant, even when using a liberal, .10 one-tailed test. The lack of significance is probably due to the manner in which this variable is defined. The assessors are instructed to assign the highest grade (5 points) to a wide range of elevations: all alps between 1,200 and 1,800 meters above sea level (see the appendix to this chapter). A point is to be subtracted for every 100 meters of altitude over 1,800 meters above sea level. The majority of alps, however, lie in the 1,200 and 1,800 meter range, and very few lie at 2,000 or 2,100 meters above sea level. Consequently, 52% of the alps in the sample received the grade of 5 for elevation, and another 32% received grades ranging from 4 to 4.9. Grades of 3.0 to 3.9 were given to 11%, grades of 2.0 to 2.9 to 4%, and grades of 1.0 to 1.9 to less than 1% of the observations. With this minor amount of variation in the data, they did not represent actual variations in elevation that exist between private and commons alps.

Contrary to the hypothesis of positive signs, surface form and location relative to market have coefficients with negative signs and large t-statistics. The strength of the negative t-statistics—the coefficients would be considered significant at the .10 level in two-tailed tests—indicates that some further explanation should be sought.

One possibility for the negative sign on location relative to market (MKTLOC) comes from this variable's being a mixture of distance from the alp to market *and* the condition of the road connecting the two. The Swiss have undertaken major projects to build good roads to their alpine areas, and there are economies of scale inherent in projects involving one or more commons alps that do not obtain as often for private alps. Because of these projects, it is possible that the commons have become on balance better connected to markets than private alps, even though the private areas are closer to the permanent settlements.

To explain the results for surface form (SFORM), it is possible that the large, expansive commons have a gentle slope and rolling terrain and the private alps lie on steeper slopes. Alternatively, the larger commons may also possess their steep areas, but users do not put them to use, whereas the constraints on size inherent in the smaller, private alps induce the farmers to use "every square inch," even the steep sections.

The other hypothesized factors in Table 6.9 cannot be shown to have significant effects on the determination of rights type. The adequacy of drinking water for the animals, the extent of the woods on the alp (for protection from inclement weather and for firewood), the danger of landslides, and the catchall category of special difficulties all have no effect.

In summary, the quality of the soil and climatic influences like exposure of the mountainside toward or away from the sun, precipitation, and wind conditions seem to have the greatest positive effects on a grazing area's being private.

Estimation of the Expanded Rights Types Model

As the section describing the data indicated, it was possible to divide the alp grazing systems into more than a simple dichotomy of private and commons rights types. Identification of ten types of private management and four types of commons management (Table 6.1) allowed the creation of fourteen dummy variables for different management types. Because estimation of single-equation systems with OLS has been shown to lead to unbiased estimates of the coefficients, it is possible to estimate expanded rights types models represented by equation (6.3). At first, I proposed doing this to overcome potential obscuration of differences in milk productivity by combining different types of private property into a single category and different types of common property into a single category, as was done in the simple model (6.1). Estimation of the simple model has already shown that there is a significant difference between all private rights types grouped together and all commons grouped together, so this fear seems to be unfounded. Various private and common property rights types, however, may still have divergent productivities, and we may still wish to expand the single-equation model to test whether the simple model is a misspecification that incorrectly constrains all private and all commons rights types to have the same estimated coefficients.

Hypotheses for the Coefficients

For the initial estimation of equation (6.3), the P-OWNER dummy is excluded from **r**. This procedure causes the coefficients on all other rights dummies to indicate performance of those rights types relative to pure, owner-operated private property. With one exception, all private rights types included in the equation deviate from owner-operated private in such a way as to indicate poorer land use or poorer milk yields. A renter or lessee has less interest in treating the land properly (P-RENTAL and P-LEASE). Owners or renters who take on most of their animals from others may have less interest in keeping the yield of those animals up (P-ACCPAN and P-ACCPRN). Private alps with a small number of multiple users (two to four), who may or may not be members of the same immediate family (P-FAMUSE and P-MLTUSE), may begin to have the characteristics of commons alps, even though they have no formal commons structure and they often obtained multiple-user status through inheritance. Grazing areas operated by a herder might have lower yields, because the herder might have less incentive to maintain the area than would the owner (P-HERDER). Alps that were formerly commons, are still owned by a township or cooperative, but are now rented to a single farmer also might show poorer yields, both because of their rental status and, if commons are poorer than private, because of their history (P-CRENT). The only private rights type that might show better yields than owner-operated private is one that includes model alps operated by some public organization, such as an agricultural school or a penal institution that uses prisoners to perform the work (P-ORGNZN). Thus, the alternative hypotheses to zero coefficients on the P-prefixed rights variables in equation (6.3) are that they have negative signs, with the exception of the sign for the coefficient on P-ORGNZN, which is hypothesized to have a positive coefficient.

Two major types of commons rights types are represented in equation (6.3): dispersed operating unit commons and cooperative commons. The primary intent of this chapter has been to compare private property with commons use. If there is no a priori reason to believe that commons perform differently than private alps, as was argued in Chapter 3, the coefficients on C-DISPER and C-COOP should be insignificant. This is the null hypothesis. With the preliminary evidence supplied by estimation of equation (6.1), which showed private to perform better than commons, as well as the argument from many economists that common property, if anything, is likely to perform worse and not better than private property, the alternative hypothesis is negative signs on C-DISPER and C-COOP, indicating a one-tailed test.

Another commons rights type is C-COOPHD. This is a cooperative commons for which the owner of some of the animals is also the herder of the alp. Because self-interest in the alp operation may alter the performance of the operation, these alps were separated from C-COOP. Relative to C-COOP, we might expect better performance. Relative to private grazing, the same one-tailed test on C-COOPHD's coefficient as for C-DISPER and C-COOP should be performed.

The final rights dummy is C-SMALL. As mentioned before, this is a dummy on a single, outlying cooperative commons of only three users. The C-SMALL observation was not included in regressions for the simple or simultaneous equation models reported earlier, which used 244 observations. Inclusion of this observation makes the number of observations for the present analyses 245. The difference between this and earlier regressions is relatively benign. Including an observation with its own dummy is almost equivalent to deleting it from the work, because the unique dummy takes up any slack between the regression hyperplane and the observed value of the dependent variable. As a consequence, results in this section are comparable to those reported before for 244 observations. The coefficient on the C-SMALL dummy, as with other commons rights types, might theoretically be zero or negative; in reality, a positive coefficient can be expected, because the dummy was constructed after it was learned that the observation was a positive outlier on average milk production and had an odd structure for a commons.

Results for the Expanded Rights Types Model

Results of estimating equation (6.3) with a full set of rights dummies and P-OWNER dropped are contained in Table 6.10. We will examine the results for the commons rights types, private rights types, and natural factors in turn.

Common property results. The most important results of estimating equation (6.3) are that both main types of common property perform more poorly on average milk production than does owner-operated private. Both the C-DISPER and C-COOP coefficients are highly negatively significant (at the .01 level in one-tailed tests), with t-statistics of -3.95 and -2.41 respectively. The estimated coefficients indicate that, other things being equal, converting an owner-operated alp to one of these two types would depress milk production by 1.26 and 1.05 liters per cow per day, respectively. With average milk production for 55 P-OWNER observations of 10.7 liters per cow per day, these amounts represent 11.8% and 9.8% decreases in production, respectively, if changes were made from private to commons.

Dispersed operating unit commons appear to perform somewhat more poorly than cooperative commons, because the value of the C-DISPER coefficient of -1.26 is larger in absolute value than that of C-COOP at -1.05. However, the difference in their performance is statistically insignificant. By dropping the C-COOP dummy instead of the P-OWNER dummy, one can evaluate the performances of other rights types relative to C-COOP. When this is done, the coefficient on C-DISPER has a t-statistic of -0.49 (Table 6.11), which indicates an insignificant difference in milk production between the two main common property rights forms.

The hypothesized advantage of the commons manager's having his own animals on the cooperative alp seems to have some validity. The C-COOPHD coefficient is not significantly different from zero in Table 6.10, an indication that it does not perform significantly differently from owner-operated private land. In contrast, C-COOP does perform significantly differently. However, C-COOPHD also does not

Table 6.10. *Estimation of the Expanded Rights Types Model,*
P-OWNER Dummy Dropped

Regressor	Coefficient	Std. Error	T-statistic
Constant	7.5890	1.0780	7.04[a]
GRDQUAL	0.0971	0.0561	1.73[a]
SFORM	0.1090	0.0876	1.25
WATER	−0.0652	0.0782	−0.83
EXPOSURE	−0.0254	0.0941	−0.27
ELEVATN	0.2486	0.1763	1.41[a]
PRCPWIND	−0.0775	0.1666	−0.47
WDSGRASS	0.0732	0.1447	0.51
SLIDEDGR	−0.0488	0.1627	−0.30
BLDGLOC	0.1825	0.1563	1.17
SPECIALD	−0.0388	0.1412	−0.27
LABORPAU	6.8460	4.3820	1.56[a]
LACTATN	1.2627	0.7204	1.75[a]
P-RENTAL	−1.1866	0.3905	−3.04[a]
P-LEASE	0.6449	0.6945	0.93
P-ACCPAN	−1.6459	0.6449	−2.55[a]
P-ACCPRN	−1.2829	0.5775	−2.22[a]
P-MLTUSE	−0.7273	0.5899	−1.23
P-FAMUSE	0.2104	0.5807	0.36
P-HERDER	2.7494	0.9600	2.86[b]
P-ORGNZN	1.3220	0.9686	1.36[a]
P-CRENT	−1.7193	0.7634	−2.25[a]
C-DISPER	−1.2608	0.3189	−3.95[a]
C-COOP	−1.0528	0.4371	−2.41[a]
C-COOPHD	−0.5759	0.6610	−0.87
C-SMALL	4.3150	1.6050	2.69[a]

Dep. var.: AVEMILK $R^2 = 28.3\%$ Regression $F = 3.46^c$

[a]T-statistic significant at .10 level. One-tailed tests are used except for the constant term.
[b]Unexpected sign. T-statistic significant at .10 level in a two-tailed test.
[c]F-statistic significant at .01 level.

perform significantly differently from C-COOP, which also can be determined from the regression in which C-COOP dummy is dropped instead of the P-OWNER dummy (Table 6.11). Thus, C-COOPHD stands somewhere between owner-operated private and pure cooperative commons, having insignificantly different average milk production from both in two separate tests.

The final cooperative dummy, C-SMALL, is positive and highly significant in Table 6.10 ($t = 2.69$). This is not surprising, since average milk production for this alp was 14.8 liters per cow per day, 4.1 liters more than the average of 10.7 liters per cow per day for owner-

Table 6.11. *Estimation of the Expanded Rights Types Model,*
C-COOP Dummy Dropped

Regressor	Coefficient	Std. Error	T-statistic
Constant	6.5360	1.1040	5.92
GRDQUAL	0.0971	0.0561	1.73
SFORM	0.1090	0.0876	1.25
WATER	−0.0652	0.0782	−0.83
EXPOSURE	−0.0254	0.0941	−0.27
ELEVATN	0.2486	0.1763	1.41
PRCPWIND	−0.0775	0.1666	−0.47
WDSGRASS	0.0732	0.1447	0.51
SLIDEDGR	−0.0488	0.1627	−0.30
BLDGLOC	0.1825	0.1563	1.17
SPECIALD	−0.0388	0.1412	−0.27
LABORPAU	6.8460	4.3820	1.56
LACTATN	1.2627	0.7204	1.75
P-OWNER	1.0528	0.4371	2.41
P-RENTAL	−0.1338	0.4804	−0.28
P-LEASE	1.6977	0.7518	2.26
P-ACCPAN	−0.5931	0.7091	−0.84
P-ACCPRN	−0.2301	0.6516	−0.35
P-MLTUSE	0.3255	0.6514	0.50
P-FAMUSE	1.2632	0.6551	1.93
P-HERDER	3.8020	1.0030	3.79
P-ORGNZN	2.3750	1.0110	2.35
P-CRENT	−0.6665	0.8049	−0.83
C-DISPER	−0.2081	0.4255	−0.49[a]
C-COOPHD	0.4768	0.7152	0.67
C-SMALL	5.3680	1.6310	3.29
Dep. var.: AVEMILK	$R^2 = 28.3\%$	Regression $F = 3.46$	

[a]Indicates C-DISPER's coefficient is insignificantly different from C-COOP's in a two-tailed test.

operated alps. Indeed, the unique dummy was used because of the unusually high milk production and notably small size of the commons (only three users, as noted).

Private property results. Besides its main conclusion, that dispersed operating unit and cooperative commons perform more poorly than owner-operated private, Table 6.10 indicates many other conclusions about the performance of other private rights types. With one exception, the *significant* nonowner-operated private rights types have the hypothesized negative signs. First, the average productivity of rental private (P-RENTAL) is significantly worse than that of owner-operated private ($t = -3.04$). In fact, with a coefficient of -1.19, it performs comparably to the commons forms. In contrast, on grazing areas where use conditions have been stabilized by a long lease or rental relationship of twenty years or more (P-LEASE), performance is insignificantly different from that of owner-operated private ($t = 0.93$). Apparently, the stable tenure situation gives the user an incentive to treat the resource with greater care.[20]

The two private systems where the owner or renter accepts most of the animals grazed from other farmers also are significantly less productive than owner-operated private. Such for-hire operations run by a *renter* have a coefficient of -1.28 ($t = -2.22$), and oddly, when they are run by the *landowner*, the change in milk production from owner-operated private is even larger at -1.65 ($t = -2.55$). The difference between the two, however, is statistically insignificant.[21]

Whereas production decreases undeniably under the two major commons management systems (C-DISPER and C-COOP), differences between owner-operated private and the private, multiple-user systems P-MLTUSE and P-FAMUSE are insignificant. The t-statistic for P-MLTUSE's coefficient is -1.23 and the t-statistic for P-FAMUSE's coefficient is 0.36 (both insignificant at the .10 level). Although both are insignificant, the coefficient on P-MLTUSE is negative and P-FAMUSE's is slightly positive. It appears that when immediate family is involved—for instance, brothers, father and son(s) and so on—multiple-user performance is better than when the consanguinity is further removed or nonexistent. This is as we might expect.[22]

The coefficient on the public organization rights system (agricultural school, prison, etc.), corresponding to the variable P-ORGNZN in Table 6.10, is positively significant (at the .10 level), as hypothesized. The greater resources, knowledge, and care given to these model alps pay off in higher milk yields—even in comparison to owner-operated

---

[20] This result contrasts with some authors' hypothesis that short-term agricultural contracts better ensure tenant responsibility, because a landlord's potential refusal to renew the contract is a more immediate threat. See Johnson (1950) or Cheung (1969).

[21] This was tested by dropping the P-ACCPRN dummy while including the P-OWNER dummy. The t-statistic on P-ACCPAN was -0.45, which indicates an insignificant difference between renter-run and owner-run for-hire operations.

[22] This conclusion cannot be solidly confirmed by testing for a significant difference between P-MLTUSE and P-FAMUSE. If the P-MLTUSE dummy is dropped instead of the P-OWNER dummy, the t-statistic for the coefficient on P-FAMUSE equals 1.21. This indicates an insignificant difference between P-MLTUSE and P-FAMUSE rights types.

private. This conclusion is based on only three alps in the sample, but this is about the number of model alps worked by public organizations that might be expected in a sample of the size considered.

The coefficient on publicly or cooperatively owned grazing areas rented to a private person (P-CRENT) is negative, as hypothesized, and significant at the .025 level. This is in keeping with the area's rental status, for as already determined, private rental land (P-RENTAL) is less productive than owner-operated areas. In fact, the coefficient on P-CRENT of -1.72 is more negative than P-RENTAL's, at -1.19. This may reflect the former's history as a commons grazing area as well.

Finally, let us look at a wrongly signed coefficient, that of P-HERDER. Under this management system, the landowner has hired an employee to tend the owner's animals and care for the alp. Although theoretically the owner can dictate the duties of the herder, it was hypothesized from a practical standpoint that the lower self-interest of the herder might lead to lower performance. In fact, the coefficient on P-HERDER is positive, large (2.75), and highly significant ($t = 2.86$). This result, however, is untrustworthy. Only three observations of this type were found in the usable sample (four in the total sample). This is probably not due to there being a limited number of such alps in the population, as was the case for P-ORGNZN. Rather, it is more likely due to sketchy reporting on whether a herder was hired in the Alp Assessments (Abteilung für Landwirtschaft 1961–73, 1978), which were the source for the determination of P-HERDER alps. Also, one of the three P-HERDER alps happened to produce the maximum observation on average milk production in the entire data set (15.8 liters per cow per day). This together with the small number of P-HERDER alps undoubtedly caused the significance of P-HERDER.

Results for the natural factors and other control variables. Again, postulating that better natural conditions (higher values on the index numbers), increased labor input, and the shift in lactation period on Justistal alps all have a tendency to increase milk productivity, we would expect positive coefficients on all these factors. These expectations are borne out among those variables that are significant in Table 6.10. The natural factors GRDQUAL and ELEVATN both have positive, significant coefficients in a one-tailed, .10 level test, and SFORM is just barely insignificant on this test. This is in contrast to the insignificance of all natural factors in the estimation of the simple model (6.1) (Table 6.4). In addition, none of the natural factors in

Table 6.10 is wrongly signed and significant. The humanly controlled factors that were significant in the simple model, labor input (LABORPAU) and lactation cycle of the cows (LACTATN), remain significant, with the postulated positive influence on milk yields.[23]

The fact that some of the natural factors are significant as hypothesized is one indication that the expanded rights types model is an improvement over the simple model (6.1). In addition, the R^2 increases from 12.9% in the simple model to 28.3% in the expanded model. The adjusted R^2 increases from 8.0% to 20.2%, even though twelve independent variables have been added. This all seems to indicate that the expanded equation with a full set of rights dummies is better than the simple model (6.1).

These facts furnish a partial explanation for the insignificance of all of the natural factors in the simple, dichotomous model (6.1). It is too simple a model. As argued in the section on econometric theory, the simplicity of model (6.1) turns out to be a misspecification. People have more choices than simple private property and some stereotypical form of common property. On the one hand, the natural factors were included in the equation to control for their possible influence on milk production. The idea was then to examine whether the rights types had an influence on milk yield. But the set of control variables can be reversed. It is necessary to control properly for the influence of rights types to determine the effects of natural factors on milk yield as well. The simple model does not do this. Lumping all of the rights categories into two systems misspecifies. The expanded equation more adequately controls for the wide range of choices made about rights systems and allows the influences of some of the natural factors on

---

[23] As I pointed out in note 18, two independent variables that should have been included in the expanded rights types model were omitted in the model that I report in the text. These were location relative to market (MKTLOC) and condition of the road to the alp (ROAD). Both of these may operate on milk productivity, because transportation costs cause farm gate price to decline as distance from market increases. Consequently, land rents fall going away from market. This may cause substitution toward land and away from cows going away from market, raising the cows' marginal and average productivities. The inclusion of these variables leads to some inconclusive results, although the basic conclusion of this study does not change. Both MKTLOC and ROAD coefficients are significant at the .10 level when included, although ROAD has the wrong sign ($t = -1.70$ for MKTLOC and $t = 2.86$ for ROAD; the expected sign for both coefficients is negative, because the poorer accessibility to market is, the lower the capital–land ratio is, and the higher marginal and average productivities are). The important result for this study, however, is that the coefficients for both major commons rights types remain negatively significant ($t = -4.34$ for C-DISPER and $t = -2.42$ for C-COOP) when these accessibility variables are included. Therefore, the basic conclusion on common property does not change.

milk yield to show themselves in the expected manner. Not only does the variability in the estimated rights types coefficients in Table 6.10 confirm that the simple model represents a misspecification, but so does examining the coefficients on the natural factors. Comparing the estimated coefficients on the natural factors in Tables 6.4 and 6.10 shows shifts in the coefficients, whereas their standard errors are fairly stable. This is typical of a comparison between an estimation that has an omitted-variable problem and one that is more inclusive and better specified.

A Model of "Pure" Rights Types

One variation on the expanded rights types model is a model of "pure" rights types. As I have argued, combining the various private rights types and commons rights types into a dichotomous categorization may obscure the differences in success between archetypical private and commons forms. Rather than including all private and commons rights types in an equation, we could test the differences between pure, owner-operated private and the two main types of common property by including only the 55 owner-operated private (P-OWNER), the 76 dispersed operating unit commons (C-DISPER), and the 27 cooperative commons (C-COOP) alps in an OLS regression. This variant on model (6.3) would be estimated with 158 observations and two rights dummies. Dropping the P-OWNER dummy would allow comparison of the productivity of the two commons rights types to that of pure, owner-operated private property.

The results of such a regression confirm the prior outcome that dispersed operating unit commons and cooperative commons perform more poorly than private, owner-operated alps on the basis of milk productivity. The t-statistics are -3.97 and -2.37, respectively—significant in one-tailed tests at the .01 level (Table 6.12). Moreover, the model seems to hold up even though the number of rights systems has been reduced to three. First, the R^2 at 26.4% is maintained at a level much closer to the R^2 for the fully expanded model (28.3%) than to the R^2 for the simple dichotomous model (12.9%). Second, the coefficients on the common property variables C-DISPER and C-COOP shift very little from the values that they take in the full, expanded model.

In addition, some natural factor coefficients are significant, as in the expanded model and in contrast to the simple dichotomous model. These include ELEVATN, SFORM, and BLDGLOC, all of which were significant or nearly so in the expanded model. GRDQUAL,

Table 6.12. *Estimation of a "Pure" Rights Types Model, Including Only 158 Observations on P-OWNER, C-DISPER, and C-COOP*

Regressor	Coefficient	Std. Error	T-statistic
Constant	7.2110	1.3380	5.39[a]
GRDQUAL	0.0752	0.0716	1.05
SFORM	0.2246	0.1184	1.90[a]
WATER	−0.1131	0.1061	−1.07
EXPOSURE	0.0092	0.1180	0.08
ELEVATN	0.2797	0.2088	1.34[a]
PRCPWIND	−0.1033	0.1958	−0.53
WDSGRASS	−0.0675	0.1821	−0.37
SLIDEDGR	−0.0286	0.2052	−0.14
BLDGLOC	0.2301	0.1755	1.31[a]
SPECIALD	−0.1101	0.1685	−0.65
LABORPAU	12.6490	4.9990	2.53[a]
LACTATN	1.1111	0.7431	1.50[a]
C-DISPER	−1.3273	0.3344	−3.97[a]
C-COOP	−1.0543	0.4453	−2.37[a]
Dep. var.: AVEMILK	R^2 = 26.4%	Regression F = 3.66[b]	

[a] *T*-statistic significant at .10 level. One-tailed tests are used except for the constant term.
[b] *F*-statistic significant at .01 level.

however, changes from before and becomes insignificant. In addition, LABORPAU and LACTATN remain significant. Despite the loss of significance of GRDQUAL, the results of this two-dummy, "pure" rights types model generally substantiate the results of the fully expanded model. Again, the main conclusion is that after controlling for other factors, commons do not have as high milk productivity as private alps.

Estimation of the Users and Rights Holders Models

Unlike other models investigated so far, model (6.4) postulates that the rights system can be measured by a continuous variable, either the number of users or the number of rights holders. Data to test this hypothesis were available from independent sources. The number of users in a grazing operation is collected as part of the information gathered for the mountain cheese subsidy. Observations for 234 alps were available with this datum as well as information on the other independent variables. The number of rights holders was determinable for some of the alps from the Alp Assessments. This figure could

Table 6.13. *Estimation of the Number of Users Model*

Regressor	Coefficient	Std. Error	T-statistic
Constant	7.7240	1.1310	6.83[a]
GRDQUAL	0.0656	0.0592	1.11
SFORM	−0.0281	0.0933	−0.30
WATER	−0.0669	0.0828	−0.81
EXPOSURE	0.0491	1.1015	0.48
ELEVATN	0.1670	0.1915	0.87
PRCPWIND	0.0171	0.1763	0.10
WDSGRASS	0.0213	0.1530	0.14
SLIDEDGR	−0.0106	0.1688	−0.06
BLDGLOC	0.2392	0.1593	1.50[a]
SPECIALD	0.0053	0.1499	0.04
LABORPAU	5.6450	4.6310	1.22
LACTATN	1.1661	0.6707	1.74[a]
USERS	−0.0311	0.0096	−3.23[a]

Dep. var.: AVEMILK $R^2 = 14.1\%$ Regression $F = 2.78$[b]

[a] *T*-statistic significant at .10 level. One-tailed tests are used except for the constant term.
[b] *F*-statistic significant at .01 level.

be ascertained for 204 alps that also had information on other independent variables. Equation (6.4) was estimated twice, once using the number of users and a second time using the number of rights holders. As before, an insignificant estimate of γ_1 in equation (6.4) would indicate no difference between private property (small numbers of users or rights holders) and common property (large numbers of users or rights holders). If, however, an increasing number of users or rights holders cause a poorer definition of property rights, poorer resource use, and lowered milk productivity, then a negatively significant estimate of γ_1 can be expected.

Results of estimating equation (6.4) for N equal to the number of users are contained in Table 6.13. The highly negatively significant coefficient on the number of users variable (USERS) is immediately apparent. Significant at the .001 level in a one-tailed test, the USERS coefficient indicates poorer milk productivity as the number of users increases.

The only other significant variables in the equation are lactation period (LACTATN) and the building's location on the grazing area (BLDGLOC). Not even labor input is significant in this model. Thus, we again find the natural factors to be insignificant. The regression F at 2.78 is nevertheless significant at the .01 level, so the model has overall explanatory power.

Table 6.14. *Estimation of the Number of Rights Holders Model*

Regressor	Coefficient	Std. Error	T-statistic
Constant	9.0650	1.3040	6.95[a]
GRDQUAL	0.0676	0.0655	1.03
SFORM	−0.0573	0.1041	−0.55
WATER	−0.1121	0.0908	−1.23
EXPOSURE	−0.0317	0.1126	−0.28
ELEVATN	0.0802	0.2174	0.37
PRCPWIND	0.0227	0.1998	0.11
WDSGRASS	0.0898	0.1709	0.53
SLIDEDGR	0.0288	0.1898	0.15
BLDGLOC	0.0757	0.1891	0.40
SPECIALD	0.1613	0.1694	0.95
LABORPAU	2.7770	5.6010	0.50
LACTATN	1.0604	0.7362	1.44[a]
RHOLDERS	−0.0108	0.0045	−2.43[a]

Dep. var.: AVEMILK $R^2 = 9.6\%$ Regression $F = 1.54^b$

[a]*T*-statistic significant at .10 level. One-tailed tests are used except for the constant term.
[b]*F*-statistic insignificant at the .05 level.

Replacing N in equation (6.4) with the number of rights holders (RHOLDERS) and estimating by OLS yields the results shown in Table 6.14. They are similar to those when the number of users is included, although the rights holders model is poorer. The number of rights holders coefficient is negatively significant at the .01 level. Again, spreading control to a larger group of people is associated with decreased milk productivity.

The rights holders model is poorer than the users model for several reasons. First, only one other variable, LACTATN, is significant in the rights holders equation, and its significance has decreased compared to estimation of the users equation. Secondly, the R^2 drops from 14.1% to 9.6%. In fact, the regression F of 1.54 is not significant at the .05 level. Apparently, the number of users is a better indication than the number of rights holders of the institutional structure's influence on resource extraction and production conditions. This is what one would expect, since in some Swiss commons situations, the rights holders are rather divorced from the actual operation of the alp (see Chapter 4). Nevertheless, both models generally indicate that commons, with their larger numbers of users and rights holders, have lower average productivity than private grazing areas.

Farmers' Adjustment to the Natural Factors

Before summarizing and drawing some conclusions about the results of this empirical investigation, I want to reflect further on the almost universal failure of the natural factors to assist in explaining milk productivity. No natural factor was significant in the simple model (6.1) or in the model that employed users or rights holders as explanatory variables. In the expanded model, loosening the constraints on the simple model's rights systems coefficients (i.e., better specifying the model) allowed the significance of some of the natural factors to show. The fact remains, however, that eight out of ten of the natural factor coefficients in estimation of the expanded model are insignificant.

A potential explanation for these facts is that the farmers adjust the number of animal units to comply with the exigencies of the grazing areas' natural conditions. If so, the farmers control for the natural factors themselves, thus making them irrelevant variables in the models estimated.[24] To investigate this idea, a new variable to measure the "loading" of a grazing area with animals was constructed to represent U in model (6.5). This was normal animal units per hectare (NAUPHEC),[25] which had the form

$$\text{NAUPHEC} = \frac{\text{total animal units}}{\text{hectares}} \left(\frac{\text{days}}{100} \right).$$

This estimate of grazing pressure meets the conditions specified for the variable U in model (6.5), which were that total animal units grazed be normalized by the number of hectares grazed and that the grazing season be normalized to one hundred days for each grazing area.

---

[24] Another possible explanation is that multicollinearity among the regressors may have inflated the standard errors on the natural factor coefficients and made their t-statistics insignificant. Auxiliary regressions (see Judge et al. 1980: 461) of the ten natural factors on all other independent variables revealed a moderate amount of linear dependence between the variables SLIDEDGR, WDSGRASS, PRCPWIND, ELEVATN, and SFORM, with auxiliary regression R^2's ranging from 49% to 66%. However, dropping one or more of these collinear variables from estimations of the expanded model (6.3) only mildly lowered the standard errors of the regressors that remained in the model, and it caused none of the included, formerly insignificant variables to become significant. Thus, multicollinearity is not a cause of the insignificance of the natural factors.

[25] To construct NAUPHEC, information on total animal units grazed was obtained from the Alp Assessments (Abteilung für Landwirtschaft 1961–73, 1978). Information on the number of days spent on the alp came from the mountain cheese subsidy data. Because different numbers of cows remain on some alps for different durations, particularly on dispersed operating unit commons, the figure for number of days grazed was a weighted average of the number of days spent by all cows.

Table 6.15. *Regression Explaining Normal Animal Units per Hectare Using the Natural Factors and the Rights Systems*

Regressor	Coefficient	Std. Error	T-statistic
Constant	−0.2317	0.1720	−1.35
GRDQUAL	0.0136	0.0090	1.51[a]
SFORM	−0.0039	0.0140	−0.28
WATER	−0.0246	0.0125	−1.97[b]
EXPOSURE	0.0210	0.0150	1.40[a]
ELEVATN	0.0669	0.0281	2.38[a]
PRCPWIND	0.0343	0.0266	1.29[a]
WDSGRASS	0.0324	0.0231	1.40[a]
SLIDEDGR	0.0571	0.0260	2.20[a]
BLDGLOC	0.0481	0.0249	1.93[a]
SPECIALD	0.0159	0.0225	0.71
LABORPAU	0.6110	0.6995	0.87
LACTATN	0.2433	0.1150	2.12[a]
P-RENTAL	−0.0407	0.0623	−0.65
P-LEASE	−0.0013	0.1109	−0.01
P-ACCPAN	−0.0864	0.1030	−0.84
P-ACCPRN	−0.3128	0.0922	−3.39[c]
P-MLTUSE	−0.2844	0.0942	−3.02[c]
P-FAMUSE	0.0371	0.0927	0.40
P-HERDER	0.0425	0.1532	0.28
P-ORGNZN	0.1800	0.1546	1.16
P-CRENT	−0.1488	0.1219	−1.22
C-DISPER	−0.1881	0.0509	−3.70[c]
C-COOP	−0.2016	0.0698	−2.89[c]
C-COOPHD	−0.1013	0.1055	−0.96
C-SMALL	−0.2207	0.2562	−0.86
Dep. var.: NAUPHEC	$R^2 = 48.5\%$	Regression $F = 8.25$[d]	

[a]*T*-statistic significant at .10 level in a one-tailed test.
[b]Unexpected sign. *T*-statistic significant at .10 level in a two-tailed test.
[c]*T*-statistic significant at .01 level in a two-tailed test.
[d]*F*-statistic significant at .01 level.

To estimate model (6.5), NAUPHEC is regressed on the natural factors. Because I suspect that better natural conditions (higher grades on the index numbers) would allow more normal animal units on the grazing area, I hypothesize positive signs on the estimated coefficients in this regression. The rights dummies also are included as regressors to control for differences of grazing pressure across rights systems.

Results in Table 6.15 indicate that seven of the ten natural factors are significant explanatory variables for NAUPHEC with correct signs. An eighth variable (WATER) is significant but wrongly signed.

Only SFORM and the catchall variable SPECIALD are insignificant. It appears that the natural factors do cause the farmers to adjust their grazing pressure.

A second regression of this type was performed with two additional independent variables: location relative to market (MKTLOC) and the condition of the road to the alp (ROAD). These were included because accessibility, measured by both distance from settlements and the transportation conditions, might affect how heavily the grazing area is used. The results in Table 6.16 indicate that MKTLOC is indeed significant. Unfortunately, the inclusion of MKTLOC makes two natural variables that were significant in the prior regression, PRCPWIND and WDSGRASS, become insignificant. Nevertheless, six of the twelve factors are significant at the .10 level and correctly signed. A seventh (WATER) is significant but wrongly signed.

It appears that the farmers adjust their herd sizes to accommodate the natural conditions. Again, with this adjustment taking place, the natural factors would be irrelevant variables in a regression explaining milk productivity. This, along with the significance of some natural factors in fully specified models, finally provides a satisfactory explanation for the insignificance of many natural factors in most models in this chapter.

Summary

In this chapter, we have examined the performance of common property in comparison to private property, using a series of econometric models to test for differences in milk productivity on cow alps managed under the two systems. The models have included a simple dichotomous model, a simultaneous equation model, an expanded model of fourteen variations on private and commons rights types, and a model that utilized the number of users or rights holders as representative of the management structure.

All of the models indicate lower average milk production for common property. The expanded rights types model, the most general model, indicates that dispersed operating unit commons and cooperative commons produce, respectively, 1.3 liters (11.8%) and 1.1 liters (9.8%) less per cow per day than owner-operated private property. Statistical significance of the relevant regression coefficients are strong. A variation on this model that includes only observations on pure, owner-operated private property, cooperative commons, and dispersed operating unit commons shows comparable results. Similarly, the simple model, which separates observations into only private

Table 6.16. *Regression Explaining Normal Animal Units per Hectare Using the Natural Factors (Including MKTLOC and ROAD) and the Rights Systems*

Regressor	Coefficient	Std. Error	*T*-statistic
Constant	− 0.2569	0.1707	− 1.51
GRDQUAL	0.0147	0.0089	1.65[a]
SFORM	− 0.0048	0.0141	− 0.34
WATER	− 0.0266	0.0125	− 2.14[b]
EXPOSURE	0.0205	0.0150	1.37[a]
ELEVATN	0.0545	0.0282	1.93[a]
PRCPWIND	0.0277	0.0265	1.05
WDSGRASS	0.0233	0.0231	1.01
SLIDEDGR	0.0476	0.0259	1.84[a]
BLDGLOC	0.0468	0.0247	1.90[a]
SPECIALD	0.0244	0.0225	1.08
LABORPAU	0.7971	0.6952	1.15
LACTATN	0.1938	0.1176	1.65[a]
MKTLOC	0.0604	0.0295	2.05[a]
ROAD	− 0.0025	0.0126	− 0.20
P-RENTAL	− 0.0372	0.0617	− 0.60
P-LEASE	− 0.0335	0.1104	− 0.30
P-ACCPAN	− 0.0972	0.1021	− 0.95
P-ACCPRN	− 0.2736	0.0924	− 2.96[c]
P-MLTUSE	− 0.2757	0.0932	− 2.96[c]
P-FAMUSE	0.0312	0.0919	0.34
P-HERDER	0.0304	0.1516	0.20
P-ORGNZN	0.1345	0.1544	0.87
P-CRENT	− 0.1891	0.1214	− 1.56
C-DISPER	− 0.2013	0.0510	− 3.95[c]
C-COOP	− 0.1887	0.0691	− 2.73[c]
C-COOPHD	− 0.1165	0.1047	− 1.11
C-SMALL	− 0.1474	0.2553	− 0.58
Dep. var.: NAUPHEC	R^2 = 50.1%	Regression *F* = 8.08[d]	

[a]*T*-statistic significant at .10 level in a one-tailed test.
[b]Unexpected sign. *T*-statistic significant at .10 level in a two-tailed test.
[c]*T*-statistic significant at .01 level in a two-tailed test.
[d]*F*-statistic significant at .01 level.

and common property and subsumes into these two categories variations such as rental property, leased property, property managed by hired personnel, and so on, indicates a higher and statistically significant average production for private property. The users and rights holders models demonstrate that productivity could even be thought of as a continuous and declining function of the number of users or rights holders of property, although the number of users model explains productivity better. Finally, the simultaneous equation model, which reflects the idea that both the rights system and productivity are dependent upon natural factors of the grazing area, collapses to the simple dichotomous model for purposes of estimation of productivity, because insufficient correlation exists in the residuals of the two equations to require a simultaneous equation estimation method.

In addition to the lower productivity of common property, a number of other conclusions emerge from the empirical investigation. First, the productivities of many private property rights types that are not pure, owner-operated private, such as operations involving rented land, private operations that accept many animals from others, and so forth, are lower than those of pure, owner-operated private. Only the model alps that are run by government-supported bodies, such as an agricultural school, have higher productivity than owner-operated private. Private, multiple-user grazing areas (two to four users) have insignificantly different productivity from owner-operated private.

Secondly, the simple dichotomous model is a misspecification. It collapses too many variations of management systems into the two categories of commons and private property. This is revealed by the considerable variability in estimated coefficients on different private and commons rights types in the expanded model, as well as the emergence of some of the natural factors as significant explanatory variables in the more fully and better specified expanded rights types model. The fit of the estimated equation also improves dramatically for the expanded rights types model in comparison to the simple model.

Thirdly, the natural conditions of a grazing area—including such things as elevation, ground quality and grass condition, precipitation and wind conditions, and exposure toward the north, south, east, or west—are not very good explanatory variables for milk productivity. Of the ten natural factors included in the expanded rights types model to control for natural variations across grazing areas, only ground quality and elevation seem to have an effect on milk productivity. Further examination indicates that the farmers adjust the number of animals grazed to accommodate varying natural conditions and maintain a certain level of milk productivity for a given rights system, thereby making the natural factors irrelevant explanatory variables in the productivity equations.

Finally, certain natural factors are significant explanatory variables for the determination of rights systems. In particular, better natural soil quality, its accompanying grass condition, and better climatic conditions favor a grazing area's becoming private property. Better accessibility to market favors common property, a finding contrary to original propositions, but consistent with the possibility that road-building projects of recent years have improved accessibility to commons. Milder slope also favors common property, a finding that is again contrary to initial expectations, but perhaps consistent with the greater expansiveness of the commons.

In conclusion, I began with the proposition that private and common property could perform as well as each other, given theoretical arguments about limited entry, limitations on individual inputs, and assurance between participants in common property. Using productivity as a proxy for grazed condition of the land, this hypothesis does not appear to be borne out in Swiss alpine grazing. In the final chapter, we examine whether the conclusion that commons are inferior economic performers is completely warranted.

Appendix: Detailed Definitions of the Natural Factor Index Numbers

As the section on the data explained, the natural factors used as control variables in the regressions examined in this chapter were index numbers collected from Bernese cantonal tax officials. Table 6.1 gave a summary of the meanings of these variables. To define the variables more precisely, this appendix provides a translation of the appropriate section in the Bernese cantonal assessment guide entitled *Bewertung der landwirtschaftlichen Grundstücke und der Waldungen* (Valuation of Agricultural Land and Woods) (Kanton Bern 1973: 52–54, my translation). At the beginning of each definition of a quality factor, I give in brackets the acronym used for the variable in the regression analyses.

II. Valuation of Land (cont.)

B. Grazing Areas in the Alps, Forealps, and in the Jura Mountains (Official form 1 b)

1. Point System (5 is the best, 1 the lowest grade)

The following factors are to be evaluated:

a) Soil Quality and Grass Condition [GRDQUAL] (3 × 5 points maximum)

Forage quality is influenced by the plant composition of the grasses. The grass condition, however, depends to a large extent on the quality of the soil.

Generally, on moderately heavy loam soils, a close, well-knit turf with a large percentage of desirable forage plants arises. In contrast, wet and heavy clay soils exhibit grasses composed primarily of undesirable plants.

The grade should indicate how the soil and grasses influence the milk productivity of the cows or the growth of the nonmilk-producing cattle.

b) Sales and Market Location [MKTLOC] (2 × 5 points maximum)

Under sales and market location are to be understood the factors that relate to sales possibilities and to obtainable prices for products. The distance and road conditions to a significant market or point where the products will be used play the most important roles. It must be realized, however, that the sales and market location does not have the same meaning here as it does when grading valley properties.

c) Surface Form [SFORM] (2 × 5 points maximum)

very good	whole grazing area is level or moderately sloped
good	majority of the area is level or moderately sloped
fair	majority of the area is rather heavily sloped
poor	majority of the area is steeply sloped
very poor	majority of the area is very steeply sloped

d) Road Conditions [ROAD] (Condition and slope of the road or path from the nearest train station; 2 × 5 points maximum)

very good	good driving road with moderate slope
good	good driving road with steep slope
fair	driving path with moderate to steep slope
poor	steep wagon trail
very poor	pack- or footpath

In making a determination, the road conditions to the lowest alp buildings are to be considered. Mountain railways or cable lifts that cannot be used for the transport of cattle are not to be considered.

e) Water System [WATER] (2 × 5 points maximum)

very good	adequate free-flowing water or good cistern water on the grazing area and by the buildings
good	adequate water by the buildings; need for more watering places on the grazing area
fair	watering places completely lacking in certain parts of the grazing area; adequate free-flowing or cistern water by the buildings

poor	water shortage or water of insufficient quality during periods of drought, or inadequate cisterns
very poor	chronic water shortage; piped water impossible or possible only with relatively high cost; or wholly unsatisfactory cisterns

f) Exposure [EXPOSURE] (2 × 5 points maximum)

Under exposure are to be understood the position relative to the sun and the duration of sunshine. It is to be judged with an eye toward its effect on forage quality. The best exposure is southwest. Full southern exposure is not entirely desirable; such grazing areas are hit hardest during long periods of dryness and the forage quickly becomes "hard."

Northern and eastern exposures are in general not so unfavorable for the [alpine] grazing areas as they are for year-round operations. This is because the grazing season occurs during the time when the sun reaches its highest point. In certain circumstances, the duration of sunshine can be just as long for eastern and northern exposures as for southern exposure. Shady-side grazing areas are to be graded unfavorably with respect to exposure when mountains or forests block the sun.

g) Elevation [ELEVATN] (5 points maximum)

The best elevation is the level between 1,200 and 1,800 meters above sea level; a grade of 5 is appropriate for grazing areas that lie in this zone. The grade is to be correspondingly decreased for higher grazing areas (approximately 1 point per 100 meters).

For forealps that lie under 1,200 meters, a grade of 5 is appropriate; in contrast, for grazing areas under 1,200 meters that remain occupied for the whole summer, the grades of 3 and 4 are appropriate.

h) Precipitation and Wind Conditions [PRCPWIND] (5 points maximum)

To be judged are the amount of precipitation; the danger of hail, snow, and frost during the summer; the prevailing winds; and the natural protection against wind.

Winds, especially the north and east winds, make the grazing areas "hard grassed" and less productive. If a natural wind barrier exists, of which forest is one kind, the grazing areas are more valuable.

i) Distribution between Forest and Grazing Land [WDSGRASS] (5 points maximum)

Woods moderate temperature extremes and break up heavy winds; they hold back snow and constitute some protection against avalanches. They offer protection to the grazing animals against inclement weather (shelter pines).

The distribution between forest and grazing land is also to be judged with an eye toward wood availability for the alp operation.

k) Danger of Landslides and Debris Accumulation [SLIDEDGR] (5 points maximum)

The existence of currently debris-covered or slumped areas is not to be judged. Rather the potential danger of such is to be evaluated.

l) Location of Buildings [BLDGLOC] (5 points maximum)

Because of the need to spread manure, the buildings should not be extremely low nor extremely high in the grazing area; rather, it is most practical for them to be in the upper third of the grazing area. The building location is also to be judged with regard to the distances that the animals must traverse from the grazing area to the buildings. Long stretches impair milk productivity or weight gain.

m) Distance from the Train Station [TRNLOC] (5 points maximum)

very good	up to 3 km or up to ½ hour on foot
good	3–8 km or ½–1½ hours on foot
fair	8–13 km or 1½–2½ hours on foot
poor	13–18 km or 2½–3½ hours on foot
very poor	over 18 km or over 3½ hours on foot

The above grade is to be raised by ½ to 1 point for regions that are accessible by bus lines, mountain railways, or cable lifts. If such transportation possibilities are limited, they are not to be considered fully in giving a grade.

n) Special Encumbrances [SPECIALD] (5 points maximum)

Only extraordinary encumbrances, excluding building maintenance, are to be considered, such as fencing requirements; public rights of way for automobile, wagon, or foot travel; and maintenance of drainage ditches and access roads. Stream bank maintenance duties are to be considered only if a maintenance agreement exists. In cases where only riparian rights holders have the duty to maintain the banks, the grade of 5 is to be entered for Special Encumbrances and a decrement for the bank maintenance duty is to be made according to the guidelines on page 22.[26] Water payments do not qualify as special encumbrances.

---

[26] The mentioned guidelines indicate that riparian parcels normally carry an annual charge for stream bank maintenance (4½% of capital value or, if no maintenance agreement exists, a certain amount per running meter of stream bank). The text here indicates that stream bank maintenance costs are included in property value through direct charges rather than through the point system I used for this study, except when a nonriparian property holder has agreed to stream bank maintenance.

CHAPTER 7

The Structure and Performance of Common Property: Conclusions

In the concluding chapter of this book, I wish to explore further the description of Swiss common property from Chapter 4 in order to generalize Swiss commons management techniques to other resource exploitation contexts and to reexamine the conclusion from the empirical work of Chapter 6 that the average productivity of Swiss commons is lower. Both these discussions draw on the theoretical discussions of Chapters 2 and 3. Accordingly, this chapter is divided into two parts. In the first, I consider some of the principles of limiting entry and user decision making that come from the Swiss grazing commons, and review the practicality of applying some of the principles to other natural resources. In the second major section, I examine the question "How well do commons work?" The empirical results of Chapter 6 seem to say that they do not work as well as private property, but the results must be interpreted with a critical eye before we reach this conclusion.

Common Property Principles in Swiss Grazing

A number of principles of natural resource control are imbedded in the practices pursued by Swiss commons users and rights holders. These include input quotas and input rights, seasonal restrictions, limiting the user group by residency or family lineage, and backward linkage or complementary input restrictions. The Swiss grazing commons also illustrate various forms of commons decision making, which have implications for the sharing and shifting of costs and the viability of user self-government.

Input Quotas and Input Rights

One of the most important principles that come from Swiss commons grazing is the idea of limiting entry by systems of input quotas or input rights. These schemes in Switzerland involve limiting the number of animal units directly rather than on the basis of personal characteristics such as citizenship. Because the cows and other animals can be considered inputs used to harvest the resource, such strategies represent input quotas or input rights.

Input quotas are found, for example, on many community alps. Limits on the total number of animal units to be grazed are set, and allocation to individual users is left to some nonmarket process. Among these are rotation, lot, historical use, and priority setting among different classes of users (citizens, residents, nonresidents, etc.).

To the economist, probably the more interesting scheme involves input rights as exemplified in grazing rights. These are input *rights* in the sense of Chapter 3, because the right to graze is transferable: It is both salable and rentable. In all but a few cases where prices are controlled, the market governs the allocation of these rights. Thus, to the extent that an unequal income distribution does not prevent it, rights go to the "highest and best use."[1] The farmer who values the services of the commons the most—whether because of lack of other feed sources, proximity to the grazing area, or his own farming efficiency—will outbid other farmers and obtain use rights.

Input quotas and input rights work in grazing because of a rigid production function between cows as capital inputs and the amount of grass harvested. There is no other direct input to grass harvest, nor will the animals graze significantly more if left on the grazing area longer each day. Thus, there is no way to intensify the harvest once the number of animal units has been fixed. Only over long periods, as the animals become larger through selective breeding, does the pro- duction relationship between animal units grazed and grass harvested change. This alteration in the production function occurs slowly, and therefore adjustments can be made periodically for increased animal size.

This is unlike the extraction process in most other jointly exploited resources, where input substitution is possible. To take the example from Chapter 3, limiting the number of boats in a fishery may result only in intensified capture through substitution of larger boats, more nets per boat, more time on the water and fuel per boat, and so on. Because it is difficult to put quotas on all inputs, and because the attempt to do so stifles technological innovation, input quotas are inadequate whenever input substitution is possible. Output quotas prove superior for many jointly used resources.

Nevertheless, the grazing right as exhibited in the Swiss commons

[1] An unequal income distribution may give rich farmers a greater ability to compete for the rights than poor farmers, in which case ability to pay impairs willingness to pay.

represents an important idea for wider application to other resource extraction processes. Grazing rights are a successful example of *transferable* common property rights. Although they are applied to inputs in Switzerland, they might be imposed on outputs for other jointly used resources, depending on the exploitative process for the resource. Thus, the idea might be transferred directly to range management in the western United States, by setting up transferable rights to grazing on federal land. Grazing in developing countries might also be controlled by a system of transferable grazing rights. In fisheries, oil and gas extraction, and groundwater pumping, transferable rights on outputs would be preferable in order to avoid input substitution. Taking the idea of transferable rights one step further and applying them to activities like hunting or recreation in national parks may be unacceptable for equity reasons. (It is usually considered important to allow access to such goods regardless of income, and instituting transferable rights that might acquire a high market price could exclude participants with low incomes. Nonmarket rationing, e.g., waiting lists, is the usual alternative.)

Where transferable rights are applied, adjustments in total resource extraction can easily be accomplished on a percentage basis when necessary. In a bad fishing year, for instance, the holding of one right might allow a person only nine hundred pounds of fish instead of the one thousand pounds allowed in a normal year.[2]

In Chapters 2 and 3, I made the distinction between symmetric and asymmetric externalities, the former being exemplified in a fishery and the latter in air and water pollution. I have concentrated on reciprocal externalities, as in the examples just given, but both types of externalities can be handled by common property solutions. A common property solution to the nonreciprocal externality case is exemplified by tradable rights apportioned to polluters to use the air's or water's assimilative capacity. The agency issuing the rights determines how much of the assimilative capacity in total should be used. Once this total amount of assimilative capacity is set, a polluter exercising a right to draw on it necessarily reduces the amount of the resource (assimilative capacity) available to other rights holders. A negative, reciprocal externality is generated. The externality, how-

---

[2] Of course, bad fishing years cannot be predicted ex ante. Adjusting the catch allowed per right must occur as the season progresses and the total catch is monitored. For instance, a right could allow a certain amount of catch in each of the first two of three thirds or the first three of four quarters of the fishing season. On the basis of fishing results, the quota per right then could be set for the final fraction of the fishing season.

ever, is controlled at the correct level because it is limited by the polluter's holding of use rights. Furthermore, the former recipients of the nonreciprocal externality—say, swimmers in a polluted river—now suffer only the reduced effects associated with the use level equal to the sum of all use rights. This level is presumably set at the socially optimal rate. Notably, the reduction in nonreciprocal externalities formerly imposed on people outside the group (e.g., the swimmers) is transformed into a set of externalities that are internalized to the group of similar users (the polluters), *and these externalities are reciprocal.* Thus, tradable pollution rights are a common property solution to a nonreciprocal externality situation whose imposition reduces nonreciprocal externalities to the appropriate level while creating new, reciprocal externalities that the user group allocates efficiently in the course of rights trading. Of course, the idea of use rights to control nonreciprocal externalities is not new, but viewing it as a common property solution is.

Seasons

A second general way in which inputs are controlled in alpine grazing is by setting the season for use through adjustment of the dates of the alp ascent and the alp descent. Indeed, many user groups deem the date of the ascent important enough to require a meeting of all users to determine it. The availability of the resource (grass) is the governing factor in the decisions on when to ascend and when to descend. Variable weather conditions cause the grass to grow at different rates, and modifying the grazing period is the major method of making annual adjustments in grazing pressure. Essentially, this approach regulates the amount of inputs applied by varying the number of days that the capital input (cows) is utilized.

Imposing seasons can be generalized to other jointly exploited resources, and it has been used in a variety of settings. Commercial and sport fishing seasons, hunting seasons, and weekly shutdown days for oil and gas pumping are a few examples. The Swiss use a variable season, depending upon resource availability. For other natural resources, seasons are often set for particular periods each year (or each week, in the case of oil and gas). One also finds variable-length seasons in other contexts, however, an example being a closing date for fishing when an annual or quarterly total production quota is reached.

Seasons have been deprecated in the literature, because they can encourage an accumulation of redundant capital inputs when used as an isolated tool to restrict resource extraction. Users may overinvest in capital inputs in order to extract as much of the resource as quickly as possible during the season. The Swiss graziers, however, combine seasons with limits on inputs. Implicitly, they recognize the need to pursue two economic goals simultaneously whenever an input is the subject of control. Both total extraction and the rate of extraction must be circumscribed. Setting total extraction is important to prevent economic overuse of the resource, and controlling the extraction rate is necessary to avoid overinvestment in inputs. Swiss graziers have limited the number of cattle to regulate the rate of extraction, and they use a season, which together with the number of animal units grazed determines total extraction. When used in this way, seasons play a valuable role in controlling total resource extraction.

Limiting the User Group by Residency

In two ways, the Swiss limit the number of users rather than, or in addition to, the amount of inputs. The first of these is a community residency requirement (formerly often a community citizenship requirement). This, of course, is only a broad limitation on the amount of use that the natural resource undergoes, and not surprisingly, imposition of the limitation was often only the first step in limiting use. Where use by citizens or residents began to overtax the resource, various forms of input quotas were introduced.

The idea of restricting the user group to residents or citizens is not unique to the Swiss commons. State fisheries regulation may limit the number of nonresident users, as has occurred in the state of Wisconsin. With many countries claiming two-hundred-mile, exclusive economic zones in their coastal waters, the status of citizenship is rapidly becoming a prerequisite for fishing a country's waters without special permission. As I have noted, this is a first step toward creating common property in pelagic fishes, even as citizenship was often the first step in limiting entry to Swiss commons. Quotas or transferable rights establishing rights and duties for fishermen who are citizens of the country in question would complete the establishment of common property in continental shelf waters.

Limiting the User Group by Family Lineage

The second way the Swiss limit the number of users is by family lineage. The primary example lies in the *Korporations*, where descent from an original user family gives one the basic right to use. A similar system exists for those alps owned by communities or community factions where citizenship is required for the right to use and community citizenship is passed from generation to generation. Like residency requirements, restriction by family lineage provides only a loose control on resource exploitation, and additional input quota restrictions are often necessary.

The use of family descent as a criterion for use rights has restricted applicability to new common property rights systems. In the United States, only if a natural resource is managed by a private community, of which there are precious few (e.g., the idealistic religious communities), or under certain Indian treaties, can one talk about restricting use to descendants. States clearly cannot restrict use to particular family lineages. State regulators may give preference to an immediate family member of a license holder when the license is transferred, as in licensing of fishermen. This is an equity consideration, however, an effort to "keep the business in the family." Its motivation does not lie in limiting use for efficiency reasons. Therefore, although this method may have untried applications in some traditional systems in developing countries, where family lineage already may have other significance, this Swiss tool for restricting use is anachronistic and probably cannot be transferred to many modern resource use situations.

Backward Linkage or Complementary Input Restrictions

The final principle used by the Swiss to limit use of their commons is a rather odd one when generalized. They limit the number of animals on the summer commons to that number that can be overwintered on hay won from the valley lands. Recall that the cattle are inputs to the harvest of summer grass. The hay or the valley land from which it comes is an input to this input. Thus, as a general principle, the Swiss restrict resource harvest through (natural) limits on inputs to an input. This might be called a "backward linkage input restriction."

This type of limitation is very specialized. It is made possible by the seasonal nature of the alpine grass harvest and by the animals' being biological organisms that must be supported through the winter on another input. Other examples of this type may exist, but they must be few. As a general principle, limiting use through restricting backwardly linked inputs has little potential for wider application. Imagine limiting wood production in order to limit the number of fishing boats or curtailing nylon production to limit the number of nets. The propositions are preposterous.

Another way to view the restriction that only overwintered cattle can go to the alp is to call the hay won from the valley a complementary input to summer grass harvest. In this interpretation, the cattle (the capital inputs) are "kept operating" or functioning in the winter in order to perform the grass harvest in the summer. The input necessary to keep the capital input functioning is stored hay. Looking at the system in this manner allows a slightly more reasonable generalization to other natural resources: limiting a complementary input to the capital input. An example might be restricting gasoline or diesel fuel used to operate fishing boats. Again, this seems like a roundabout way to control resource extraction. The possibility of input substitution also remains, unless the complementary input is essential and there is a rigid production relationship between its use and extraction of the resource. For instance, in developing countries one might find grazing systems where limitation of a complementary input such as hay or water could help control overinvestment in the capital input. Thus, the Swiss principle of restricting use through limits on backwardly linked or complementary inputs seems at best to have occasional applicability to other resource use systems.

Conclusions on Limited Entry Principles

Whereas some principles employed in Switzerland to limit use, such as family lineage and restrictions on backwardly linked or complementary inputs, do not seem to be practical for many other jointly exploited resources, other principles do seem to have general usefulness. These include residency or citizenship requirements, seasons, and transferable use rights. The last possibility is probably the most engaging idea. It could have wide applicability in jointly used resources, from fisheries to grazing to surface water allocation to groundwater pumping to air and water pollution. Policy makers have already begun to use this method of limiting and allocating use rights to jointly exploited resources, and applications to more cases are likely to arise.

User Decision Making

As explained in Chapter 4, the Swiss have adopted two voting rules to facilitate their decision making, one person–one vote and voting proportional to use rights. Often the former rule is used for less important decisions, and the latter may be reserved for weightier questions. Although the one-person–one-vote rule promotes greater equality among people of unequal financial means, the proportional-to-rights rule may be more in tune with economic efficiency. If costs are borne proportionally to rights and decisions are made on a one-person–one-vote basis, the potential exists for small users to shift costs to larger users. This danger of shifted costs may even extend to the decision regarding setting or changing the maximum number of animal units. Under proportional-to-rights voting, the larger users can better prevent decisions that will unduly shift costs to them and possibly reduce total net benefits from the grazing area.

As a final principle, the Swiss commons exemplifies the overall viability of user participation in decision making. The modern tendency in government regulation of natural resource extraction is to limit severely the involvement of users in decision making. In Swiss grazing, the users not only participate, but they have complete control over decisions regarding the corporately managed resource. This indicates that user participation in decision making can work, and it might be explored with greater energy for other jointly used resources. An example of this is already occurring in the Commercial Fishing Board in the state of Wisconsin's limited entry program. Composed partially of commercial fishers, this board assists the state Department of Natural Resources in regulatory decisions.

Of course, how well user decision making works is tied to the question "How well do commons work?" Using the results from Chapter 6, I explore this question next.

How Well Do Commons Work?

The coefficients on the commons dummy variables are repeatedly negative and significant in the models of Chapter 6. I hypothesized that this would indicate poorer grass condition and poorer management under common property. In this section, we examine more closely whether the conclusion that the commons are more poorly managed can be drawn.

There are two sides to the argument. First, we scrutinize possible insufficiencies in the analysis that caution against concluding that commons performance is inferior. Secondly, with these caveats in mind, we use theory and the empirical results of Chapter 6 to examine whether commons do not work as well as private property.

Econometric Control of the Natural Factors

The first caution against concluding that commons perform inadequately arises from a possible inadequacy in the data. Common prop-

erty and private property in Switzerland may operate under such
different conditions that they are incomparable. Some Swiss argue,
and one model in Chapter 6 attempted to show, that common property grazing areas often are found in a different environment than
are private grazing areas. Thus, the natural productivity of the land
may be more important in determining the rights system than the
rights system is in determining the land's productivity. Because of
this, in the places where common property is used, it might not work
ideally, but at least it works. Under the same conditions private property might not work at all (Hafner 1979).

Although the models in Chapter 6 attempted to put the two systems
on an equal footing by controlling for natural conditions, perhaps the
econometrics do not fully capture the difference between the two
environments or the ways in which the farmers react to them. One
reason to doubt the measures of natural suitability used in the econometrics is that they are subjective grades, assigned by different sets of
people in different townships. Although written guidelines marshal
the assignment of grades, one might question the ultimate compara-
bility of the grades. If they are poor measures of the natural factors,
the statistical analyses in Chapter 6 that indicated poorer commons
performance may have been inadequate.

If common property emerges in poorer, remoter areas in ways for
which the econometrics could not control, the care necessary to raise
their average product to the level of private alps may not make economic sense. An example of this reasoning emerged in an interview
with Georg Donau, president of the community of Peist in Graubünden, a farmer and an alp user himself (Donau 1979). Improvements of Peist's alp are really an economic question that the farmers
have weighed and decided against pursuing beyond a certain point.
As Donau explains:

> The elevation is one natural factor that hinders the pasture's productivity,
> since the better sections of the grazing area lie at 2,000 to 2,200 meters above
> sea level. Another factor is the great distance from the village to the alp,
> which makes even getting to the alp for improvement work difficult. A third
> is that the alp is so extensive in area that it is difficult to care for it all. . . .
> As I mentioned, it takes a long time just to reach the alp, and the farmers
> are already pressed for time in the summer. There is not that much that can
> be done profitably with the alp anyway. One could apply artificial fertilizer,
> but the growing season is too short to try to pull the maximum out of the
> ground. . . . It may be wiser to put that fertilizer on the village-level fields,
> where you get more hay and avoid all the transportation costs.
> [To get rid of the weeds and] to change the plant composition to include
> mainly edible plants would simply require too great a time investment. The

relationship between time invested and the benefits received is out of balance. . . . For instance, we tried to spray the *Blacken* [a weed]. We thought we had had a great success. But after a couple of years, they were back just as they had been before. . . . The effort was greater than the benefit received. (My translation)

From this account, it is evident that the farmers judge the marginal productivity of inputs applied in different locations—mainly their own labor, but also such things as fertilizer and herbicides—and come to the conclusion that their efforts and funds are better spent on valley land. The same mental calculations for the more accessible and more naturally favored private alps may justify greater investments of time and money. This process would result in a higher average product on the private alps, the result found in Chapter 6, without the commons users' having given economically inadequate attention to their alps.

The Genetic Uniformity Assumption

A second way in which the econometrics of Chapter 6 might have failed arises from the assumption that the cows on commons alps are inherently as productive as those on private alps. (This is the assumption of genetic uniformity with respect to milk-producing capabilities across herds of cows on different types of alps.) As has already been pointed out, if the farmers generally send poorer milk-producing animals to commons alps than to private ones, this would depress the coefficient on common property rights types. In fact, an omission of inherently different milk-producing capability from the equation might introduce missing-variable bias into the estimated coefficients on all of the variables in the equation.

Lack of genetic uniformity, therefore, would seem to be a potentially serious problem. Given the results obtained, however, genetic uniformity is not crucial. If the farmers send poorer cows to commons than they do to private alps, they likely do so for one of two reasons. Either the farmers might not wish to send their better animals to the poorer natural conditions on commons alps, where their milk-producing capacity would be hampered, or the farmers might not want to give their better animals over to common property management, because they do not trust the unfamiliar alp personnel or because common property has caused a poorer grazed condition of the land. Neither of these reasons for a divergence in genetic makeup of herds would cause major problems for the current analysis.

The first reason is not a problem, because all equations controlled econometrically for the natural factors. If, for the sake of argument, we assume that the contentions in the previous section are false and the natural factor variables accurately reflect natural conditions, and if the genetic quality of cows is a function of the natural quality of the grazing areas, then controlling for the natural factors econometrically also effectively controls for genetic milk-producing capacity. Of course, the effect of the omitted genetic variation would have been absorbed into the coefficients on the natural factors, and thus would have biased them. But it would not have affected the results on the rights system dummy variables, which were the primary results sought.

Secondly, it is not a grave problem if the farmers send poorer cows to commons because they do not like giving their animals to unfamiliar alp personnel or because they perceive that a poorer grazed condition has resulted from commons management. If this is the case, the genetic inferiority of commons cows would depress the coefficients on the commons dummies, but only for the reason that negative coefficients on the commons dummies are obtained in the first place—poorer commons management. In this case, it would be preferable to separate the effects of genetic variation from the pure effects of commons management, but it is not essential.

In summary, the assumption of genetic uniformity in the analysis was a safe one. If it is not accurate, the global conclusions about different rights systems' productivities would not be altered.

Overexploitation

In this and following sections, I turn to theoretical discussions that use the empirical results of Chapter 6 to examine whether the Swiss grazing commons perform more poorly than the private grazing areas. The negatively significant commons dummies of Chapter 6 indicate lower average milk production on the commons after controlling for natural factors, which I hypothesized would reflect poorer grass condition and hence poorer management under common property. In current arguments, I take the analysis a step further. I examine and vary revenue and cost conditions under common and private property, employing the graphic (static fisheries) model of Chapter 2, to see how the variations fit the results obtained in Chapter 6. Viewing the problem under different revenue and cost conditions corresponds to three cases associated with common property: current overgrazing, including previously omitted costs, and underinvestment in common improvements (or overgrazing in the past). Here I consider current overgrazing.

To begin, assume the simplest arrangement, namely that commons and private grazing have the same total product and total cost curves. Under these conditions, one easily can compare the two systems for overgrazing, which is defined as grazing more animal units than would result in the maximum sustainable economic yield. Under similar revenue and cost conditions, the theoretical case can be built that Swiss commons graziers exploit beyond the optimal point, whereas private graziers do not. I will make this case first and then examine the empirical evidence from Chapter 6.

Users of commons may exploit beyond the maximum economic yield because, as was argued throughout Chapter 4, they tend to set and maintain limits on use when an area reaches carrying capacity. Carrying capacity is equivalent to exploiting at maximum sustainable yield in the static open access fisheries model, which of course is beyond the economic optimum.[3] On the other hand, if the typical private owner exploits at a rate corresponding to the economic optimum, as most economic theory supports by saying that the private individual has the incentives to seek and find the optimum, then under similar cost and return structures, common property users exploit the resource beyond the optimal level while private users do not.

This is a theoretical argument. What empirical evidence can be brought to bear on it? First, average milk production (average product) is, *ceteris paribus*, lower under common property than it is under private property, as the negative coefficients on the commons dummies in Chapter 6 indicate. The implication for inputs (cowdays)[4] applied to the grazing area is that they should be greater under common property. This can be seen by again employing the static fisheries model of Chapter 2. Refer to Figure 7.1, a reproduction of Figure 2.2 with the average and marginal product curves drawn in. The model shows that the average product (*AP*) declines as effort (input level) increases throughout the entire range of effort. Applied to grazing, if commons operate at a lower point on the *AP* curve than private holdings and both have the same average product curve, the depressed

---

[3] See the sections entitled "Definition of Overuse" and "Graphic Models of Open Access" (specifically, the subsection "The General Static Fisheries Model," especially Figure 2.3) in Chapter 2.

[4] The composite input whose average product is being measured is "cowdays," i.e., the number of cows times the number of days on the alp. The reason for this is that the dependent variable AVEMILK was formed by taking total milk production from the grazing area and dividing it by the number of cows and by the number of days grazed.

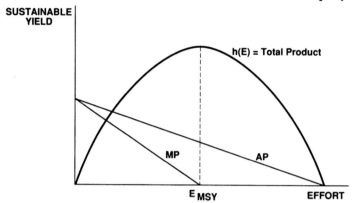

Figure 7.1. Average and Marginal Products in the Static Model

average product of commons must be due to the application of greater effort measured in cowdays.

Reconsidering findings of Chapter 6, however, discloses that common property grazing systems in general do *not* apply greater grazing pressure to their land. In the final modeling section of Chapter 6, a model was constructed to explain the grazing pressure put on the land, in which the measure of grazing pressure was normal animal units per hectare (NAUPHEC). The explanatory variables for the regressions were the natural factors *and* the rights systems. In that section, the question was whether farmers adjust the number of normal animal units to account for natural conditions. The same regressions, however, can be used to evaluate whether common property or private property applies more grazing pressure to the land by examining the signs on the coefficients for the rights systems. Because the rights dummy for pure, owner-operated private land (the P-OWNER dummy) was excluded from the equation, the coefficients on the included rights dummies, which involved among others dummies for both cooperative and dispersed operating unit commons, indicate grazing pressure in normal animal units relative to owner-operated private property. Inclusion of the natural factors as regressors controls for natural conditions that may make any one of the rights systems stock the grazing area more or less heavily.

Referring to Table 6.15, we see that the coefficients on the dispersed operating unit and cooperative commons, C-DISPER and C-COOP, have t-statistics of -3.70 and -2.89, respectively. They are negatively significant at the .01 level. Similarly, in Table 6.16, when market location and road conditions are added as regressors, the t-statistics are -3.95 and -2.73 for the coefficients on C-DISPER and

C-COOP, respectively. Again, they are negative and highly signifi-cant. *This indicates that the commons are grazed less intensively than owner-operated private property.* Controlling for other factors, fewer normal animal units per hectare are grazed on common property.

This result directly contradicts the idea that common property's lower average product is caused by excessive inputs under a structure of costs and returns similar to private property's. Pure overgrazing cannot be blamed for the lower average product of commons. How can the simultaneous results of lower average product and lower graz-ing pressure for commons be reconciled? We will explore this ques-tion further by varying first the cost and then the revenue curves of private and common property.

The Problem of Omitted Costs

In Chapter 6, I used a physical productivity measure, average milk production, to compare common property with private property. This approach considers only the production side, or equivalently, the rev-enue side, of the operations' economic computations. In judging the efficiency of economic systems, economists are interested in compar-ing the profit that each returns; they are interested in maximizing the difference between total revenues and total costs. Therefore, because Chapter 6 used only a physical productivity measure to compare com-mon property with private property, it ignored an essential element of the economic calculus: costs.

Because of this, one might argue that the performance of common property relative to private property cannot be definitively deter-mined from the work described in Chapter 6. The productivity on the commons seems to be lower, but so may be the costs. On a net basis, common property may perform equally as well as private property. The case is not difficult to make that costs on common property are lower. Fewer fences must be built to divide the land, labor input per animal is lower on commons that collect many owners' animals into a single operation, fewer buildings may be needed, and other econo-mies of scale may exist. The transportation costs from commons may be lower also, given the advantage in market location for common property alps found in the Chapter 6 regression that used the natural factors to explain where common and private property grazing areas are located.[5]

---

[5] Recall that this did not mean that commons were located closer to market but that they had better road connections.

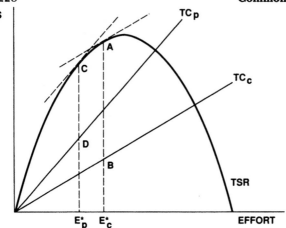

Figure 7.2. Effort and Rents under a Lower Commons
Cost Structure

Under a lower cost structure for commons, it is possible to show
better performance (higher profits) from common property than for
private property, even though the result from Chapter 6 of a lower
average product on commons obtains. Figure 7.2 is a reproduction of
Figure 2.3 with two total cost curves drawn in, one for commons (TC_c)
and one for private property (TC_p). The less steeply sloped total cost
curve for commons indicates that it has lower marginal costs than
private property. The optimal level of effort for common property
under these conditions is E_c^*, because at this level of effort a line
tangent to the total sustainable revenue curve is parallel to TC_c. The

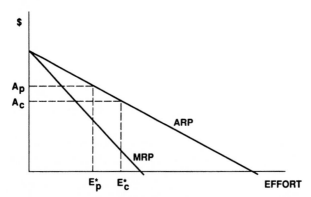

Figure 7.3. Effort and Average Revenue Product under
a Lower Commons Cost Structure

optimal level of effort for private property is E_p^*, determined in a similar way using the TC_p curve. Rents accruing to common property are AB and those to private property are CD. Since AB is greater than CD, common property rents exceed private property rents. Concomitantly, average product (AP) under commons will be lower. This can be seen in the average and marginal graph, Figure 7.3. Given optimal private effort E_p^*, the average revenue product (ARP) is A_p. The optimal commons effort E_c^* results in average revenue product A_c, which is less than A_p. Because ARP is proportional to AP (differing only by a factor equal to the price of output), the commons AP lies below the private AP, a result consistent with the econometric results of Chapter 6. In this model this is due to the lower cost structure for commons, which encourages greater effort. That is, E_c^* exceeds E_p^*. The greater effort under commons decreases the average product.

Unfortunately, this analysis requires effort under common property to be greater than under private property, a condition that we found in the previous section to be contrary to empirical results. Therefore, simply varying cost conditions does not result in a theory that is consistent with all of the facts either. One parameter has not yet been varied, the total product or yield–effort function. It is also possible that the total product curves for common property and private property diverge. This idea is explored next.

Past Underinvestment or Overgrazing

Controlling for the natural factors in the econometrics of Chapter 6 constituted an attempt to give commons and private property equivalent original resource bases from which production proceeds. At least from the standpoint of the natural factors, this would give the two use systems the same yield–effort functions. It is possible, however, that human management has caused the yield–effort functions under the two institutional structures to diverge. If there is less invested in maintenance or common improvements under common property, the resource base itself will be different under common property, even in places where the natural conditions are the same. Similarly, past overgrazing could depreciate the resource base, even though commons grazing pressure since has been adjusted below that of private property. In either case, this would be reflected graphically in a depressed yield–effort function (total product curve) for common property. The entire total product curve in Figure 7.1 would be shifted down. Consequently, the AP curve would be lower (shifted toward the origin) along its entire length. This is shown in Figure 7.4.

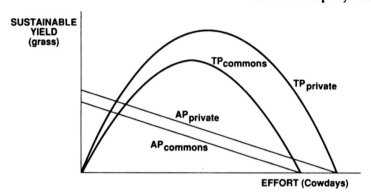

Figure 7.4. Total and Average Products in the Case of Lower Commons Yield

At any given level of effort in this case, no matter what that level might be, a lower *AP* results under common property.

If the total product curve under common property is shifted down far enough, it is possible that effort under common property is less than under private property, while common property's average product is simultaneously less. Assume that the total product curve for commons is shifted down so that when it is multiplied by a constant market price, it has a total sustainable revenue curve (TSR_c) that lies under private property's total sustainable revenue curve (TSR_p), as in Figure 7.5. Given the total cost curve for private property TC_p, optimal private effort is E_p^*. Assuming for simplicity that commons has the same total cost curve, optimal commons effort is E_c^*. This is less than E_p^*. It is even possible with a sufficiently depressed total sustainable revenue curve like the one in Figure 7.5 that economic overgrazing occurs on the commons—say, at its maximum sustainable yield E_c—while less effort is applied than the private optimal rate E_p^*.

This scenario is the only one that allows reconciliation of the dual results of lower average product *and* lower effort on the commons. Underinvestment in common improvements to the land may well have caused the total product curve for commons to lie below the total product curve for private property. Alternatively, overgrazing in previous years may have caused the grazing area to deteriorate, and commons graziers may have compensated subsequently by reducing grazing pressure to an intensity below today's private level.

It is hard to say from any direct evidence that I analyzed whether investment in common improvements is lower under common property than under private. The alp regulations described in Chapter 4 that require users to fertilize properly, help in debris cleanup, per-

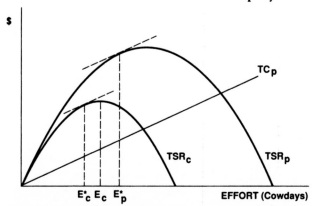

Figure 7.5. The Case of Simultaneously Lower Commons Effort and Average Product

form a work duty, and so forth are designed to elicit adequate individual efforts toward common improvements. Yet the users set these rules themselves, and they may have set them too low. Besides, it is always possible to slight one's duty if one is not truly interested in contributing.[6] The attentuation of individual benefit in a group situation makes both of these results possible.

Although I did not investigate directly the empirical question whether investment in common improvements is lower under common property than under private, further research might provide a straightforward answer. Some data on investments in commons and private grazing land could be collected. How much labor is expended on grazing area improvements? Is manure collected and spread? Is commercial fertilizer purchased? If so, how much per hectare? How much time and money is spent on weed control? Does the grazing area include noticeably weedy areas owing to overfertilization or lack of weed control? These are a few empirical indicators, some of them quite measurable, regarding the effort expended on common and private improvements.

The alternative explanation that previous overgrazing deflated the yield–effort function for commons would be difficult to substantiate, because reductions in grazing intensity have occurred on commons

---

[6] In this regard, Frödin (1941: 55) makes the following comment about community alps: "The communal alps with use limited to estimated carrying capacity may be protected from being "mined" by overgrazing. However, this form of communal alpine grazing is hardly conducive to awakening individual interest to promote the [group] operation or to improving the yield of the alp through personal efforts" (my translation).

for other reasons. As explained in Chapter 4, adjustments have taken place whenever natural forces have destroyed parts of grazing areas, and commons alps also have corrected the number of animal units as the animals have become larger through selective breeding. It would be hard to separate these influences from potential compensations for previous overgrazing. I surmise that underinvestment in common improvements is a more likely reason for a lower commons output in any event. This is both because it is easier to shirk improvement duties than to get around group-imposed grazing limits and because one would have to show substantial reductions in grazing pressure for commons to go from a grazing pressure level above to one below that of private property. For whatever reason, whether lack of common improvements to the grazing area or past overgrazing, a depressed yield–effort function for commons appears to be the most likely explanation for the simultaneously lower average product and lower common property grazing pressure observed.

Further Research

The conclusions drawn thus far have opened up questions that further research could resolve. The thorniest problem, of course, is the omission of costs. To resolve this question, an approach quite different from the empirical analysis of Chapter 6 could be used. First, one might select pairs of grazing areas, one commons and one private, that exist under similar natural conditions. Where possible, adjacent grazing areas under the two rights systems should be chosen so that they have similar environments. Then an exhaustive survey of costs and returns could be taken by individual interview to determine net returns for each grazing area. After one had performed analyses for ten to fifteen such pairs, a pattern might emerge indicating which rights system produces a better net return.

Although conceptually simple, this approach is fraught with problems. I conducted a small number of such surveys, but the problems that arose and limits on time have prevented analyzing the results. The first problem is finding pairs of private and commons alps that exist under similar natural conditions. To find potentially comparable alps, I used the Alp Assessments (Abteilung für Landwirtschaft 1961–73, 1978), which contain descriptions of the grazing areas. Having chosen pairs (and some triplets, namely of private land, cooperative commons, and dispersed operating unit commons), I visited the alps, often only to find that the dissimilarities in natural setting were greater than the similarities. Reading the Alp Assessment descriptions had been a poor substitute for firsthand observation. A second problem is that many private graziers keep no records of expenditures, and one must ask the farmer to guess what costs were. This procedure does not provide data in which one can have great confidence. Finally, for dispersed operating unit commons, one may have to survey five, ten, or fifteen operations to obtain complete cost and returns data for a single alp. Despite these problems, estimation of net returns for a moderately sized sample of alps under different rights types may be the best available means of shedding further light on the relative efficiencies of commons and private alps.

Another method of comparing commons and private performance would be to tap the economic information contained in the market prices for rights on share rights alps. A right's price reflects the quality of a grazing area and implicitly considers both costs and returns. From the market prices and the numbers of rights, one could determine the capitalized values of the grazing areas. After controlling statistically for natural factors, one might compare these values to the market prices for private alps. The comparison would give another indication of commons performance, at least for share rights alps. The main problem here may be the lack of transfers, both of private alps and of grazing rights for commons, from which market price data could be acquired.

Finally, closely related to the overall question of optimal resource management would be investigation of the subsidiary questions of overgrazing and underinvestment in improvements on commons and private property. One could appraise grazing areas for overgrazing by examining their plant composition and condition. A survey across rights types by a range management expert would provide information on how well each does on overgrazing. Regarding underinvestment, asking questions about time and effort spent on care and improvement of the alp, some of which were suggested in the previous subsection, would give empirical evidence about whether underinvestment occurs on common property.

Conclusion

My results do not give a definitive answer about common property's efficiency, but they do provide a strong indication of its performance relative to private property's. The results are not definitive because of the omission of costs. If we assume that common property costs are equal to those of private property and that the commons overall total sustainable revenue curve is lower (which, again, could happen if commons invested less in grazing area care or if overgrazing occurred in the past) the theoretical result is consistent with the observed outcome of both lower average product and lower grazing pressure on commons. Such a scenario necessarily leads to lower rent for the commons.[7] What happens, however, if care of the commons is poorer *and* costs are lower for commons? Both the total product and the total cost curves diverge between commons and private property. Results become ambivalent and definitive conclusions cannot be drawn. For this reason, work on the cost side of the question is needed. Only a net revenues analysis will completely answer the question about commons' relative efficiency.

The discussion in this chapter does indicate, however, that common property in Switzerland can perform as efficiently as private property only under fairly restricted circumstances: much lower costs than private property. This conclusion follows from the same simultaneous results of lower average product and fewer variable inputs (less grazing pressure) on the commons. Because these dual results are consistent only with a lower total sustainable revenue curve for commons, costs would have to be sufficiently lower to make up for not only the lower total revenue generation potential (lower yield–effort function) but also the lower observed level of variable inputs to generate those revenues. Moreover, the indicated lower yield–effort function for commons resulting from less investment in grazing area care or past overgrazing is itself evidence that commons are not as well managed. This means that the results cannot refute the conventional wisdom that group control of a natural resource leads to a poorer outcome than private control, and the results may even give the customary view guarded support.

Whether or not an eventual net revenues analysis indicates that commons management is generally poorer than private management, common property will still have its place in specific instances. In Switzerland, natural conditions exist under which only commons will work, regardless of the general incentives inherent in commons management. Particularly the remote areas are unsuitable for private management. Because of the costs of managing the resource privately at these locations, rents under common property may well be higher. Thus, even if generally poorer performance of common property is

---

[7] This can be seen in Figure 7.5 by observing that any distance between TC_p and TSR_c is necessarily smaller than the distance between TC_p and TSR_p, the latter distance measured at the optimal private effort E_p^*.

found in a net revenues analysis, not all commons will be inferior, nor can the conclusion be reached that all commons should be converted to private property. This notion parallels the more general idea that particular resource configurations exist—from fisheries to the atmosphere—for which we are compelled to find common property rather than private property solutions.

References

Abteilung für Landwirtschaft. 1961–73, 1978. *Land- und alpwirtschaftlicher Produktionskataster*. 44 vols. from the canton of Bern. Bern, Switzerland: Abteilung für Landwirtschaft des eidgenössischen Volkswirtschaftsdepartements.

[Aeschlimann, Fritz.] 1973. *Land- und alpwirtschaftlicher Produktionskataster der Gemeinde Grindelwald*. Bern, Switzerland: Abteilung für Landwirtschaft des eidgenössischen Volkswirtschaftsdepartements.

[Aeschlimann, Fritz.] 1978. *Schweizerischer Alpkataster: Die Land- und Alpwirtschaft im Berner Oberland, Emmental und Schwarzenburgerland*. Bern, Switzerland: Abteilung für Landwirtschaft des eidgenössischen Volkswirtschaftsdepartements.

Alchian, Armen A., and Harold Demsetz. 1973. "The Property Rights Paradigm." *Journal of Economic History* 33(1): 16–27, March.

Alp Geilskummi. 1936. "Reglement für die Alp Geilskummi." Adelboden, Switzerland, May 1. Photocopy.

Alpkorporation Sellamatt. 1958. "Alpreglement der Alpkorporation Sellamatt." Alt St. Johann, Switzerland, January 19. Mimeograph.

Alp Krinnen. 1975–79. "Krinnenbergrechnung." Gsteig, Switzerland. Handwritten.

Alpschaft Ober-Egerlen. 1950. "Reglement für die Alpschaft Ober-Egerlen." Frutigen, Switzerland, January 12. Photocopy.

Amemiya, Takeshi. 1981. "Qualitative Response Models: A Survey." *Journal of Economic Literature* 19(4): 1483–1536, December.

Anderegg, Werner. 1976. "Die Alpwirtschaft im Obertoggenburg und ihre Entwicklung zur heutigen Form am Beispiel von Alt St. Johann." In *Toggenburger Annalen 1977: Kulturelles Jahrbuch für das Toggenburg und Umgebung*, 4th annual ed., ed. Paul Widmer, 29–38. Uzwil, Switzerland: Buch- und Offsetdruck Zeno Fischers Erben.

Anderson, Lee G. 1977. *The Economics of Fisheries Management*. Baltimore: Johns Hopkins University Press.

Anderson, Terry L., and P. J. Hill. 1977. "From Free Grass to Fences: Transforming the Commons of the American West." In *Managing the Commons*, ed. Garrett Hardin and John Baden, 200–216. San Francisco: W. H. Freeman and Co.

Atkinson, Scott E., and T. H. Tietenberg. 1982. "The Empirical Properties of Two Classes of Designs for Transferable Discharge Permit Markets." *Journal of Environmental Economics and Management* 9(2): 101–21, June.

Ault, David E., and Gilbert L. Rutman. 1979. "The Development of Individual Rights to Property in Tribal Africa." *Journal of Law and Economics* 22(1): 163–82, April.

Ault, Warren O. 1965. "Open Field Husbandry and the Village Community." *Transactions of the American Philosophical Society* 55(7): 5–102, October.

[Bäbler, R.] 1962. *Schweizerischer Alpkataster: Kanton Glarus.* Bern, Switzerland: Abteilung für Landwirtschaft des eidgenössischen Volkswirtschaftsdepartements.

[Bäbler, R.] 1965. *Schweizerischer Alpkataster: Kanton Nidwalden.* Bern, Switzerland: Abteilung für Landwirtschaft des eidgenössischen Volkswirtschaftsdepartements.

Bacharach, Michael. 1977. *Economics and the Theory of Games.* Boulder, Colo.: Westview Press.

Baker, Alan R. H., and R. A. Butlin. 1973. "Conclusion: Problems and Perspectives." In *Studies of Field Systems in the British Isles,* ed. Alan R. H. Baker and Robin A. Butlin, 619–56. Cambridge: Cambridge University Press.

Becker, Lawrence C. 1977. *Property Rights: Philosophic Foundations.* Boston: Routledge and Kegan Paul.

Bergschaft Lombach. 1928. "Alpreglement der Bergschaft Lombach." Goldswil, Switzerland, March 24. Photocopy.

Bigler, H., M. Boller, U. Bundi, H. Gloor, U. Hüni, W. Leuener, H. Spetzler, and E. Weinmann. 1969. "Alp Palfris SG." Senior thesis, Institut für Kulturtechnik, Eidgenössische technische Hochschule, Zürich.

Bishop, Richard C. 1983. Personal communication, March.

Bishop, Richard C., and Scott R. Milliman. 1983. "Bioeconomic Foundations for Fisheries Management." Department of Agricultural Economics, University of Wisconsin–Madison. Invited paper presented at the annual meetings of the American Fisheries Society, Milwaukee, Wisconsin, August 17.

Bottomley, Anthony. 1963. "The Effect of the Common Ownership of Land upon Resource Allocation in Tripolitania." *Land Economics* 39(1): 91–95, February.

Braden, John B. 1985. "Uncertainty and Open Access: Implications from the Repeated Prisoners' Dilemma Game." *American Journal of Agricultural Economics* 67(2): 356–59, May.

Bromley, Daniel W. 1986. "Closing Comments at the Conference on Common Property Resource Management." In *Proceedings of the Conference on Common Property Resource Management,* April 21–26, 1985, prepared by the Panel on Common Property Resource Management, Board on Science and Technology for International Development, Office of International Affairs, National Research Council, 593–98. Washington, D.C.: National Academy Press.

Bromley, Daniel W. 1989. *Economic Interests and Institutions: The Conceptual Foundations of Public Policy.* New York: Basil Blackwell.

Büchi, Walter G. 1972. "Oberlugnez: Wirtschafts- und Siedlungs-Entwicklung vom Ende des Mittelalters bis zum 20. Jahrhundert." Dissertation, Universität Zürich.

Bundesamt für Landestopographie der Schweiz. 1986. 1:500,000 backpiece: "Politische Gliederung" (political divisions). CH-3084 Wabern, Switzerland.

Camenisch, Emil. 1924. "Geschichte der Großalp in Safien." Reprint from the *Bündnerisches Monatsblatt*. Chur, Switzerland: Buchdruckerei Sprecher, Eggerling und Co.

Carlen, Louis. 1970. *Das Recht der Hirten*. Studien zur Rechts-, Wirtschafts- und Kulturgeschichte, ed. Nikolaus Grass, Universität Innsbruck, no. 7. Aalen, Germany: Scientia Verlag.

Cheung, Steven N. S. 1969. *The Theory of Share Tenancy*. Chicago: Chicago University Press.

Cheung, Steven N. S. 1970. "The Structure of a Contract and the Theory of a Non-exclusive Resource." *Journal of Law and Economics* 13(1): 49–70, April.

Cheyney, Edward Potts. [1901.] *An Introduction to the Industrial and Social History of England*. New York: Macmillan Co.

Christy, F. T., Jr. 1973. "Fishermen's Quotas: A Tentative Suggestion for Domestic Management." University of Rhode Island, Law of the Sea Institute Occasional Paper 19.

Ciriacy-Wantrup, S. V. 1952. *Resource Conservation: Economics and Policies*. Berkeley and Los Angeles: University of California Press.

Ciriacy-Wantrup, S. V. 1971. "The Economics of Environmental Policy." *Land Economics* 47(1): 36–45, February.

Ciriacy-Wantrup, S. V., and Richard C. Bishop. 1975. " 'Common Property' as a Concept in Natural Resources Policy." *Natural Resources Journal* 15(4): 713–27, October.

Clark, Colin W. 1976. *Mathematical Bioeconomics: The Optimal Management of Renewable Resources*. New York: John Wiley and Sons.

Clawson, Marion. 1974. Comment on "Managing the Public Lands: Assignment of Property Rights and Valuation of Resources" by Anthony Fisher and John Krutilla. In *The Governance of Common Property Resources*, ed. Edwin T. Haefele, 60–63. Baltimore: Johns Hopkins University Press for Resources for the Future.

Coase, R. H. 1960. "The Problem of Social Cost." *Journal of Law and Economics* 3:1–44, October.

Cordell, John. 1978. "Swamp Dwellers of Bahia." *Natural History* 87(6): 62–72, June–July.

Crommelin, Michael, Peter H. Pearse, and Anthony Scott. 1978. "Management of Oil and Gas Resources in Alberta: An Economic Evaluation of Public Policy." *Natural Resources Journal* 18(2): 337–89, April.

Crutchfield, James A., and Arnold Zellner. 1963. *Economic Aspects of the Pacific*

Halibut Fishery. Fishery Industrial Research 1(1). Washington, D.C.: United States Government Printing Office.

Cunningham, Roger A., William B. Stoebuck, and Dale A. Whitman. 1984. *The Law of Property.* St. Paul: West Publishing Co.

Dahlman, Carl J. 1980. *The Open Field System and Beyond: A Property Rights Analysis of an Economic Institution.* Cambridge: Cambridge University Press.

Dales, J. H. *Pollution, Property and Prices.* 1968. Toronto: University of Toronto Press.

Dasgupta, Partha S., and Geoffrey M. Heal. 1979. *Economic Theory and Exhaustible Resources.* Welwyn, England: James Nisbet and Co. and Cambridge University Press.

Davidson, Paul. 1963. "Public Policy Problems of the Domestic Crude Oil Industry." *American Economic Review* 53(1): 85–108, March.

Demsetz, Harold. 1967. "Toward a Theory of Property Rights." *American Economic Review* 57(2): 347–59, May.

Dodgshon, Robert A. 1980. *The Origin of British Field Systems: An Interpretation.* London: Academic Press.

Donau, Georg. 1979. President of the community of Peist. Interviews with author. Peist, Switzerland, June 21 and 22 and August 19.

Dorfman, Robert. 1974. "The Technical Basis for Decision Making." In *The Governance of Common Property Resources,* ed. Edwin T. Haefele, 5–25. Baltimore: Johns Hopkins University Press for Resources for the Future.

Elliott, G. 1973. "Field Systems of Northwest England." In *Studies of Field Systems in the British Isles,* ed. Alan R. H. Baker and Robin A. Butlin, 41–92. Cambridge: Cambridge University Press.

Ely, Richard T. 1914. *Property and Contract in Their Relations to the Distribution of Wealth.* 2 vols. New York: Macmillan Co.

Frehner, Otto, ed. 1925. *Das Alpbuch der Schwägalp in Appenzell Außer-Rhoden.* Trogen, Switzerland: Otto Kübler.

Frödin, John. 1941. *Zentraleuropas Alpwirtschaft.* Vol. 2. Oslo: H. Aschehoug und Co.

Genossenschaft Grosse Schwägalp. 1976a. "Alp- und Sennenreglement der Genossenschaft Grosse Schwägalp." Gais, Switzerland, April 27.

Genossenschaft Grosse Schwägalp. 1976b. "Entschädigungs- und Bussenordnung." [Gais, Switzerland,] April 27. Photocopy.

Gordon, H. Scott. 1954. "The Economic Theory of a Common Property Resource: The Fishery." *Journal of Political Economy* 62(2): 124–42, April.

Gruner, Erich, and Beat Junker. 1972. *Bürger, Staat, und Politik in der Schweiz.* Basel: Ameba-Druck GmbH.

Hafner, Pius. 1979. Doctoral candidate in ethnology, Universität Fribourg. Interview with author. Fribourg, Switzerland, February 2.

Hallowell, A. Irving. 1943. "The Nature and Function of Property as a Social Institution." *Journal of Legal and Political Sociology* 1(3–4): 115–38, April.

Hardin, Garrett. 1968. "The Tragedy of the Commons." *Science* 162(3859):

1243–48, December 13. Reprinted in *Managing the Commons*, ed. Garrett Hardin and John Baden, 16–30. San Francisco: W. H. Freeman and Co., 1977.

Haveman, Robert H. 1973. "Common Property, Congestion, and Environmental Pollution." *Quarterly Journal of Economics* 87(2): 278–87, May.

Heckman, James J. 1979. "Sample Selection Bias as a Specification Error." *Econometrica* 47(1): 153–61, January.

Henderson, James M., and Richard E. Quandt. 1971. *Microeconomic Theory: A Mathematical Approach.* 2nd ed. New York: McGraw-Hill Book Co.

Hoffman, Richard C. 1975. "Medieval Origins of the Common Fields." In *European Peasants and Their Markets*, ed. William N. Parker and Eric L. Jones, 23–71. Princeton, N.J.: Princeton University Press.

Hohfeld, Wesley N. 1919. *Fundamental Legal Conceptions.* New Haven: Yale University Press.

Honoré, A. M. 1961. "Ownership." In *Oxford Essays in Jurisprudence*, ed. A. G. Guest, 107–47. London: Oxford University Press.

Hoskins, William George, and L. Dudley Stamp. 1963. *The Common Lands of England and Wales.* London: Collins.

Howe, Charles W. 1979. *Natural Resource Economics: Issues, Analysis, and Policy.* New York: John Wiley and Sons.

[Imboden, Adrian.] 1969. *Land- und alpwirtschaftlicher Produktionskataster der Gemeinde Visperterminen.* Bern, Switzerland: Abteilung für Landwirtschaft des eidgenössischen Volkswirtschaftsdepartements.

[Imboden, Adrian.] 1972. *Die Land- und Alpwirtschaft im Oberwallis.* Bern, Switzerland: Abteilung für Landwirtschaft des eidgenössischen Volkswirtschaftsdepartements.

Imboden, Adrian. 1978. Specialist in surveys for mountain and alpine agriculture, Swiss Federal Department of Economics, Division of Agriculture. Interview with author. Bern, Switzerland, October 3.

Imboden, Adrian, Willi Schohaus, and Martin Schmid. 1951. "Alpfahrt." In *Kommentare zum schweizerischen Schulwandbilderwerk*, 2nd picture seq., 3rd ed., picture 10. Schweizerische pädagogische Schriften series, notebook 79. Zürich: A. G. Fachschriften Verlag und Buchdruckerei.

[Indergand, R.] 1963. *Schweizerischer Alpkataster: Kanton Obwalden.* Bern, Switzerland: Abteilung für Landwirtschaft des eidgenössischen Volkswirtschaftsdepartements.

Johnson, D. Gale 1950. "Resource Allocation under Share Contracts." *Journal of Political Economy* 58(2): 111–23, April.

Johnson, Norman L., and Samuel Kotz. 1972. *Distribution in Statistics: Continuous Multivariate Distributions.* New York: John Wiley and Sons.

Judge, George G., William E. Griffiths, R. Carter Hill, and Tsoung-Chao Lee. 1980. *The Theory and Practice of Econometrics.* New York: John Wiley and Sons.

Juergensmeyer, Julian C., and James B. Wadley. 1974. "The Common Lands

Concept: A 'Commons' Solution to a Common Environmental Problem." *Natural Resources Journal* 14(3): 361–81, July.

Kanton Bern. 1973. *Bewertung der landwirtschaftlichen Grundstücke und der Waldungen (Landwirtschaftliche Schätzungsnormen).* Pt. 1 of *Amtliche Bewertung der Grundstücke und Wasserkräfte.* [Bern, Switzerland:] Kantonale Schatzungskommission, September 17.

Katzman, Martin T. 1974. "The Von Thuenen Paradigm, the Industrial-Urban Hypothesis, and the Spatial Structure of Agriculture." *American Journal of Agricultural Economics* 56(4): 683–96, November.

Kmenta, Jan. 1971. *Elements of Econometrics.* New York: Macmillan Co.

Korporation Uri. 1916. *Allmendbuch der Korporation Uri.* Vol. 4, pt. 1, of *Landbuch des Kantons Uri.* Altdorf, Switzerland: Buchdruckerei Huber.

Korporation Uri. 1952. *Sammlung der Gesetze, Verordnungen, und Beschlüsse der Korporation Uri (soweit sie im Landbuch IV nicht enthalten sind).* Altdorf, Switzerland: Buchdruckerei Gisler und Cie.

Kreps, David M., Paul Milgrom, John Roberts, and Robert Wilson. 1982. "Rational Cooperation in the Finitely Repeated Prisoners' Dilemma." *Journal of Economic Theory* 27(2): 245–52, August.

Krupnick, Alan J., Wallace E. Oates, and Eric Van De Verg. 1983. "On Marketable Air-Pollution Permits: The Case for a System of Pollution Offsets." *Journal of Environmental Economics and Management* 10(3): 233–47, September.

Leamer, Edward E. 1983. "Let's Take the Con Out of Econometrics." *American Economic Review* 73(1): 31–43, March.

Libecap, Gary D. 1981. *Locking Up the Range.* Cambridge, Mass.: Ballinger Publishing Co.

Linggi, Josef, Sr. 1979. Alp overseer for the Stossebenalp, canton of Schwyz. Interview with author. Brunnen, Switzerland, July 2.

Luce, Robert D., and Howard Raiffa. 1957. *Games and Decisions.* New York: John Wiley and Sons.

McCay, Bonnie M., and James M. Acheson, eds. 1987. *The Question of the Commons: The Culture and Ecology of Communal Resources.* Tucson, Ariz.: University of Arizona Press.

McCloskey, Donald N. 1975. "The Persistence of English Common Fields." In *European Peasants and Their Markets,* ed. William N. Parker and Eric L. Jones, 73–119. Princeton, N.J.: Princeton University Press.

McFadden, Daniel. 1974. "Conditional Logit Analysis of Qualitative Choice Behavior." In *Frontiers in Econometrics,* ed. Paul Zarembka, 105–42. New York: Academic Press.

McGartland, Albert M., and Wallace E. Oates. 1985. "Marketable Permits for the Prevention of Environmental Deterioration." *Journal of Environmental Economics and Management* 12(3): 207–28, September.

Maddala, G. S. 1983. *Limited-Dependent and Qualitative Variables in Econometrics.* Cambridge: Cambridge University Press.

[Marti, Ernst.] 1966. *Schweizerischer Alpkataster: Die Land- und Alpwirtschaft im*

Kanton Schwyz. Bern, Switzerland: Abteilung für Landwirtschaft des eidgenössischen Volkswirtschaftsdepartements.

[Marti, Ernst.] 1970. *Schweizerischer Alpkataster: Die Land- und Alpwirtschaft im Kanton Uri.* Bern, Switzerland: Abteilung für Landwirtschaft des eidgenössischen Volkswirtschaftsdepartements.

Medicus, Ludwig W. 1795. *Bemerkungen über die Alpenwirthschaft auf einer Reise durch die Schweiz.* Leipzig: Heinrich Gräff.

Menet, Hannes. 1979. Treasurer of the Grosse Schwägalp, canton of Appenzell Ausserrhoden. Interview with author. St. Gallen, Switzerland, June 16.

Messmer, Elizabeth. 1976. *Scharans: Eine Gemeindestudie aus der Gegenwart.* Schriften der schweizerischen Gesellschaft für Volkskunde, vol. 59. Basel: Verlag G. Krebs AG.

Meyer-Mayor, Rosalie, and Fritz Früh. 1961. "Pachtvertrag zwischen Frau Rosalie Meyer-Mayor als Verpächterin und Herr Fritz Früh, Landwirt, als Pächter." Neu St. Johann and Matt, Switzerland, August 14. Typescript.

Mill, John Stuart. 1878. *Principles of Political Economy with Some of Their Applications to Social Philosophy.* People's [6th] ed. London: Longmans, Green, Reader, and Dyer.

Mittelberg-Genossenschaft. 1931. "Statuten der Mittelberg-Genossenschaft." Sigriswil, Switzerland, March 1. Mimeograph.

Moloney, David G., and Peter H. Pearse. 1979. "Quantitative Rights as an Instrument for Regulating Commercial Fisheries." *Journal of the Fisheries Research Board of Canada* 36(7): 859–66, July.

Montgomery, W. David. 1972. "Markets in Licenses and Efficient Pollution Control Programs." *Journal of Economic Theory* 5(3): 395–418, December.

Muhsam, H. V. [1973] 1977. "An Algebraic Theory of the Commons." In *Managing the Commons*, ed. Garrett Hardin and John Baden, 34–37. San Francisco: W. H. Freeman and Co. Reprint of appendix to "A World Population Policy for the World Population Year," *Journal of Peace Research* 10(1–2): 91–99.

Neff, Karl. n.d. "Lebendige Demokratie: Die Oberallmeind, die grösste Korporation der Schweiz." Oberallmeind-Korporation Schwyz, Schwyz, Switzerland. Mimeograph.

Netting, Robert M. 1976. "What Alpine Peasants Have in Common: Observations on Communal Tenure in a Swiss Village." *Human Ecology* 4(2): 135–46, April.

North, Douglass C., and Robert P. Thomas. 1977. "The First Economic Revolution." *Economic History Review*, 2nd ser. 30(2): 229–41, May.

Oberallmeind-Korporation Schwyz. 1940. *Auftriebs-Verordnung der Oberallmeind-Korporation in Schwyz.* Schwyz, Switzerland: Emil Steiner, Buchdruckerei.

Oberallmeind-Korporation Schwyz. 1974. *Verordnungen der Oberallmeindkorporation Schwyz.* Schwyz, Switzerland: Triner.

Odermatt, Josef. 1926. *Die Emmentaleralpen und ihre Wirtschafts- und Rechtsgeschichte.* Doctoral dissertation, Universität Bern. Huttwil, Switzerland: Buch- und Akzidenzdruckerei Joh. Schürchs Söhne.

Orwin, C. S., and C. S. Orwin. 1954. *The Open Fields.* 2nd ed. Oxford: Clarendon Press.

Ostrom, Elinor. 1977. "Collective Action and the Tragedy of the Commons." In *Managing the Commons,* ed. Garrett Hardin and John Baden, 173–81. San Francisco: W. H. Freeman and Co.

Ostrom, Elinor. 1986. "Issues of Definition and Theory: Some Conclusions and Hypotheses." In *Proceedings of the Conference on Common Property Resource Management,* April 21–26, 1985, prepared by the Panel on Common Property Resource Management, Board on Science and Technology for International Development, Office of International Affairs, National Research Council, 599–615. Washington, D.C.: National Academy Press.

Ostrom, Vincent, and Elinor Ostrom. 1977. "A Theory for Institutional Analysis of Common Pool Problems." In *Managing the Commons,* ed. Garrett Hardin and John Baden, 157–72. San Francisco: W. H. Freeman and Co.

Panel on Common Property Resource Management, Board on Science and Technology for International Development, Office of International Affairs, National Research Council. 1986. *Proceedings of the Conference on Common Property Resource Management,* April 21–26, 1985. Washington, D.C.: National Academy Press.

Pejovich, Svetozar. 1972. "Towards an Economic Theory of the Creation of Property Rights." *Review of Social Economy* 30(3): 309–25, September.

Pigou, A. C. 1932. *The Economics of Welfare.* 4th ed. London: Macmillan and Co.

Pollock, Frederick. 1896. *The Land Laws.* London: Macmillan and Co.

Rhoades, Robert E., and Stephen I. Thompson. 1975. "Adaptive Strategies in Alpine Environments: Beyond Ecological Particularism." *American Ethnologist* 2(3): 535–51, August.

Rhyner, Hans. 1980. President of the *Ortsgemeinde* (community faction) of Buchs, canton of St. Gallen. Interview with author. Buchs, Switzerland, March 26.

Roberts, B. K. 1973. "Field Systems of the West Midlands." In *Studies of Field Systems in the British Isles,* ed. Alan R. H. Baker and Robin A. Butlin, 188–231. Cambridge: Cambridge University Press.

Rostow, Eugene V. 1948. *A National Policy for the Oil Industry.* New Haven: Yale University Press.

Rubi, Chr. 1979. "Die Bäuert Weissenburg Berg: Älter als Kirchgemeinden oder Gerichtsbezirke: Aus der Geschichte einer simmentalischen Allmendgenossenschaft im 17. und 18. Jahrhundert." *Der Bund,* no. 16 (January 20), no. 22 (January 27), and no. 28 (February 3).

Runge, C. Ford. 1981. "Common Property Externalities: Isolation, Assurance, and Resource Depletion in a Traditional Grazing Context." *American Journal of Agricultural Economics* 63(4): 595–606, November.

Runge, C. Ford. 1986. "Common Property and Collective Action in Economic Development." In *Proceedings of the Conference on Common Property Resource Management*, April 21–26, 1985, prepared by the Panel on Common Property Resource Management, Board on Science and Technology for International Development, Office of International Affairs, National Research Council, 31–60. Washington, D.C.: National Academy Press.

Samuelson, Paul A. 1947. *Foundations of Economic Analysis*. Cambridge, Mass.: Harvard University Press.

Samuelson, Paul A. 1983. "Thünen at Two Hundred." *Journal of Economic Literature* 21(4): 1468–88, December.

Say, Jean-Baptiste. [1821] 1964. *A Treatise on Political Economy, or the Production, Distribution, and Consumption of Wealth*. 4th ed. Trans. C. R. Prinsep. New York: Augustus M. Kelley, Bookseller and Sentry Press. Reprint of 1880 New American ed., trans. and ed. Clement C. Biddle. Philadelphia: Claxton, Remsen and Haffelfinger.

Schallenberg, Fritz. 1980. Alp master of Alp Krinnen, canton of Bern. Interview with author. Gsteig, Switzerland, July 28.

Schuler, Karl. 1951. "Entstehung, Sinn und Zweck der Oberallmeind." Reprint from the *Landwirtschaftlicher Genossenschaftskalender der Zentralschweiz*, vol. 28. Oberallmeind-Korporation Schwyz, Schwyz, Switzerland. Mimeograph.

Scott, Anthony D. 1955. "The Fishery: The Objectives of Sole Ownership." *Journal of Political Economy* 63(2): 116–24, April.

Sen, Amartya K. 1967. "Isolation, Assurance, and the Social Rate of Discount." *Quarterly Journal of Economics* 81(1): 112–24, February.

Sidgwick, Henry. 1883. *The Principles of Political Economy*. London: Macmillan and Co.

Slater, Gilbert. [1907] 1968. *The English Peasantry and the Enclosure of Common Fields*. Reprint. New York: A. M. Kelley, Publishers.

Smith, Adam. [1786] 1880. *An Inquiry into the Nature and Causes of the Wealth of Nations*. 2nd ed. Reprint of Smith's 3rd ed., ed. James E. Thorold Rogers. Oxford: Clarendon Press.

Solenthaler, Alfred. 1979. President of the Grosse Schwägalp, canton of Appenzell Ausserrhoden. Interview with author. Gais, Switzerland, May 26.

Stebler, F. G. 1901. *Ob den Heidenreben*. Zürich: Buchdruckerei Aschmann und Scheller.

Stebler, F. G. 1903. *Das Goms und die Gomser*. Supp. to the Yearbook of the Schweizer Alpen Club, vol. 38. Zürich: Buchdruckerei Fritz Amberger.

Tawney, Richard H. 1912. *The Agrarian Problem in the Sixteenth Century*. New York: Burt Franklin.

Thirsk, Joan. 1964. "The Common Fields." *Past and Present* no. 29:3–25, December.

Thirsk, Joan. 1973. "Field Systems of the East Midlands." In *Studies of Field Systems in the British Isles*, ed. Alan R. H. Baker and Robin A. Butlin, 232–80. Cambridge: Cambridge University Press.

References   245

Thürer, Georg. 1978. "Die Genossenschaftsidee im schweizerischen Staat." In *75 Jahre Raiffeisened*, ed. Schweizer Verband der Raiffeisenkassen, 68–71. Baden, Switzerland: Buchdruckerei AG Baden.

Townsend, Ralph, and James A. Wilson. 1987. "An Economic View of the Tragedy of the Commons." In *The Question of the Commons*, ed. Bonnie M. McCay and James M. Acheson. Tucson: University of Arizona Press.

Turvey, Ralph. 1964. "Optimization and Suboptimization in Fishery Regulation." *American Economic Review* 54(2): 64–76, March.

Viner, Jacob. 1931. "Cost Curves and Supply Curves." *Zeitschrift für Nationalökonomie* 3:23–46. Reprinted in *Readings in Price Theory*, American Economic Association, George J. Stigler and Kenneth E. Boulding, Selection Committee members. Chicago: Richard D. Irwin, Inc., 1952.

Vinogradoff, Paul. [1923] 1967. *Villainage in England: Essays in English Mediaeval History*. Reprint. New York: Russell and Russell.

Wagner, Ernst. 1924. *Die obertoggenburgischen Alpkorporationen*. Doctoral dissertation, Universität Bern. Thalwil, Switzerland: Buchdruckerei Dr. Tellenbach.

Waldmeier-Brockmann, Anni. 1941. *Sammelwirtschaft in den Schweizer Alpen: Eine ethnographische Studie*. Dissertation Universität Zürich. Basel: Helbing und Lichtenhahn Verlagsbuchhandlung.

Warming, Jens. [1911] 1981. "On 'Land Rent' of Fishing Grounds." *Fisheries Economics Newsletter* no. 12., Fisheries Economics Research Unit, Edinburgh, Scotland, November. Translation by Rognvaldur Hannesson and Lee G. Anderson of "Om grundrente af fiskegrunde," *Nationaløkonomisk Tidsskrift* 49:499–505. Also reprinted as Staff Paper no. 81-13, Department of Resource Economics, University of Rhode Island, Kingston.

Weiss, Richard. 1941. *Das Alpwesen Graubündens: Wirtschaft, Sachkultur, Recht, Älplerarbeit, und Älplerleben*. Erlenbach-Zürich: Eugen Rentsch Verlag.

Weitzman, Martin L. 1974. "Free Access vs. Private Ownership as Alternative Systems for Managing Common Property." *Journal of Economic Theory* 8(2): 225–34, June.

[Werthemann, Andreas.] 1969. *Schweizerischer Alpkataster: Kanton Graubünden*. Pt. 1. Bern, Switzerland: Abteilung für Landwirtschaft des eidgenössischen Volkswirtschaftsdepartements.

Wiggins, Steven N., and Gary D. Libecap. 1985. "Oil Field Unitization: Contractual Failure in the Presence of Imperfect Information." *American Economic Review* 75(3): 368–85, June.

Wilckens, Martin. 1874. *Die Alpenwirthschaft der Schweiz, des Algäus und der westösterreichischen Alpenländer*. Vienna: Wilhelm Braumüller, K. K. Hof- und Universitätsbuchhändler.

Wohlfarter, Richard. 1965. *Die Besitz- und Ertragsstruktur der Tiroler Alp- und Weidewirtschaft*. Innsbruck: Amt der Tiroler Landesregierung, Abteilung III d4, and Imst, Austria: Egger Druckerei.

Index

Lightning Source UK Ltd.
Milton Keynes UK
UKOW02f1204241016

285994UK00001B/241/P